CHANCE GOVERNS ALL

CHANCE GOVERNS ALL

A Memoir by Marmaduke Hussey

MACMILLAN

First published 2001 by Macmillan
an imprint of Pan Macmillan Ltd
Pan Macmillan, 20 New Wharf Road, London N1 9RR
Basingstoke and Oxford
Associated companies throughout the world
www.panmacmillan.com

ISBN 0 333 90256 4

Typeset by SetSystems Ltd, Saffron Walden, Essex
Printed and bound in Great Britain by
Mackays of Chatham plc, Chatham, Kent

Chaos umpire sits,
And by decision more embroils the fray,
By which he reigns: next to him high arbiter
Chance governs all

Milton: *Paradise Lost*

To Sue

Who loyally supported me
through some tumultous times

Introduction

This book began as something rather different. Indeed, if I had realized that I might one day end up writing my memoirs, I would probably never have got involved in the first place.

Its origins lie in my friendship with Frank Gillard, a Somerset man and one of the most distinguished of our war correspondents. Field Marshal Montgomery so trusted Frank that, from the moment of his arrival in the Western Desert, he ordered him to set up his broadcasting unit never more than 600 yards from headquarters. 'I want you beside me always,' Montgomery told Frank, 'because through you I will be the first army commander in the history of war to speak simultaneously not only to the men under my command but also to their wives, girlfriends and to the great British public.'

After the war, Frank returned to the BBC where he was a distinguished director of BBC Radio. When he retired, he was asked by the Director-General to interview all the leading executives of the BBC as the basis for the corporation's radio and television archive. When I became Chairman of the Governors in 1986 I met Frank for the first time, though heaven knows how often I had heard his voice on the radio. All together he interviewed me some fifteen times over my ten years at the BBC and we became very close friends, usually winding up a two-hour session with a bottle of champagne at his club or mine.

We exchanged many reminiscences and he persuaded me, against my will, to record my experiences at Anzio and as a prisoner of war. I was wounded within four days of landing at Anzio. I did not even have time to meet the fellow officers of my battalion. And for forty-two years I was ashamed of my war because all my contemporaries in the army, at school and at Oxford had done so much and I had done so little. I even avoided regimental reunions because I thought I should be an anonymous stranger. But in the end I gave Frank the story.

The writer Christopher Booker, who lives two miles away from me in Somerset, knew that I had made a tape with Frank and was anxious to hear it, so I asked him and his wife to lunch. When she dropped out, I invited another neighbour in her place, Amanda Markham. I didn't really want to listen to it with just one other person. After lunch we sat down and put on the tape. It was the first time that I had heard it and I am bound to say that, by the time it had finished, I had found it quite interesting. I looked up and both Christopher and Amanda seemed moved. He immediately persuaded me to let him send it to the *Daily Telegraph* with a strong recommendation that a transcript should be published.

I was very apprehensive and thought nothing would come of it, but, as with many things in my life, I was proved wrong. On Saturday 9 May 1998 the *Telegraph* published an edited version of the tape over two pages. The contents of this tape are reproduced from the *Telegraph* version, give or take a word or two, in the following chapter. Suddenly old friends, colleagues and relatives were ringing and writing to me about it. My whole view of a crucial time in my life was turned on its head. Something I had at heart regarded with embarrassment and about which I had kept quiet for over four decades was being celebrated by people whose opinions and judgement I valued.

A year later Macmillan approached me and suggested that the *Telegraph* article might make a good basis for writing my memoirs. Eventually, with great doubt and apprehension, I was persuaded to say yes. I still have grave doubts but my life falls easily into three phases: the war and the five years of hospital that followed it; the newspapers – the *Daily Mail*, *The Times* and *Sunday Times* (and their year-long shutdown); and my spell as Chairman of the BBC.

Writing this in my own words has forced me to be clear about what this book is and what it is not. And what it is not is an annotated autobiography with a long list of sources and references at the back. It is not a document of record. If you want to know about the role of the Grenadier Guards in the Second World War or a history of Fleet Street since that war, or, above all, the developments and turbulent trials of the BBC, you should look elsewhere. The main source of this book is my memory, aided and abetted by valued friends like Arthur Brittenden, Phyllis Cunningham, Clare Denman, Lord Ferrers, Carole Haynes, Lady Penelope Robson, Lord Rees-Mogg, Mike Mander, Sir Edward Ford, John Grigg, Rowan Wadham, Daphne Dempster, Michael Stevenson, Patricia Hodgson, John McCormick and, above all, Frank Gillard, who died in October 1998 on the night that the German Ambassador gave a dinner in my honour to which he had been hugely looking forward. If there is any merit in this book it stems from Frank, and it is for that reason that I dedicate it to him, along with my family.

So here it is – a strictly personal account of my life as I saw it at the time and of the controversial events in which I have been involved. I claim no credit for what has happened to me. As the title of the book seeks to convey, I believe that all our lives are decided by chance and I have simply been one of the lucky ones, blessed throughout my life with more good luck than bad.

Marmaduke Hussey
Somerset, May 2001

Chapter One

It was still dark. Norman and I, along with two guardsmen, jumped into a deep, very heavily brambled gulley. A German came up to the gulley and said: 'We know you are down there. Unless you come out and surrender we will throw grenades into the ditch and fire a machine gun down it.' And I am bound to say that at that moment I was beginning to think enough was enough, but Norman said: 'Oh, no, no, we will sit this one out.' So the German gave a count of three and we lay very, very close to the earth. Down came the grenade, then the machine-gun fire. It was a dicey moment, but, somehow or other, because of the brambles we didn't get a touch. Amazing.

We could hear the Germans milling all round us and lay there for about two hours. We thought we should try to get back to battalion headquarters. We knew roughly the direction it was in, and decided to do this immediately before dawn. We took off our distinctive steel helmets and our packs, so that we were stripped down to our uniforms with nothing on our heads. I had a grenade and a revolver. I think Norman had the same, and we started off when it was still dark, trying to wend our way through the German lines.

We got through one German position rather successfully. We were challenged. Norman was ahead, I was at the back, with two guardsmen in between, and I can remember quite clearly saying: '*Offizier, gute Nacht!*' I don't speak any German but hoped for the best. I could have put my hand on the head of the

Spandau gunner as we walked through. That was the first lucky bit. The second was less fortunate.

It was beginning to get light when we came to what we thought was the front-line trench – which is exactly what it turned out to be. We decided to charge and jump over the trench. I thought I might drop the grenade on them as I jumped over, but I decided it was rather dangerous to take the pin out of a grenade, so I didn't. I cleared the Germans but on landing – I suppose because I was rather tired – I slipped. It was now light, and I was in the unfortunate position of being on the ground about three yards away from a trench full of Germans. I can remember it flashing through my mind, 'I've had it now. Should I say *Kamerad* and surrender?' Surrender was unthinkable. I just couldn't do it. I suppose it comes down to one's training, being in a good regiment and the way one had been brought up.

I thought I would get up and go for it. As I was getting up off the ground, I was hit by the burst of fire. That's why I was hit in the way I was – through my right hand, one through my right leg, and the one that later caused me so much trouble, in my spine between the fourth and fifth lumbar vertebrae. I was lucky. I was brought down by the worst shot in the German army. He couldn't miss but he didn't kill me. I suppose I am one of very few people who has been hit by a burst of machine-gun fire from three yards and who knew it was about to happen. Initially it wasn't as bad as one would expect. It was like a great big thump. The pain immediately afterwards was acute and I fell unconscious. When I regained consciousness it was broad daylight and there were Germans standing all round me. They carried me back into their trench.

We were a close family. My father had spent his life as a colonial civil servant, mainly in Africa. In those days it was not unusual for fathers, or indeed both parents, to be abroad, separated from their children for one or two years at a stretch. Britain had an enormous empire to be governed and defended. To do so large numbers of the armed forces and the Indian, Sudan and colonial services went abroad as a lifetime career. It made for a difficult home life as children did not see their parents for long stretches.

Many were sent to school back in England which was an equally arduous separation.

The only time we were abroad together as a family was in Uganda, between 1925 and 1929. My father later described those years in his memoirs as among the happiest of his life and cited part of the pleasure as 'having my family around me'. He was Director of Education and my sister Helen was born in Kampala in April 1926. I was almost three at the time. When my father was promoted to do the same job in Nigeria, the first time there had ever been a single Director of Education for the whole of that large country, we did not accompany him. The climate was considered too bad for English families and there was schooling for my sister and me to organize. So it wasn't until much later that we lived together again as a family – and then in England

I hardly remember Uganda. It must have been a comparatively comfortable life with a fairly large house and plenty of servants. My father always loved the Africans and they him. My earliest memory is being taken out in a pushchair by my nanny when an old African came forward and presented me with a double banana, two stuck together and very rare – a special gift for the Director of Education's son. My mother enjoyed Uganda but tried to keep English traditions going, so in our last year she bought a turkey for Christmas lunch. It was delivered a month early to be fattened up. We all became very fond of that hapless bird. Mummy could hardly bear to kill it so, to soften the blow, gave it a shot of whisky. As my father said, we must have been the only family in Uganda and possibly the world to celebrate Christmas with a whisky-flavoured turkey.

My father went to Nigeria for spells of eighteen months at a time, with my mother joining him every other year for six months. So I hardly knew him. I remember him coming to say goodbye when I was at my prep school. We went for a gloomy walk around Virginia Water, me in floods of tears, but that was the life that many people lived. His sister Dorothy was a missionary in India, spent her whole adult life there and died there. She had hardly ever been home.

Children were parked out with various relations. By today's

standards this sounds odd, if not inhuman, but there were plenty of cousins to look after us and my father was in touch as much as communications in those days permitted. One Christmas, which we spent with our cousins the Shirleys in London, he promised me a python skin as a present. Every morning for weeks I rushed downstairs to greet the postman. It arrived in the end, a fairly moth-eaten python, about fourteen feet long, but I treasured it. On another occasion, he sent a crate of pineapples to my prep school, considerably enhancing my popularity.

Because of the nature of my father's work, there was no one family home that was a constant in my life. When I was at prep school, we lived in 49 Palace Gardens Terrace in Kensington and I would come back and join my mother and my sister there for the holidays. It was a rented house and we borrowed the furniture from various relations because we had little of our own. In those days, Kensington was considered very downmarket and therefore cheap, well to the west of Mayfair. How times change.

I can remember the house well. It had 126 stairs and, by some weird coincidence, from the fourth-floor nursery window I could look across into the nursery of the house opposite, where many years later my brother-in-law, William Waldegrave, raised his family. At that time, domestic service was one of the major industries in the United Kingdom and very poorly paid. A reasonable cook cost £50 a year. We had a cook, a parlourmaid and a nanny. But then there were no washing machines, dishwashers, tumble driers, fridges, freezers, electric irons, hoovers or, above all, central heating, so it was coal fires, everywhere. More exciting, we could hear the bells of the muffin man as he walked down the street with his square basket balanced on his head and the Wall's ice-cream man on his bicycle. We rushed down, hopefully, for both!

My father retired from the colonial service in February 1936 and became Secretary of the National Society, the body which oversaw all Anglican schools in England and Wales. He was, someone once put it, the Church of England's own Minister for Education. Schooling started in England and for that matter all over Europe not as a state but as a church responsibility. It was only in 1870 that our government became involved. When my father took up his post, there were some 9,000 Church of England schools in the country, educating more than 20 per cent of all children.

His was then an important job and had a grace and favour flat which went with it in Great Peter Street in Westminster. So we gave up the house in Kensington and my parents lived simultaneously in the new flat and in the small house he had bought in Littlehampton, Sussex, for £1,600 because he could foresee the war and thought it would be safe there.

Littlehampton was fine. We all loved bathing in the sea which was only 400 yards away. There was a tennis club and a golf club where my mother was captain of the ladies' team. But safe it was not! It turned out to be approximately the left-hand landing beach if the Germans had invaded, with only the ill-armed Home Guard to defend us. It may seem unlikely now, but we watched the dogfights in the sky, cheering when a German plane fell. We rushed out on our bicycles to see the wreckage and once to watch the Germans dive-bombing Ford Aerodrome nearby.

But we had no roots in Littlehampton and it was, funnily enough, only three years ago that I felt I belonged anywhere when I went to see the church and Old Rectory at Pimperne, near Blandford in Dorset. A friend of a neighbour of ours in Somerset had bought it and invited us to stay. This was where my grandfather, James Hussey, had been vicar for twenty years from 1886 onwards. It is a beautiful, large, double-fronted Georgian house with a very big garden, luxurious by today's standards, although my grandparents were far from well off. The house came with the job and my grandfather was Low Church, indeed unfashionably so at a time when the High wing of the Church of England was in the ascendant. But luckily Martha Hussey, my grandmother, had inherited a little money to ease the strain of six children. Her family, the Hewetts, were successful lawyers and unsuccessful brewers in Reading but fortunately the lawyers' fees made up for the indifferent beer.

When I stayed at the Old Rectory, I slept over the porch in

what must have been my father's room when he was growing up and knelt in St Peter's Church at Pimperne on a tapestry kneeler with the name James Hussey woven into it. My father's middle name was James. It is my middle name and my son's name. So four generations were united by that kneeler. Sadly, my grandfather died in 1920, followed soon afterwards by my grandmother, and before my parents' marriage, so my mother never met them.

My aunt Hilda, another of my father's sisters, wrote a brief account of her memories of Hussey family life at Pimperne. She recalls an isolated place – 'the journey to Blandford by our pony and donkey cart was quite an undertaking on rough roads, stones just laid down and left there for carriage wheels to grind into the surface'. Of the family itself, she writes: 'Our life was very self-contained. We made our own bread; Mrs Barnett came in on a Monday to cope with our laundry. Over the road from the Rectory we had a large walled garden, which provided us with fruit and vegetables. We kept cows, pigs and chickens, so that all we had to buy were supplies of fresh meat, fish and groceries.' The Good Life!

My mother's family had lived from 1897 at Parkgate House – sometimes known, rather misleadingly given its size, as The Cottage – on the Knebworth estate of Lord Lytton in Hertford-shire. She adored it. Her father, Noel Morley, was one of two brothers who married two sisters, Jessie (my grandmother) and Alice Ford. Looking back over various family documents and birth, marriage and death certificates, my grandfather used various descriptions of his occupation. When my mother was born, he called himself a Manchester warehouseman, but later, when she married, he was a director of companies. I believe he and his brother William owned a textile mill in Yorkshire and then sold up to work in the City to which my grandfather went in the morning in his dark suit and bowler hat. He was full of ideas for making money – none worked! The one of which I was always told was a substitute for rubber. 'It looks like rubber, it feels like rubber, it even tastes like rubber.' Unfortunately it didn't work like rubber. It was one of the several unhappy ventures which impoverished my mother's family.

When they left Knebworth in 1906, they built what they thought was rather a pokey house just by the eighth tee on the Worplesdon Golf Course. They were all good golfers and my grandfather had a single-figure handicap. His golf was better than his business and the pokey house, Lychwood, now seems a very substantial one. I have some photographs of it, and it looks lovely with some very good furniture. I don't know what happened to that. Not much of it came to us anyway when the house was sold in 1929 after my grandfather died. My grandmother ended up living in a genteel ladies' hotel on Queen's Gate in Kensington where I used to visit her and have brandy snaps for tea. She had a soft spot for grandsons. Very Victorian.

We were just all right financially but had to live carefully. The exciting relations were my Morley grandmother's family, the Fords. They were perhaps more glamorous than rich, though they were solid, professional and comfortably off by the standards of their times. My great-grandfather was a successful London solicitor with ten children and a large house in Sussex Square near Paddington. He sent all his sons to public school at Repton in Derbyshire (where my father went on a scholarship) and they all excelled there. All but one was head boy; they were all good at games and all went on to Cambridge.

They didn't all, however, live up to their early promise. They became, variously, a schoolmaster, a provincial solicitor, a singer, an England cricketer and an artist. Henry, the artist, was well known in Pre-Raphaelite circles in equal measures for his talent and his close friendship with the actress Mrs Patrick Campbell. He featured in a recent Royal Academy catalogue. I have two of his paintings. One is an excellent oil of the Needles near the Isle of Wight. The other, a classic Pre-Raphaelite painting of an elegant and beautiful naked lady, floating across a starlit sky, was his wedding present to my mother. She never hung it because she thought it was indecent, but I have.

The penultimate Ford son, Lionel, became headmaster of Repton, then Harrow and finally Dean of York. It was Lionel who introduced my parents to each other. My father had been at Repton from 1899 to 1904, and was head boy when Lionel was headmaster. When he later revisited his old master on leave from the Sudan, he said regretfully 'I'm afraid I will never marry.' Lionel replied: 'You have yet to meet my niece, Christine.'

There was a seven-year age difference between my parents. My father was born in April 1885; he was thirty-seven and my mother thirty when they married at Holy Trinity Anglican church in Sloane Street in Chelsea in July 1922. Almost at once they went out together to the Sudan where my father was then working as a district commissioner. My mother enjoyed that part of her life in the colonies. She used to describe buzzing around on a motor bike and long journeys riding a camel across the empty, flat desert. This could create an embarrassing problem. When she wished to 'retire', my father would instruct all the natives to turn to the left which they did with dignity. With equal dignity, my mother turned to the right.

She was born in 1892 and was usually known as Chrissie, though her older sister Hermione and her husband occasionally called her Twip. One of three children, she also had a younger brother Marmaduke. Hermione – known to my mother as Peter – married Viscount Tamworth, later 12th Earl Ferrers, and was a wonderful, warm, generous woman. She went with my grand-father to India for six months after the First World War, as young unattached women often did. There were many unat-tached men in India and few in England. It was there that she met 'Tam'.

We spent the last two Christmases before the second war at Staunton Harold, Hermione and Tam's home in Leicestershire. The Shirleys were a very old Saxon family with a line which goes back beyond the Norman Conquest. Robin Hood was rumoured to be a connection. Less reputable was the unmarried 4th Earl who was the last peer ever to be executed, for murder-ing his butler. He died in great state, driving to Tyburn gallows in his coronation coach, and was hanged by a silken rope.

Staunton was a huge Georgian mansion set in 3,000 acres and alongside was the only High Church Anglican place of worship built during Cromwell's Commonwealth. It had cost the Shirleys' ancestor, Sir Robert Shirley, dear. He was imprisoned in the Tower of London and died there. But the church had a most memorable and much-quoted dedication: 'In the year 1653, when all things sacred throughout the nation were either demolished or profaned, Sir Robert Shirley, Baronet, founded this church whose singular praise it is to have done the best things in ye worst times, and hoped them in the most calamitous.'

The church was beautiful. The household would walk over for the morning service on Sunday, with my aunt and uncle bringing up the rear. The pews were arranged into boxes, with a door at the side. The men sat on the left, women on the right. It was magical going to Staunton with its priceless setting overlooking a lake, butlers, coal fires everywhere, but no electricity. After the Second World War, the cost of upkeep was too great and Tam decided to sell it. It broke his heart and he died in 1954 on the night before the sale, leaving it to his son Robin, my cousin. It is now a Ryder-Cheshire Home. Robin himself has added lustre to the history of the Shirleys, taking up his seat in the House of Lords when twenty-six and winning, as I can vouch myself, popularity and respect from all sides of the chamber. In 1999, when it came to electing a number of hereditaries to retain their seats in the reformed House, Robin came top and in reply to my letter of congratulation wrote: 'I can't believe it. I have never been top of anything before, even at school.'

Hermione lived on until 1969 and our cousin, Edward Ford, who served both King George VI and the present Queen as assistant private secretary with great distinction, remembers her as 'a great expansive lady, always laughing'. About my mother, by contrast, he says, 'You always had to make her laugh.' Another cousin, Clare Denman, recalls her as 'awe-inspiring'. Edward says she was very good, very sound but slightly formidable at just under six foot, a fraction taller than my father. I remember her differently, of course, as a warm, affectionate mother, always telling me a story before I went to sleep.

The Shirleys and the Husseys grew up together, living close together in London, the Shirleys in Victoria Road with their three children, Elizabeth, Penelope and Robin. We spent our summers together in Littlehampton, hiring adjoining houses and bathing every day – before my parents bought their house there. Often the Troutbecks, other Ford cousins, would join us.

I was called Marmaduke after my mother's brother who was killed on the first day of the Battle of the Somme. He had been to Winchester and Cambridge and was a friend of Tam's which was the connection. He was commissioned in the Yorkshire Light Infantry. I still have some of his letters from the Front, written in pencil. I can hardly bear to read them. In January 1916, he wrote from the trenches: 'Oh! This is the life. I love it, not the fighting because I don't know anything about that, but just being out here. And I'm not twenty-one yet. Everything is just right for me. It's the finest school in the world and as you do this war, so you'll do everything for the rest of your life.' But for him there was to be no more life.

My mother never forgot the arrival of the telegram, saying he was missing. My grandmother's face and her words when she opened the telegram remained with her always: 'I am afraid. Very afraid.' When it became increasingly obvious that another war was brewing, that memory became especially poignant.

The two sisters – Chrissie and Hermione – had little expectation of marriage after the first war with so many young men killed, but they promised their mother that if either of them had a son, the first one would be called Marmaduke, after their brother. My grandmother, however, could never bear to call me Dukie – which was what Marmaduke was always called – and preferred Jimmy, my second name.

It is difficult now to understand the devastating effect of the First World War casualties. England had fought many wars, won most of them, but always as an away game on the Continent. The last invasion was in 1066. We sent our small armies to Europe to fight the strategic wars, but largely with foreign armies for which we paid – mercenaries by any other name. Even at Waterloo, the English forces made up less than half of Wellington's army. Being an island, our concentration was on the sea, and the great naval battles down the ages involved far fewer people than a land war.

The appalling casualties of the First World War left virtually no family unscathed. As well as my mother's brother, Harold Hussey, my father's only brother, was also killed fighting in Mesopotamia after he had survived the Somme. His body was never found.

After her brother was killed, my mother went out to France with the VADs – the Voluntary Aid Detachment. In both world wars, many women joined the VADs. It was a hard, stressful but invaluable nursing service. I was looked after marvellously by them in Roehampton Hospital. In the First World War, many of the recruits were young women accustomed to wearing gloves whenever they went out, accompanied by servants to carry their parcels. Suddenly, they upped sticks and went to France. In less than a week they were transferred from a leisured life of comfort to nursing, sometimes under fire, in huge wards, crammed with many terribly injured men, few drugs and only primitive medical aids. It was a rough, tough life and they were a gallant and wonderful service. My wife's great-aunt, Hermione Hichens, was one of them. She had a lovely voice and used to sing and give concerts to the wounded. She once told Sue and me that one day when she returned to France from a week's leave the train stopped and she saw three of her old dancing partners on the platform. They had an hilarious lunch. Within a week all three men were dead.

The loss of a sibling was one of the things my parents had in common. Another was a shared interest in sport. My father had been an outstanding athlete. At Repton in his final year he won seven of the ten main athletics events, setting various records into the bargain. Later he was president of the Oxford University Athletics Club for two years. He was awarded his Blue for athletics in his first year and later ran the hurdles in the Olympic Games in London in 1908. He got through one round but, in those days, only the winner of each heat progressed so he never made it to the podium. I like to think now that, under the modern system with fastest losers also getting through to the next round, he might, with a bit of luck, have got a bronze. He also played soccer for Oxford.

In March 1907 the university magazine *Isis* featured him as

one of its 'idols', remarking that despite his many achievements
in sport he was 'a cheery companion, warm-hearted and open,
whose friendship all may win, whose enmity none need fear'.
He evidently spent so much time on games and socializing that
he only got a third when he left Hertford College; I believe this
was a matter of great distress to his father, though quite why, I
don't know, since he also only got a third – in theology in 1874.

My mother, like all her family, had a good eye. She was an
excellent golfer, had a handicap in single figures in Africa and, I
think, ten in this country. When they played together, to my
father's intense irritation, he would address the ball with all the
enthusiasm of an amateur boxer and belt it. It would bounce
along the ground for about seventy-five yards. My mother would
then step up and with an effortless swing send her ball soaring
towards the green.

My father was a deeply religious man but I don't think it
ever occurred to him to follow his father into the church. The
moral side came out in his work in the colonial service. Edward
Ford, who knew him well and used frequently to lunch with
him, likens him to Eric Liddell, the clean-living runner, who
went on to Olympic glory and whose story was told in the film
Chariots of Fire. Edward and my father used to lunch at each
other's clubs, my father's being the Athenaeum where, after the
second war, he took me. Sometimes we saw a small, rather slight
man with a moustache lunching alone. It was the Prime Minister,
Clement Attlee. Wouldn't happen today.

It was after leaving Oxford in 1908 that my father joined the
Colonial Civil Service. In those days, the various colonial services
had the pick of the best young men from Oxford and Cambridge. The Indian was perhaps the most highly prized, but the
Sudan Political Service, established by Lord Cromer in 1899,
came a close second. It had a reputation for recruiting Oxbridge
graduates who had excelled on the sports field – it was dubbed
'the land of blacks ruled by blues'. My father joined it and
initially worked as a tutor at Gordon College in Khartoum. The
attraction to idealistic young men like him was that they could,
while still in their twenties, effectively run large swathes of
Africa on enlightened principles.

He was certainly enlightened. After four years at Gordon College, he was seconded as a District Commissioner at Sennar. He also served as Senior Inspector in the Education Department in Khartoum and went on a special mission to Somaliland in November 1920 to advise on education. He moved to Uganda in 1925, having earlier compiled a report on how its education service might be improved. He had this great feeling for Africans, but that went down badly with bureaucrats. He was at pains to learn their language – Arabic in the case of the Sudan – and he told his masters, for instance, that it would be much better to teach people in British Africa how to till their land more effectively rather than waste time teaching the intricacies of parliamentary democracy. Looking back now, the history of Africa after decolonization would have changed greatly for the better if there had been more concentration on the land and less on the politics.

While in Uganda, he struck up a particular rapport with J.H. Oldham, the highly influential secretary of the International Missionary Council. Together they were firm advocates of the 'adaptation theory' of African education which, broadly speaking, meant avoiding trying to westernize pupils in African schools. Another pet subject of my father was the need to educate African women, which met with resistance from all sides. While in Nigeria, he was able to appoint the first female schools' inspector. 'I felt,' he later commented, 'that it was only when African women were holding positions of importance in the country that the population as a whole could be led to value a good education for their girls.'

On a broader point, writing later of his time in the Sudan, he described what he called the 'paternalistic' style of government – a handful of whites telling Africans what was best for them. 'There must in the future be more and more devolution of power and authority to local people,' he urged, 'in view of the vastness of the territory, the multiplicity of languages and the widely differing modes of life and forms of rule.' Another bad mark with the bureaucrats and another good mark for him.

And with his interest in sport, he believed that as soon as we taught the Ugandans and Kenyans how to run round a track, they would win all the medals in the Olympic Games. That was thought to be heresy, though now at Uganda's national athletics championships they still compete for a Hussey Shield. I often think how pleased he would be to see his words come true, though he would not, of course, take any pride in his own powers of prophecy. Later in life he was a contributor to *African World* magazine and the then editor, James Gray, summed my father up well when he wrote: 'He was an educationalist of distinction . . . a living example of how much a man can accomplish if he does not care who gets the credit'. Not, I fear, true of me.

Michael Okorodudu, a Nigerian chief, remarked at the time that my father was the first colonial official he had encountered who wore shorts and an open-neck shirt and sat down to eat Nigerian meals with Nigerian boys and girls.

The African legacy still occasionally visits me. A few years ago, I was telephoned by a man of property from the Sudan. He wanted to meet me and, when he did, it was to explain that when he was a small boy he developed a very badly infected leg. He was effectively dying of the poison. But my father took him into his house, kept him there and changed his dressing every day. He lived.

If my father had to choose between saying what he thought to be true or what was expected of him, he would always do the first. That did not help promotion. He got to be an acting Governor in Nigeria but never held a top job. He wasn't ambitious enough for himself, or at least his ambition was tempered by his determination to do what was best for the Africans. He retired at fifty when it was clear he was never going further. He didn't fit in. But his memory lives on as a man who always wanted to change any system he believed was wrong and counter-productive.

When I was Chief Executive of Times Newspapers, I entertained a member of the Nigerian cabinet (I think we were after the advertising). He was very struck by my name and asked if I was a relation of Eric Hussey. He had been educated at the university college in Nigeria that still bears my father's name, and had run for Hussey cups. Later I was invited to a reception at the Nigerian Embassy. When I was about to leave, I was taken to one side because the ambassador and minister wanted to have a private word with me. I waited. They then came in with this fantastic offer. The ambassador referred to a forthcoming visit to be made by the Queen to Nigeria at which my wife would be in attendance, as lady-in-waiting. They had been on the telephone to the president who wished to invite me to Nigeria, at their expense, over the period of the royal visit, so that I could see my wife and visit the university college named after my father. A marvellous and moving gesture. Sue was at Balmoral at the time and so I thought I would ring her in the morning. I listened to the news at 8 a.m. The first item was that there had been a coup in Nigeria and the president had fled the country. What cruel timing.

Once back in London and working for the National Society, my father continued to hanker after Africa and succeeded in returning when in August 1942 he was sent by the British government to Ethiopia to assist the restored Emperor Haile Selassie in rebuilding his country's education system. Later, after the war, he was for three years in charge of the Middle East department of the British Council where I was on the boards much later, for ten years.

He was, of course, sad not to have got further in the colonial service, as was my mother on his behalf. Looking back, I'm not surprised his views were unpopular. He was at least fifty years ahead of his time.

There were two sorts of people in my family: decent, easy-going good Christians like my father and the ambitious go-getters like me. I don't think I fully appreciated his true virtue. He was a good man, a kind man, with no thought of self and no thought of ambition. He had great charm. Once, when home from Nigeria on leave, he was driving through the centre of Oxford when he saw through a shop window an African he knew. He stopped his car in the middle of the street and went in to talk to him. When a policeman came along to remonstrate, my father replied that he was used to the wilds of Africa where you stopped your car anywhere. He got away with it.

He was godfather to my cousin Penelope who remembers

him well. He was always cheerful, always energetic, sweeping her up and throwing her into the air. She says he must have passed on his energy to me. What he certainly passed on to me in large measure was his love of sport. I was surrounded by sportsmen on both sides of the family.

The Fords were outstanding, especially at cricket. In 1942, when I appeared for Oxford, I was the fourth successive generation of the family to have played in the Varsity match. First came G. J. Ford who played for Oxford in 1839 in only the fifth-ever Varsity match. Then there were his nephews, A. F. J. Ford, who batted number eleven and bowled for Cambridge in the 1878 fixture, and his brother Francis Ford – F. G. J. Ford – who took three wickets in the 1887 match, then moved up the order and by 1890 was one of the Cambridge openers and its captain. Next in line was their nephew, Neville Ford, who played for Oxford between 1928 and 1930. Neville was my mother's first cousin.

Of them all, Francis Ford was the most distinguished. When I was Chairman of the BBC, a friend rang up and said, 'Do you know your great-uncle still holds the record for the fastest hundred ever made at Lord's in a first-class match?' I didn't so I rang up Brian Johnston, as *Test Match Special* was on, and asked him.

'Oh, that will be F.G.J. Ford, Cambridge, Middlesex and England,' said Brian.

'That's the chap.'

'It doesn't sound very likely to me.'

'It doesn't to me either. Why don't you ask the bearded wonder (Bill Frindall, the scorer) and ring me back?'

He did. 'Do you want the good news or the bad news?'

'I'll take the good news.'

'Well, it's true, 112 in 55 minutes in 1897.'

'What's the bad news?'

'The opposition wasn't very good. It was the Gentlemen of the United States of America.'

'Oh Lord.'

Five years later, the Prime Minister, John Major, gave a dinner in my honour to mark my retirement as Chairman of the

BBC. Knowing how keen he was on cricket I thought I would tell the story, but knowing what an ace he was on statistics I thought I should check first. So I rang John Woodcock, the distinguished *Times* cricket correspondent, and asked him. He rang back two days later and said: 'Well, it's absolutely true. The only thing that's wrong is that it wasn't the Gentlemen of the USA, it was the Gentlemen of Philadelphia.'

'That makes it even worse.'

'No, it doesn't, it's the other way round. At that time, Philadelphia had a superb cricket team including the best fast bowler in the world, J.B. "Bart" King, which reflects a great deal more credit on your uncle Francis but ruins the story, so I'd leave it out if I were you.'

I did.

Like many sons, I suppose I was closer to my mother than my father who was often away. My mother was staunch and when we lived in our tiny house in Littlehampton, she got on with it. She was capable – chairman of the local hospital there and later at Cuckfield when they moved. During the war she ran all the hospital libraries in Sussex, a bigger job than it sounds.

We lived very simply. My parents had just enough money for the school fees. We hardly ever had wine and only one glass of sherry on Sundays. For a long time we didn't have a car until my father bought one for £10. My mother made new covers for the seats. Taxis, never.

However, Uncle Charles Hewett, one of my Hussey grandmother's relatives, had left some money which my father's sister, Hilda, discovered by looking up his will at Somerset House. It turned out that Charles – a successful Reading lawyer some thought to be the model for Soames Forsyte in John Galsworthy's *The Forsyte Saga* – left a nice fortune to be divided between my father and his surviving sisters Hilda and Ella on the death of his second wife, Amy. My father always talked hopefully of his ship coming home, but probably only a canoe! Sadly, Amy died two days after he did in 1958, so he never knew the size of his legacy, which was about £30,000, a large sum in those days. It went first to my mother and then on to my sister, Helen.

I was not very close to Helen. She was someone for whom life never really went well. She was never strong, always white and washed out, as one of my cousins recalls. My mother put it down to being born in Africa and not getting the right nourishment as a child. She was rather in my shadow. While I captured prizes and won races, she struggled and then later was dominated by my mother who, particularly as she grew older, wasn't always sympathetic. Helen was shy and awkward but she had a simple, gentle character. When she died we were touched by the number of people in Cuckfield who came to her funeral and all that they said about her. She loved animals and, in her will, left legacies to twenty different animal charities. As her executor, I doubled them in her memory.

In her quiet way, she had a good brain and once achieved the top letter in *The Times* with a characteristic, but caustic, political comment. Later, she was diagnosed with Alzheimer's. I kept her out of hospital for as long as possible because she loved her house in Cuckfield and above all her dog. Fortunately its death and her departure to a superb Alzheimer's hospital in Haywards Heath coincided.

My parents were ambitious for me and I was for myself. So they sent me to a well-known kindergarten, Rene Ironside's in Elverston Place. I had to walk there from Palace Gardens Terrace every day and back through Kensington Gardens and round the Round Pond. Seventy years later it is still a walk I enjoy.

At eight, I went on to an excellent prep school – Pinewood, in Hampshire – as a boarder. My father's best man, Richard Young, was an old school friend from Repton who had represented England at both football and cricket. He had then become a housemaster, teaching maths and cricket, at Eton. I was put down for his house, but I didn't want to go to Eton. I wanted to go to Rugby. I'm not sure why – probably because of games. Anyway, I went there and my father got a reduction in the fees from £60 a term to £50 because I was considered to be promising. Luckily, I passed in top and Pinewood got a half day's holiday to celebrate. There was no trouble getting in all the teams but, despite being unable to sing in tune, I turned my attention to the choir because they had the best annual picnic which much encouraged any boy with a trace of musical talent. I did some research and qualified by volunteering to pump the school organ at every service. Up and down, up and down – exhausting, but the picnic was well worth the effort.

Rugby was a good school. I liked the ethos, a place to train empire-builders, clergymen, teachers, public servants, public-spirited individuals – all the things that were part of my own childhood. Most of my contemporaries were from similar backgrounds. There were some who were rich but we were unaware of any difference.

It was also a tough school. Rugby had very high academic standards and regularly won many scholarships at Oxford and Cambridge. I was in both the school cricket XI and rugby XV for two years. My old school friend, Rowan Wadham, who was also in both XIs, remembers my sporting achievements in terms of my size and speed – jumping higher than anyone else in the line outs and then running like a scalded cat is how he puts it. I was better at rugby than cricket where I oiled my way into the team as a slow left-arm bowler. When I was a child, my mother got a telegram from my great-uncle Francis, scorer of that fastest century, saying: 'Chrissie, if your Dukie is left-handed, don't change it. A slow left-arm bowler is the easiest way into any cricket side.' He was right. It got me into the Oxford team.

Rugby was a secure, happy environment, but the war broke out while I was there. It didn't affect us directly at once, although some old Rugbyans who had been at Dunkirk in 1940 came down to the school a week later to play cricket. We looked at them in awe. War began to impinge on our consciousness. As a schoolboy I filled sandbags to put around the hospital at Littlehampton in 1938 when war was imminent. Later we listened in our studies to Churchill's famous speech about fighting them on the beaches. I was in Lower Sixth Classified (for six terms which must have been a record) and within a week we had translated passages from the text into Latin and Greek. I don't think my generation shared the appalled apprehension of our parents. On the cusp between adolescence and

adulthood, we were old enough to find war exciting but too
young to understand what it meant in terms of human lives.

It slowly hit us. We spent the night in the cellars while
Coventry, ten miles away, was bombed to rubble. Wirty Hin-
gley, captain of the Rugby XV in 1940 and a scholar, left in the
middle of summer term and was killed before the next cricket
season had started.

In the June of that year, Churchill issued the call to join the
Local Defence Volunteers – later renamed the Home Guard.
Younger television viewers will never realize how true to life
Dad's Army is. My father commanded a platoon in Littlehampton – their job was to defend the coast with the equivalent of
one gun, some pitchforks and anything else that was handy. My
mother was in the Red Cross and my sister in the Observer
Corps. In my summer holidays I worked on the land – probably
my greatest contribution to the war effort. It was a real family
affair, though there was nothing unusual in this. War service in
some form or other embraced every family.

At Rugby we all had to do fire-watching. All the senior boys
were in the Home Guard. Every night four of us and a master,
armed with loaded rifles, stood guard on Rugby Water Tower.
We were waiting for the parachutists, perhaps, we had been
told, disguised as nuns.

I really don't think that the Rugby Water Tower was high on
the list of German objectives.

Chapter Two

In November 1941, I sat the scholarship examination for Trinity College, Oxford. As luck would have it, I had been concussed in a school rugby match the week before so had spent three days in the sanatorium, the best preparation, I suspect. If I'd been fit I would have swotted like crazy and probably failed. I was a history specialist, but in addition to the standard history papers all entrants had to write an essay. The chosen theme was always one word. In my case, Luck. In retrospect that was appropriate and prophetic, my argument being that everyone has good luck and bad luck. I illustrated it with several historical examples like that of Frederick the Great. On 5 January 1762, Frederick was at war simultaneously with the full might of the Austrian and Russian armies. Over 100,000 of his troops had been killed and he was desperate. Then the Empress Elizabeth of Russia died and was succeeded by Peter III, a great admirer of Frederick's who lifted the siege at once. 'A miracle,' Frederick said. I call it luck. The trick is to capitalize on good luck. Looking back on my life, chance has played a major part in it – as it does in many lives – and in my case most of it has been good.

I did well in the examination and was offered an open scholarship. When I heard, I went to thank my history tutor at Rugby, a brilliant teacher called Rob Watt. He was also a great exponent of the put-down. He just said: 'Why don't you thank the games master?' In those days, if you wanted to go to Oxbridge from a good school, you just went there. It was a question of choosing the college and applying. And some colleges certainly favoured those who were good at sport. But a scholarship had to be won. It was worth £100 a year, a lot of money.

That Christmas I found myself hovering between three worlds – school, Oxford and the army. Before taking the Oxford exam, I had gone, in the autumn of 1941, to Wellington Barracks in Birdcage Walk, in London, for an interview with the Grenadier Guards. As Christopher and Edward Ford were already in that regiment, it seemed the obvious thing to do. They were twins, first cousins of my mother and sons of Lionel Ford. They had encouraged me to apply as did their mother. 'Dukie,' she said, 'when you join the army it is important to join a good regiment like the Grenadiers. You get the best NCOs.'

For all my contemporaries, the choice was usually a simple one between the army, navy or air force. I do remember three who, all having won classical scholarships to Oxford, went to train as Japanese interpreters. It didn't sound very dangerous. I just hope that I never said as much when we met again after the war. It wasn't until the 1980s that I learnt that all three had been at Bletchley – the highly secret code-breaking centre.

At that stage I was just eighteen and the Grenadiers suggested that joining straightaway might be too early. While they had suffered casualties at Dunkirk in 1940, none of their three infantry battalions was then in the main theatres of war in Africa or the Middle East. Their three tank battalions were being trained in England for the future invasion of Europe. So casualties were light. They could afford to suggest a year at Oxford before joining up. Looking back I think there was a recognition in the army that too many young men of eighteen had been killed in the first war, especially the young officers whose prime responsibility was to lead from the front. Second time round, they tried to hold them back a bit. But, of course, that didn't survive the landings in Europe. By 1945, when casualties were heavy, such scruples were abandoned.

In my case, once the news of my scholarship came through just before Christmas, it meant that I could look forward to a year at Oxford. I went up in January 1942. Had there not been a war, I would have started the following September and stayed three years. My father had planned for me to go to the Sorbonne

in Paris for a year before Oxford, his typically progressive idea
to teach me a language and give me a well-rounded education.
The war put a stop to that.

The year at Oxford was magical. My rooms at Trinity were
in the Garden Quad looking over the beautiful lawns designed
by Sir Christopher Wren. In those days, there were still scouts
to look after you. They would lay a coal fire every day and serve
meals in your rooms. Oxford was divided between students who
were working – there were many medics because of the urgent
need for doctors – and those like myself who were spending a
year at university having a ball before going into the forces. We
had tutorials, and I apparently passed two exams though heaven
knows how. Life was very relaxed as if in anticipation of what
lay ahead. Anything might happen. So work at our books did
not seem a high priority. Why not enjoy life.

We were told which lectures to go to – though I don't
remember always following the advice. Two afternoons a week
were given over to the Officer Training Corps – OTC – and then
there were games. In winter, rugby, and in summer, cricket. My
left-arm bowling got me into the university XI. I still have the
cuttings from *The Times* and the *Sunday Times* for the Varsity
cricket match in June 1942. According to *The Times*, 'M. J.
Hussey was the only bowler who could get the ball past the bat.'
Its stablemate was more mixed: 'Hussey, a long-legged, left-
armed bowler whose run-up suggests a floral dance had Matthews [the Cambridge opening batsman] all but stumped and
alone of the bowlers kept a length.' It was the best bowling
performance I ever managed, but Cambridge still won. It stood
me in good stead, however, because all through 1943, before I
went off to Italy with the Grenadiers, I used to get invited to
play cricket or rugby nearly every Saturday, thereby missing the
battalion parade to the fury of my fellow subalterns.

In the Michaelmas term of 1942, I was poised to achieve my
life's ambition to play rugby for Oxford against Cambridge. I
was much better at rugby than cricket. The match was scheduled
for a Tuesday and the following Monday I was due to join my
regiment at Pirbright, the Guards' depot. A couple of weeks
earlier playing for Oxford I tackled an English international

three-quarter, who handed me off hard. I fell and fractured a small bone in my right hand. It was painful, but the Oxford captain still wanted me to play against Cambridge, even with my hand bound up. I went to see a doctor to check this out.

'What chance do I have of getting through this game?' I asked.

'Well, you certainly have no better than an even chance of ending the game with your hand in no worse state than it is now,' he replied.

I said: 'That might mean that I can't join the army on my arranged date.'

'That's a matter for you and the army.'

So I told the captain of the team that I couldn't play. It broke my heart. My life's ambition and I ended up as a touch judge. Of course I could have played but in December 1942, with the war gathering pace, to play a rugby match and to postpone joining the army seemed the wrong order of priority. It is strange how some comparatively minor events assume greater significance with hindsight. At that time, there was a great pressure to speed up the commissioning of young officers and get them out to Africa or Italy as soon as possible. It was a conveyor belt. A great friend, the historian John Grigg, another Grenadier, pointed this out to me. 'That changed your life. If you'd been delayed, you would never have been wounded at Anzio.' I replied: 'I could have been killed in the drive up through Italy. It's all a matter of how you look at things.' Chance again.

I travelled to Pirbright for eight weeks of pre-OCTU – Officer Corps Training Unit – training with a Trinity colleague, Paddy Matthews, who was joining the Irish Guards and was later badly wounded in the stomach. We stopped off at Waterloo to share a bottle of disgusting Algerian wine and then apprehensively boarded our train. We took a taxi from the station to the guardroom, but thought it might look rather bad turning up in a taxi, so we made it stop 300 yards short, and walked in carrying our suitcases. We had eight weeks there. Sheer hell. Up at six each morning. Followed by an hour, maybe an hour and a half, every morning on the square, being drilled by an ex-prison warder who was alleged to have flogged the Mayfair playboys. Whatever they had done, they had my sympathy.

In among all the drills, the marching, the discipline and no free time there was one unlikely startling element of adventure. One night our squad of officer cadets, dressed in denims with rifles, helmets, maps but no money, were sent on an exercise. We were each pushed out of the back of the truck, in darkness, and told to find our way to a map reference by 5 p.m. the next afternoon. As Perry Worsthorne, later a distinguished editor of the *Sunday Telegraph*, disappeared, he thrust a piece of paper in my hand and said: 'Try to get to this address.' So that became my objective.

The first thing was to raise some money which I managed to do by borrowing £3 from someone at a pub who took pity on my plight. Technically, we were not meant to cadge money – it wouldn't have been so easy behind enemy lines. But once I had it I got to a train station and bought a ticket to London. Once there it was not difficult to find my way to the address Perry had given me in Campden Hill Road in Notting Hill.

I arrived and pressed the bell, which was answered by a butler. 'Mr Hussey I assume. You are expected, sir, but first of all you might wish to change.' I went upstairs, took off my denims and changed into a silk dressing gown and pyjamas, then went down for dinner. Perry was looking very much at home, not surprisingly as it was the home of his mother, married then to Sir Montagu Norman, the Governor of the Bank of England.

We had a delicious dinner and the next day we consulted each other on what to do next.

'Well,' said Perry, 'we don't have to get to Reading until about 5 p.m. so we can have an easy morning, then go and have lunch in Soho at Au Jardin des Gourmets.' This was an insight to a lifestyle which was totally foreign to my experience, but I was happy to go along with it. I'd never been to a restaurant in Soho before, certainly nowhere of that calibre. Even in the war it was extremely luxurious. We parked our rifles and helmets in the Gents, and had a very good lunch after which we took a taxi (of course) to Paddington where we caught the train to Reading.

When we got there I said, 'What do we do now?'

'Oh,' said Perry, 'we take another taxi out to the map reference.'

We may not have been good soldiers, but we were good map readers, so we had no difficulty locating exactly where to go. Again, arrival by taxi wasn't quite in the spirit of the exercise, so we stopped it about 400 yards short, muddied our uniforms and hands, put on our rifles and steel helmets and marched in, aping with some difficulty the exhaustion of twenty-four hours or more on the road. When we passed the platoon commander, he remarked: 'Good heavens, Worsthorne and Hussey. You're the first. That is a real surprise.'

We got great credit from our officers, but rather less from our colleagues, most of whom slogged through fields and ditches in the dark and arrived absolutely exhausted – except for another small group of the more affluent who, I suspect, spent the night in the Dorchester.

After four months at the OCTU at Aldershot, in June 1943 I was gazetted as a second lieutenant in the Grenadier Guards and sent to Victoria Barracks, Windsor, their training battalion. I was proud to have been commissioned in the regiment and my father supplemented my military pay with £150 per annum which he said he would have given me for Oxford.

Being absolutely hopeless at anything mechanical – then and now (the internet has got me beat) – I opted for the infantry, with my feet on the ground. It was hard but, as the adjutant said, 'If anything really important happens, like a girlfriend coming to London, you can have a late pass.' The term girlfriend was different in those days. It could literally be a friend who was a girl. But as we were all going abroad soon discipline was relatively light. Except for the Saturday morning battalion parade which was a two-hour drill followed by the battalion run. To the fury of my fellow subalterns, I kept missing it because I was always being asked to play in some match. Then came the day when no one asked me to play.

This run was all round Windsor Great Park and ended with the whole length of the Long Walk up to the castle itself. I realized that because I had been absent so often I needed to make a special effort, but was appalled at the pace set by the tough old sergeants. Especially as it was a warm October day. I just about managed to keep up with the leading group as we turned onto the Long Walk. A drill sergeant shouted at me: 'Keep at it, sir, hold your head up, sir, show some guts, sir, pull yourself together, sir.' I kept going. Soon there were just three of us left, the other two previous winners. The first fainted and then the other fell out. I was completely knackered and slowed down. I could see the finishing post 300 yards away, with a group of senior officers standing there. I pulled myself together to stagger the last 150 yards. I think I was the only officer to win the run for ages. As I tottered past the Commanding Officer, he said, 'Disgraceful. Just because you're a good athlete, there is no need to show off. Report to the adjutant in the morning.' Julian Lyttleton told me that it served me right.

While we were in Windsor in 1943, the Italian campaign began in September, involving three battalions of the Grenadiers. On the fourth anniversary of Britain's entry into the war, the Allies established their first foothold on continental Western Europe since Dunkirk, with General Montgomery and his Eighth Army landing at Reggio on the toe of Italy and advancing up the Adriatic side of the peninsula. On the Mediterranean side, a combined British-American force, the Fifth Army, which included the Grenadiers, landed at Salerno. They met stern German resistance and so people began to disappear from Windsor pretty fast to reinforce our troops and within a few weeks we would see their names in the casualty lists.

In December 1943, after six months at Windsor, I was given embarkation leave and spent Christmas with my mother in Littlehampton. My father had by that time gone to Ethiopia to work with Haile Selassie on rebuilding the education system. Embarkation leave is not a picnic. You rush around trying to see as many people as possible, knowing that your mother is regretting that you are not spending the entire time with your immediate family. I was relieved when it was over.

I reported back to Windsor after an exceptionally boozy dinner with some old friends. They had to send a lorry to pick me up at the station and take me to the barracks. No one referred to it the next day. Then we were given one final day's leave. We weren't allowed to say we were about to go abroad but everyone knew we were. My mother and Helen came up to London and we went to a service at Westminster Abbey, then to the National Gallery. It was a difficult day, not least for my mother who must already have been reliving her memories of her brother, my namesake, in the first war.

There was a hilarious departure from Windsor. First of all we were addressed by the Major-General, Sir Arthur Smith. He was short on imagination and known as 'Bible' Smith. He stood up to address us: 'The first thing you must all realize is that within two or three months many of you will be dead.' Not encouraging. Then we all got ready to go. The six officers who were leaving were given dinner in the mess and plied by our colleagues with port and brandy and anything else available. The men went through roughly the same process and at midnight, marching with some difficulty, we set off, supposedly in dead silence, to the station. My aunt May, mother of the Ford twins, who lived in St George's Chapel Cloisters at Windsor Castle, heard us go. It was a very, very noisy march. There was nothing secret about our departure.

The journey, by ship, lasted about a fortnight. We went from Liverpool, through the Atlantic and via the straits of Gibraltar. I remember hanging over the stern of the ship with Julian Lyttleton, a modest, clever and courageous man who enlivened and enriched any company in which he found himself. It was a beautiful night, we could see the great black shape of the Rock to our left and the lights of neutral Tangier to our right. It sticks in my mind because as we sailed through it was as if we were passing the last outpost of peace – Tangier – and entering the war zone proper, the Mediterranean.

In Italy, the Allied forces had made slow progress and indeed had ground to a halt at a seemingly impenetrable line the Germans had established across the whole peninsula some eighty miles south of Rome. It wouldn't be breached until April 1944. Casualties were heavy. The strategically important Monte Cassino, known to troops as 'Murder Mountain', had been captured at the end of October 1943 after two great battles involving the 6th Battalion of the Grenadiers. Their losses were so heavy that the flow of reinforcements could not keep pace. The battalion was merged with my own battalion, the 5th, after our equally heavy casualties at Anzio.

At a meeting on Christmas Day 1943 in Tunis, the Allied leaders had agreed a bold new strategy to try to break the impasse – a landing, behind the German lines, at Anzio, about thirty miles south of Rome. They landed on 22 January just as we were arriving in Naples, which had by then been captured.

We went up to the Guards' reserve camp at Rotundi. While we were on the ship we had heard about the Anzio landing; rumours began to come back of heavy casualties. In fact in two weeks of fighting there between 25 January and 10 February, the battalion lost 29 officers out of 35 and 575 other ranks out of 800. The figures illustrate the violence of the battle. The Germans managed to contain the Anzio landing – 'the Anzio abscess' Hitler called it – but never to expel it. It remained a battlefield until the spring of 1944 when the Germans started to retreat. Rome was eventually captured in June 1944.

After four days at Rotundi, I was suddenly told to parade for the beachhead in an hour and a half. The day before I had been for a long walk over the hills with Julian. I can remember saying to him: 'I don't really mind if I am killed, apart from its effect on my family and everything. What I do not want to be is badly maimed, a cripple.' He said he had never heard such nonsense in his life – it would be a great relief to all my friends if I were, so I could concentrate on my brain instead of my games. It was the last time I saw him. Julian was killed on 11 October at Battaglia. I only learnt of his death much later when I was in hospital in England. I wrote to his parents and received a reply straightaway from his mother, telling me how much Julian had spoken of me in his letters and enclosing a pile of books for me to read. She had, she explained, always sent books to Julian, so it seemed appropriate now to be sending them to me.

An urgent request had come from the beachhead for a company commander plus three platoon commanders. Four were chosen – Norman Johnstone and Anthony Courage who had both been in action before, Duncan Boulton and Jonathan Savill who had been out in Italy a little longer than me. They couldn't find Savill, however, so the colonel, getting a bit impatient, said: 'Well, send Hussey then.' It wasn't until fifty years later that I was to learn for the first time what had happened. Jonathan Savill went on to have a distinguished war, winning the Military Cross in 1945. He subsequently became a most successful painter, gaining a considerable reputation for landscapes and portraits. Sue asked him to paint my portrait and, at a party in August 1999 at my house in Somerset to celebrate its completion, he told some friends about that day in Italy. He had been sent by his company commander in a truck to try and scrounge some eggs and chickens from nearby Italian villages and farms. He had been successful, but, unaware of the Anzio reinforcements, he had got back so late that he missed the boat – literally – and I caught it. That's how it goes.

We sailed in a landing craft from Castiglione. The mood was not so much of excitement but of relief that at last we were going to be part of the battle. It was a ten-hour journey and the Royal Navy kept us well supplied with creature comforts throughout. We landed in peaceful conditions and went to the base camp where I learnt that earlier in the day my cousin, Christopher Ford, had been buried. He had died, along with two fellow officers and a guardsman, on 28 January when three jeep-loads of Grenadiers strayed across the front line by accident and were mown down or taken prisoner by the Germans. It was four days before the Germans were driven back and Christopher's twin, Edward, was able to recover his body. One of the men under Christopher's command later wrote of him: 'He was a powerful influence for good wherever he went. He created a greater impression on all officers and men than anyone else I have known; and no truer Christian ever walked.'

After two days, Bill Sydney, who was to win the VC three days later, appeared at my tent. I had just taken my platoon – a sergeant and thirty-six men – for a tough route march to make certain they were fit after the journey at sea. He said: 'Oh Duke, I've got some good news for you.' I thought, whoopee he's going to send me back to Naples with a message. But he said: 'We had a bit of a problem in the night. There is a gap in the line, the platoon commander has been killed and I'd be very grateful if you could take your platoon up to fill it.' I said, 'Well, of course, how marvellous', trying to mask my apprehension. This was about midday. I had assumed that I would go up under cover of darkness, but he looked at his watch and said, 'It's 12 o'clock now, I'd like you in the line by quarter to one.'

Many years later, Bill Sydney, by then a distinguished ex-Governor-General of Australia and government minister, told me, 'Every time I see you, oh Duke, I always feel such a terrible shit putting you in that position where you were bound to be hit.' I said: 'Well, I don't think you need to. After all we are both here to talk about it.' Soon after his death, his son invited me to step into Bill's shoes and speak to a mixed group of German and British soldiers who had all been blinded and lost both hands. To survive such appalling injuries takes exceptional courage and great character. You could see both etched indelibly on their faces. Indeed, some had so overcome these disabilities they had had successful careers in industry and the law. I was asked to make a speech. What can you offer to such people except deep and humble admiration.

We went by truck to within a mile of the front line, and then marched along the road to battalion headquarters. There was spasmodic shellfire. As I arrived the adjutant shouted, 'Get those f—ing men off the road.' I rapidly dispersed my troop. I was very green but thought I had better look efficient and unafraid, so we had marched up in close formation. Not the best thing to do, because Anzio stood in the shadow of the Alban Hills. From this vantage point the Germans could see every movement.

There I met Paul Freyberg, the only officer left in the company, who took me up to my platoon position. The platoon followed later. Paul and I went up under mortar fire – one landed slap between us – we were only five yards apart – but neither of us was hit. We grinned at each other – it was an immediate and lasting bond. He later wrote of that first meeting and generously described me as 'an imperturbable young officer'.

We had about three days there, and then we were told there was an adjustment of line and we had to move. We got into new positions at night. It was dune-like country. We were on the reverse side of a hill and occasional shells or mortars arrived. Then came the night of the 7th and 8th of February. We had been joined by Tommy Gore-Browne, the company commander who had been wounded but had come back. He ordered me out on patrol to a position the Scots Guards had vacated to discover whether the Germans had reoccupied it. I remember saying, 'But they're firing on us from that position', but he brushed that aside.

Looking back, I realize that they always sent young officers on patrol as soon as possible to accustom them to life in the line. A form of training, but in action. I took three men and we crawled slowly and carefully towards the position about 500 yards away. It was a bright moonlit night and so we were lying very close to the ground. I suddenly heard and then saw a close-knit column of Germans marching past me about 100 yards away. Clearly they were going to attack our left flank. I knew that I must warn the battalion as fast as possible since no one was expecting a night attack. I ran back to our line and risked the noise.

If the Germans saw or heard me, they did nothing about it. I got back to company headquarters to report that I suspected a heavy attack was coming in on the left. I think, to be honest, they thought I had panicked and it wasn't true. They were certainly sceptical about my report. Not for long though. We heard heavy shelling and rifle fire mainly from the left-hand company. Then we came under fire and Tommy was wounded again. Total confusion.

Ronnie Taylor, a Grenadier who has written extensively in the *Guards Magazine* about the Anzio campaign, describes it as the battle that came closest, in the Western European theatre, to a first war battle. That is, it was mainly an infantry slog.

Paul and I were ordered to retake a small hill in the middle of our company position. So we formed up our two platoons, gave the order to fix bayonets and charged. I think we both thought the Germans had vacated that position. Happily we were right. Half an hour later Paul joined me and said that we were now surrounded but the orders were to hold the position, no matter what. I went round every man in my platoon, explained what the orders were and reassured them that there would be artillery support and a counter-attack coming to back us up. My platoon sergeant, much more experienced in battle than me, took me to one side and said: 'There isn't going to be a counter-attack, is there, sir? And there won't be any artillery support either, will there?' I admitted that I didn't think there would. 'Don't worry, sir,' he replied, 'we will do our stuff.' I never knew what happened to him until years later, when I was appointed Chairman of the BBC. He wrote to me from Wales and said that he had been watching the news that night when I had appeared on it and he turned to his wife and said, 'I always thought Hussey had had it, but Hussey hasn't had it. I've just seen him on the news. He's the bloody Chairman of the BBC.' I met up with him soon afterwards and subsequently invited him and his wife to my first BBC dinner in Wales and another ten years later.

Back to the battle. It wasn't too bad, although there was a lot of noise. There was little shelling but plenty of small-arms fire. The Germans were now about 300 yards away. For some reason, we were told to move off our hill into another position, so I got my platoon together and we ran straight into the enemy. By then, there was machine-gun and small-arms fire all around us and we had been joined by Norman Johnstone who had commanded the company on our left. It was a total muddle. He told me that both Duncan and Anthony had been killed. We were now surrounded by Germans calling on us to surrender. Most of the men were taken prisoner, including Paul.

It was still dark. Norman and I, along with two guardsmen, jumped into a deep, very heavily brambled gully. A German came up to the gully and said: 'We know you are down there. Unless you come out and surrender we will throw grenades into the ditch and fire a machine gun down it.' And I am bound to say that at that moment I was beginning to think enough was enough, but Norman said: 'Oh, no, no, we will sit this one out.' So the German gave a count of three and we lay very, very close to the earth. Down came the grenade, then the machine-gun fire. It was a dicey moment, but, somehow or other, because of the brambles we didn't get a touch. Amazing.

We could hear the Germans milling all round us and lay there for about two hours. We thought we should try to get back to battalion headquarters. We knew roughly the direction it was in, and decided to do this immediately before dawn. We took off our distinctive steel helmets and our packs, so that we were stripped down to our uniforms with nothing on our heads. I had a grenade and a revolver. I think Norman had the same and we started off when it was still dark, trying to wend our way through the German lines.

We got through one German position rather successfully. We were challenged. Norman was ahead, I was at the back, with two guardsmen in between, and I can remember quite clearly saying: '*Offizier, gute Nacht!*' I don't speak any German but hoped for the best. I could have put my hand on the head of the Spandau gunner as we walked through. That was the first lucky bit. The second was less fortunate.

It was beginning to get light when we came to what we thought was the front-line trench – which is exactly what it turned out to be. We decided to charge and jump over the trench. I thought I might drop the grenade on them as I jumped over, but I decided it was rather dangerous to take the pin out of a grenade, so I didn't. I cleared the Germans but on landing – I suppose because I was rather tired – I slipped. It was now light, and I was in the unfortunate position of being on the ground about three yards away from a trench full of Germans. I can remember it flashing through my mind, 'I've had it now. Should I say *Kamerad* and surrender?' Surrender was unthinkable. I just couldn't do it. I suppose it comes down to one's training, being in a good regiment and the way one had been brought up.

I thought I would get up and go for it. As I was getting up off the ground, I was hit by the burst of fire. That's why I was hit in the way I was – a bullet through my right hand, one through my right leg, and the one that later caused me so much trouble, in my spine between the fourth and fifth lumbar verte-brae. I was lucky. I was brought down by the worst shot in the

German army. He couldn't miss but he didn't kill me. I suppose I am one of very few people who has been hit by a burst of machine-gun fire from three yards and who knew it was about to happen. Initially it wasn't as bad as one would expect. It was like a great big thump. The pain immediately afterwards was acute and I fell unconscious. When I regained consciousness it was broad daylight and there were Germans standing all round me. They carried me back into their trench.

They removed my watch and my revolver – unhappily it was a German Mauser which had been nicked and which I had borrowed from a fellow officer. I was then carried into a barn, which doubled as a regimental headquarters and first-aid post, where I was joined by Norman Johnstone. He had been brought down by a nasty wound to the thigh, and had been wounded in the shoulder by our own artillery as he was lying on the grass. We had one night and two days in that barn. They couldn't get us out. They couldn't get any of their own wounded out either.

The Germans were kind. We were bombed, shelled and mortared by our own side for the whole time. Every now and then, someone in the barn was killed and the Germans asked us to make the sign of the cross which we did, wondering 'who next?' There was virtually no medical treatment. I can remember the Irish Guards counter-attacking. They got so near to retaking the barn that half the Germans in it were already surrendering to us. There was a group of four still firing a Spandau from the door of the barn but inside they were actually surrendering to Norman and myself. We were lying on the floor, and Norman was telling them where to stack their rifles, when suddenly the Irish Guards retreated.

It's one of those things about a battle: the moment of victory, the moment of defeat, separated by a few seconds. The German Red Cross men were very considerate. There was not much they could do but they did give us cigarettes – though I didn't smoke. Norman did and indignantly complained that they weren't Turkish. The hand wound didn't seem to worry me very much. I wasn't really conscious of the wound in my back – I suppose the bullet had deadened the pain or something. The leg was very painful.

Two days later, I was carried out by Italians on a stretcher. There was shell and mortar fire going on and whenever it got close the Italians would drop the stretcher on the ground and jump into a ditch, leaving me somewhat exposed. Then I was put into an ambulance for a very uncomfortable journey to the CCS (Casualty Clearing Station), where I lay on the floor for the best part of a day. That was the only time I suffered some modest ill-treatment. I was kicked hard by a German officer and sworn at. I responded with equally violent military language.

Obviously, as a prisoner, I was at the end of the queue but eventually, after several hours, they took me into an operating theatre and a German who spoke a little English told me he was going to amputate my leg. I said, 'Is that necessary?' and he said, 'Yes, you have the poison. It is here . . .' he pointed to the lower half of my right leg. 'By tomorrow morning it will be here . . .' and he pointed to my thigh. 'And by tomorrow night you will be dead.' So I said, 'In that case you had better go ahead.'

He tied me down onto the operating table – it was a pretty grim room, splashes of blood in all directions. Frankly, I thought I wasn't going to get an anaesthetic and got a bit windy. So I asked him. 'Yes, yes,' he said, and produced a flannel, put it over my face and poured chloroform over it. I drank it down like a champagne cocktail.

When I came round, everything felt all right. I lifted up my left leg and that was there, so that reduced the odds. I lifted up my right leg, but of course it wasn't there. Even now, after all these years, I can still sort of wiggle my toes on my right leg. Or imagine I am. I don't like doing it. It's rather a creepy feeling and anyway, what's the point?

Chapter Three

The next day I was taken by ambulance to a large emergency hospital in Rome. There were about a hundred people in the ward and, so far as I could see, I was the only non-German. Norman Johnstone was there for twenty-four hours and then sent off to a prisoner-of-war camp. But I was treated like every other patient. There was a German pianist who used to play late at night and always finished with 'J'attendrai'. I remember thinking that, if I ever got out of that place, I would have 'J'attendrai' played to remind me that, whatever happened to me, I had to be better off than when I first heard it. I'm happy to report I had it played in many nightclubs in the years that followed.

It was at that point that a German Lutheran priest came to see me and offered to take down a letter to my mother. I had of course been desperate to let her know I was alive. He accordingly posted the letter in the Vatican and, indeed, it was the first news my mother had that I was alive. I couldn't write myself, and she didn't know who the letter was from since she did not recognize the handwriting. It was only when she got to the end and saw 'Dukie' written in very clear script that she realized it was me.

I still have the letter. It carries a great big Red Cross stamp and is dated Rome, 11 February 1944. 'My dear parents, I am save [sic] and well, wounded three times [he got that wrong – it was places] right hand; behind [slightly] and right leg worse and amputated just below the knee. Please don't worry as I am very well looked after and am suffering very little indeed. When you get my offlag address can you sent [sic] anything that the Red Cross suggests. I was captured with nothing at all and have not got boots. With all very best loves and wishes.' He took down another letter from me a few days later – a very Christian pastor.

My mother had learnt that I was missing when she received a telegram on 20 February. From then, for her as for so many others, it was a terrible time. My father had been abroad when I was reported missing, but headed home from Ethiopia as soon as he could. Before he arrived she received, on 31 March 1944, that first letter from me.

Much later, after her death, I found the file of correspondence she had kept from that agonizing period. There were letters to and replies from the headquarters of the Grenadier Guards searching for information, plus letters from friends and relatives expressing concern and sympathy. One letter from the Regimental Adjutant, dated 22 February 1944, offers hope and adds, in a postscript: 'I need not say how much I hope we may have good news of your boy who has shown such promise as an officer and has made many good friends in the regiment.' The last was a standard phrase. They were hardly going to tell a worried mother that her boy had been deeply unpopular even if he had been. As late as 20 March, however, she was told that since the Germans held the ground where I had gone missing, there had been no opportunity to check for my dead body.

Before she got my letter from Italy telling her that I was alive, all she had to go on was the telegram – an exact replay of what happened to her own mother in the First World War and indeed to my father's mother at the same time when Harold was reported missing in Mesopotamia. Mummy got up every night, like so many wives and mothers, to listen to the broadcasts on the German radio of prisoners who had been taken at Anzio. She was searching newspaper pictures of the wounded prisoners being marched through Rome to see if I was among them. Among her correspondence are enlargements of photographs that she had obtained from the *Evening Standard* to check if she could spot me.

The doctors at the Rome hospital decided to change the dressing on my stump. The amputation had been what is called a guillotine operation. In other words they just cut straight down – like a guillotine. The Germans used this method often. It was quick and effective although it needed a re-amputation later to arrange the flap of skin to heal over the stump. So they warned me and ripped the dressing off the raw flesh. Two days later, they tried to get the bullet out of my back and failed. I hadn't actually realized there was one there.

While I was in the hospital I thought I might try to escape; it sounds an unlikely enterprise, given the state of my health, but we had all been told that if we were ever taken prisoner our best bet was to head for the Vatican which was officially neutral territory. Paul Freyberg had also been captured but not wounded. He managed to give his captors the slip a few days later and made his way through their lines to the Pope's summer residence, Castel Gandolfo, in the Alban Hills outside Rome and not far from Anzio. Since it was papal property, the Germans couldn't touch him there. Then he was smuggled in a delivery van, hidden under a pile of vegetables, into the Vatican City itself, where he remained until the liberation of Rome on 4 June. After that he rejoined the battalion for the advance up Italy. While he was in the Vatican, he used to wander around St Peter's Basilica looking like a priest and he told me that German soldiers often asked him for a benediction. He raised his hand, mumbled a few words, but not, I think, the sentiments they were expecting.

In hospital there was a very Anglophile Italian girl who brought me something to read – as far as I remember by P.G. Wodehouse. She used to come and talk to me. I said, 'Look, I keep on going off for an operation, why don't you wheel me out of the ward, find a friendly Italian ambulance driver and persuade him to drive me to the Vatican? When I get there I'll try and talk myself in.' I never saw her again. I've always been sorry that it didn't come off. It would have been a great coup.

After three days in Rome I was put on a German ambulance train carrying the wounded north. For most of the journey I believed I was the only prisoner on board, though, at a station stop, I did catch a glimpse of someone else in our uniform. It was a nightmare journey. The whole train was laden with wounded men on stretchers with only a few orderlies to look after them. My recollection is that it took two days but my memory of it is hazy.

Medical care or provisions were extremely scarce. There was little food and we were down to about a tumblerful of water a day. I can still remember the thirst. I would dream that someone was giving me a glass of water and would even wake up, with my hand outstretched, to take it – but it vanished.

The journey was rough but the Germans themselves were not. Their wounded on the train were, I must say, very decent. When we stopped at stations, those who could walk would get off and find water and bring me a cupful together with any fruit they managed to buy. The basic point was that we were all wounded soldiers. We were all comrades in trouble. Another example of my good fortune. Prisoners under the care of the Gestapo or Security Forces suffered heavily for it.

After two days, they emptied the train and sent us up to a convent-run hostel in the Italian Alps. We were given some soup – the first hot drink I had had since I had been wounded. There, on 15 February, I had a very unusual experience. It turned out to be a very important one, perhaps the crucial moment of my life. I was still in the same uniform I had been wearing when I set out for Anzio and was in a small room which I remember clearly. There were four beds – occupied by three Germans and me. As I lay on the bed, with sheets, the first I had seen for days, I suddenly had an overwhelming urge to lie back and go to sleep. I had slept very little since I had been wounded and sleep would have been bliss. But however overwhelming the temptation, I was at the same time convinced that if I gave way, I would never wake up. It would be the end and I was determined that would not be so. So I forced myself up with my arms into a semi-sitting position – difficult in view of my back and my leg. I kept myself awake for as long as I could manage. Though I went to sleep in the end, I did wake up.

That was the moment, I think, when deep in my subconscious I knew that I could conquer this, whatever it was. It was the turning point – that belief never left me. When, after the war, I was at Oxford with an open wound and still going to hospital every day for dressings, Ro Wadham (we were later each other's best man) says that everyone around me – family, tutors, doctors and friends – thought I could not survive, but I never doubted that I would.

Two days later I was put on another train, through the Alps to Germany. It stopped at Salmünster station. There were about seven Allied prisoners and some German wounded as well. We were lying on the platform and some of the walking British wounded were being manhandled by the Germans. I shouted, '*Offizier!*' at them, pointing at my officer's stars and then told them in very firm Anglo-Saxon to stop it. The Germans are an extraordinary race. They jumped to attention and obeyed. The others were put in an ambulance, and I was taken off in a horse and cart to Stalag 9B in Bad Soden, about five miles outside the historic town of Fulda, final resting place of Saint Boniface, a West Countryman who converted the Germans to Christianity in the eighth century.

I spent the next seven months there. The word *Stalag* for the post-war generation conjures up images of Colditz and the TV series, but literally it means a camp. 9B was part of a number of connected hospitals, the biggest for wounded Germans, and 400 yards up the hill was a small prison camp, housed in a convent. It was for British, Commonwealth and American prisoners who were either blind or had severe eye injuries and was run with great sympathy and Christian charity by the Catholic Sisters of Saint Vincent de Paul.

Ralph Smith, the Quaker orderly who was to look after me at Bad Soden and who saved my life there, remembers my arrival well. He had been a non-combatant Quaker and had been captured in Greece while serving with the Friends' Ambulance Unit.

Duke Hussey did not have anything wrong with his eyes and we had no idea why he had been sent to an eye hospital. We were totally unequipped to cope with anybody with major wounds. I was, of course, kept inside the barbed wire that surrounded the hospital while his fate was discussed. Neither the senior British officer nor the German colonel for these reasons wanted to admit him and said he should be

sent on to a major POW hospital four hours away. The
German doctor and the guards who had brought him up
from the station on a cart were standing there arguing about
this when from nowhere out popped one of the sisters –
Sister Egberta was her name to the best of my recollection.

She was very young and very pretty and in a sense quite
pro-British. She went round to the back of the cart that
Duke Hussey was on, gave him a quick looking over, then
turned to the German doctor and said: 'You must admit this
patient to this hospital because there is no way that he is
going to survive another four hours' journey. If you do send
him on, he will almost certainly die on the way. There will
be an enquiry about his cause of death, an investigation
will be carried out by higher authorities and you will have
to explain why you did not admit him in accordance with
orders that you have received from the guard and why you
sent him on. And if he dies, and you don't have a good
explanation, then I reckon you are going to get sent to the
Russian Front.'

That, Ralph recalls, was enough to swing it. I was seen by a
British doctor, Captain Harries, who brought me a cup of coffee.
My back was discharging pus very heavily and I had had very
little food for three weeks. He and Major Charters, the other
English doctor there, had both been taken prisoner – in France
and Greece respectively – and had refused repatriation in order
to remain looking after the wounded captives. Charters was an
eye specialist, so all the surgical treatment was done by a
German colonel who used to prod me with his hand and say,
'Schmertz, Schmertz?' – 'Pain, pain?'

The German doctor told Ralph that I would be dead in
fourteen days. I had septicaemia as a result of the botched
amputation and they had no antibiotics. 'I didn't think so,' Ralph
said later. 'He had a glint in his eye and I was always impressed
with his will to live and his sense of humour. It must have been
an extremely painful business for him, but he never complained.'

Because of the danger of the septicaemia spreading to other
patients, Ralph was detailed to concentrate exclusively on me.

The first thing was to test my blood, a procedure he had never done before. When he saw the result, he thought he had done it wrong because it was so low. So he checked it with a more experienced orderly who said, 'This man is dead.' Ralph replied: 'Oh no he isn't. He's in room 12 and we've got to save him.'

They concluded that I needed a blood transfusion immediately, but there was no blood in the hospital as it was all being sent to the Russian Front. Ralph checked the medical records of all the patients and staff and found four suitable to give a blood donation, and – though, again, he had never done one before – gave me a transfusion. It was the first of many over the next six months.

My position was complicated by bad bedsores because I couldn't turn over in the bed and was weak and thin. But the British doctors, the German doctors and the nuns nursed me devotedly, frequently sending me for X-rays in the main hospital which meant being carried down the hill to the German hospital on a stretcher and back up again. With the company of my fellow prisoners, and the treatment I was receiving, I never lost hope, nor did I regret the loss of my leg. I just concentrated on trying to keep going – and remembered what Julian had said.

Landing at Bad Soden was an immensely lucky stroke because, since my head was about the only part of me which was uninjured, I had no right to be there. The Red Cross, primarily through the neutral countries of Switzerland and Sweden, organized parcels for all prisoner-of-war camps and, once the system had started, it worked extremely well. They were packed with coffee, tinned ham, dried fruit, and above all, cigarettes. Moreover in every batch there were one or two especially for the very sick. Most of the other patients – about thirty in total – had eye and face injuries, but were relatively fit. So they would pass on the extras from their Red Cross parcels to me. I got the cream, as it were, and drank so much dried milk, Horlicks and Ovaltine to give me strength that I have never touched any of them since.

The nuns were wonderful, and wizards on the black market. I didn't smoke so they used to barter the cigarettes from my parcels to get eggs. Sister Egberta did me one other favour. She took away my filthy uniform so that, when later I left Bad Soden, it reappeared clean and freshly pressed. I was probably the best cared for and treated prisoner in the whole of Germany. How lucky can you get.

I had kept a compass with me, no doubt with some vague hope of escaping, and managed to smuggle it into the camp, together with a few revolver bullets. I gave them all to the senior British officer. I hope they were helpful to someone. Bad Soden was only thirty miles from Frankfurt and so we lay awake at night listening to the heavy Allied bombing with somewhat mixed feelings. Just as long as a stray bomb didn't come our way. The American Air Force also bombed by day and Ralph Smith described one day seeing one of their planes being brought down with the crew floating to the ground by parachute. So close to the action, I deeply regretted that my own war had been so short and that I had not had the opportunity to fight for longer.

One of the men with whom I shared a room at Bad Soden, an American called Carl Thinnes, contacted me out of the blue a year ago. He had been shot down and badly burnt in the face and was thought likely to lose his sight, but once back in America it had been saved. 'You were very close to making your exit at that time,' he wrote. 'You had had twelve transfusions and had stopped taking nourishment. An Anglican priest had come by to give you the last rites. I well remember that because we were both asleep when he arrived and, with my eyes being bandaged and my battered body in evidence, he erroneously deduced that I was the Anglican ready to depart. He had the little table with candles, etc., set up next to my bedside. Fortunately I woke up in time to inform him that you were the one who needed the last rites, not me.' I was totally oblivious but I do remember a clergyman coming to see me and we said the Lord's Prayer together.

Thanks to the efforts of the Red Cross, I was also able to receive and send occasional letters. My first letter to my mother, dated 5 March 1944, was taken down by a fellow patient, a bagpipe-playing New Zealand major, Geoff Bedding, who was in charge of physiotherapy at the hospital. It was full of reassurance about my wounds. It also shows how much I was looking forward to being home and to peacetime. 'I am sure that you ought to start house-hunting in earnest,' I told my mother, 'because after the war it will be impossible, while if you get one too small it can be enlarged. I should start exhaustive enquiries whenever you tour the country.'

She had first heard about my whereabouts in Germany by telegram on 28 April. Subsequently she also received my medical reports, which became increasingly gloomy. There was always a time lapse of several months before they reached her which can only have increased the anxiety. In a report dated March 1944, for instance, Major Charters reported via the Red Cross that I was 'firmly on the road to recovery' but the next month he was indicating that my family 'should be warned of the serious nature of his condition'. In July he wrote again that my condition had been 'extremely serious for many weeks', though the report did add, it 'is now beginning to make progress'.

The Red Cross prisoner-of-war department was extremely efficient and even managed to get a special parcel to me containing what they thought I needed, complete with rubber ring to relieve my bed sores. And in the chaos of war, it arrived.

I recall very distinctly my first card from home – from my mother – which, sadly, I haven't kept. She said that I must remember my scars were honourable scars. She was doing her best to cheer me up.

After about six months, the prisoners decided to have a party. For reasons that I can't now fathom, each of us received small sums in pay, presumably organized through the Red Cross in Switzerland. The other patients had had more opportunity to spend theirs than me, so when it came to organizing the party, I had a good credit balance and volunteered to pay for a large barrel of beer. It was the least I could do. The prisoners were more ingenious. They wanted to supplement the beer. Our parcels were always stuffed with raisins and prunes – the last things we needed incidentally – and so they put them into a huge container and fermented them. Then to give it an extra

kick, they poured in surgical spirit. By the end there was hardly
a man standing.

The next morning Major Charters came through to see me.
'I've got some good news for you,' he said. He still called me
Mr Hussey. They were very formal in those days. 'You are to
be repatriated with two of the blinded prisoners. You will be
leaving the hospital tomorrow.' The exchange of badly wounded
prisoners from each side took place three times in the war. Mine
was the third and last. It was supervised and organized entirely
by the Red Cross. Everyone to be repatriated had to pass a
medical examination with the Germans in attendance. The
principle was that you had been so badly wounded that you
could not fight. Again, I was fortunate. I would not have survived
another eight months in the camp until the end of the war.

My departure was deeply moving. As I was carried out on
my stretcher, the whole camp was there including all the nuns
and the German colonel. They each filed past to say goodbye.
Then, as I was carried through the gates, a tiny POW band
struck up and played 'Happy Birthday to You'. The German
colonel called out the guard to salute. The date was 29 August
1944, my twenty-first birthday.

I was put on an ambulance train and taken to Obermassfeldt
which was an enabling centre for those being repatriated. I was
placed in 'Bed Pan Alley', reserved for the worst wounded.
There was a New Zealander and an Australian, but the rest were
American, one a very badly wounded Texan who had had a
double amputation. He was a man of great courage who carried
on laughing while he was dying.

After him I was the worst. I was next door to this American.
He had been in the Junior American Davis Cup tennis team. He
kept us all awake one night crying because he couldn't serve
overhead again. In the circumstances, it didn't seem to me a
major problem. They are amazing people, the Americans. I was
the only Englishman and kept quiet. The next morning the rest
of the ward gave my neighbour a real going over. They were fed
up with him. The young Englishman next door, they said, was
far worse off and hadn't said a word. It was a savage verbal
assault.

Then we were taken, again by ambulance train, to Rugen on the north-east German coast, close to the present border with Poland. The train got stuck in Berlin for about four hours. In those days the Allies were bombing Berlin every day and every night. Just our luck, we thought, if we all get hit now just as we are on our way home. There was a remarkable moment when the train stopped. Three Allied prisoners were working in the fields under the care of a dozy old German. They asked us where we were going. 'Back to England!' my companions shouted. Without a word, they turned on the German, knocked him out with their spades and climbed on board. They got home. A great escape!

We were taken by ferry to the Swedish port of Trelleborg, and then by train to Gothenburg. Sweden was neutral in the war. They had backed the Germans at first but now were supporting the Allies. So at every crossroads there would be groups of children standing waving the Stars and Stripes and Union Jacks. As soon as we were in the hands of the Swedish Red Cross, we were fed scrambled eggs heavily laced with butter. I was terribly sick.

We sailed back to England in a British liner, marvellously cared for in comfort and luxury by trained New Zealand nurses. We docked in Liverpool and I was the first off the ship and was transferred to Mostyn Hall, a military hospital near Chester. It was 15 September, I think, two days before the start of the airborne operation at Arnhem.

I stayed in that hospital for three to four months. At first my family was waiting in London. They were told not to come up, that the hospital would try to get me to London instead, but I was too ill to be moved. So they eventually made the journey. Before they arrived, David Henley Welsh, who was at Trinity and in the Oxford XI with me, suddenly appeared at the end of my bed looking immensely elegant as a Fleet Air Arm pilot. He was the first person I saw whom I actually knew. I asked him what on earth he was doing. He said he didn't know really. The station commander had summoned him and apparently said, 'There is a friend of yours who has just come back from Germany who looks as if he may be dying. You'd better take the day off and go see him.' We have never discovered who set this up or how they knew.

Eventually I was moved south to Roehampton Hospital. I was flown down and they took me via Rugby and did a circle over the school. The problem was not the amputation. That was all right. It was the wound in the spine. An Irish surgeon at Chester called Somerville-Large got the bullet out. Like a fool I threw it away – out of the window. I felt I'd had enough of that bullet. I rather regret that now, but it had set up osteomyelitis which went all over the spine. That's a gangrenous decay of the bone. They can cure it now but they couldn't then. It quickly spread all over my back and subsequently my stomach. I spent the next five years fighting it.

Before moving on what I want to emphasize is this. You would expect care and comfort from your own countrymen, particularly if you were wounded, and to be a wounded soldier during the war and in the years immediately afterwards was to be a rather glamorous figure. But from the moment I was wounded, right through to the end, when my back wound finally healed in October 1949, I was treated marvellously well. From the soldiers in the Anzio barn, who offered us cigarettes, to the Germans who cared for me in Rome and the Italian girl who came to see me, the Lutheran priest who wrote the letters, the nuns who nursed me so devotedly and used their black-market skills to get me extra food, and the German colonel who called out the guard – all those people showed mercy. Christian charity accepts no political or military boundaries.

After the war I always wanted to go back to that German hospital to express my heartfelt gratitude. It wasn't until many years later, when I had to go to Frankfurt on business, that I had the chance. When Sue and I arrived, I recognized the place immediately. I could remember the hill from my many stretcher journeys up and down for X-rays. We were given a huge tea by the sisters while they looked up the records. They produced a little old nun in her eighties who couldn't have been more than five foot tall. It was Sister Egberta. She bent down and lifted my trouser leg and said: 'I remember now, so young, so ill.' She took my hand and burst into tears. So did we.

The most moving moment was when they took us to the chapel, where they had recorded in a book on the altar the names of all the people who had died in the hospital. The Mother Superior found my name, Lieutenant M. J. Hussey, Grenadier Guards. They did not believe that I could have lived. She pulled out her pen, put a stroke through my name and wrote: 'Married, with two children.'

Chapter Four

In December 1944, I arrived at Roehampton Hospital in south-west London and spent the next six months there. In the bed opposite me on Ward B was Major Harry Grenfell. He must have been forty and had been badly wounded in Burma. In fact it had taken longer for him to get to Roehampton than the ten months it did for me, via Germany. I wondered how an old man like him had got mixed up in this affair.

He was the stepbrother of my future mother-in-law, Mary Waldegrave. That is how I came to know the family. All together, there were six children including Harry's elder brother Reggie who married the comedienne Joyce Grenfell. Their father, Arthur Grenfell, a great character whose fortunes went up and down like the tide, had once owned Roehampton House before it was converted into the hospital in which we were both now lying.

We were nursed by VADs and frequently fell for them. I did and Harry did. Come Christmas 1944, while I was in a wheelchair, Harry's stepmother, Hilda Grenfell, a woman of great character, arranged a Red Cross hospital ambulance to take Harry, also in a wheelchair, and me up to her home for lunch on Christmas Day together with a nurse to look after us. I was very nervous about this. They were all strangers. The nurse, of course, turned out to be Harry's girl. When we arrived at the house in Chesham, Hilda, arranging the seating plan, said, 'Well, we will put Duke here with his friend next door to him.' She meant the nurse. I could have slaughtered Harry.

The Grenfells played a large part in my life. They were connected to my mother's family, the Fords, through marriage,

and two of Harry's sisters used to come to visit us and push us
in our wheelchairs down the hill to the Roehampton Club for
tea – and back up afterwards. They were tough girls. And
Ward B was a pretty sparky place. In spite of the many
operations and, sadly, occasional deaths, we were thirty-two
young wounded officers ready for anything. Most nights we set
off with the VADs to the pub. Then we'd retire to the sluice –
where they emptied the bedpans – and played poker. Bizarre
but fun.

In February I had my first bath for a year – bliss. Then they
gave me a rudimentary wooden leg called a pylon. It was made
of a plaster cast round the stump attached to two bits of wood
going down to the floor with no foot at the end – just like the
leg of a chair. Cheap, easy and effective. The first time I wore it,
no problem. I got up, took two sticks and was away.

It gave me freedom – enough to go up to London in the
evenings. For one trip with a fellow patient, John Maxwell, who
had been badly wounded – he had one leg off and severe injuries
to an arm – we hired a Rolls-Royce and driver from a local taxi
service (the only car they had), took two nurses out for a good
dinner and then dropped them back at the nurses' home. When
we arrived at the hospital, the gates were locked. It was 12.30
a.m. They closed at 10 p.m.

John and I looked at each other: 'What do we do now?' So
we thought we had better try to climb over the gates. John with
an amputated leg and a very dicky arm and me with my right
leg amputated and a bad spine started to clamber up the gates.
A light went on and there were two policemen standing there.
'What are you doing?' one said. John replied: 'Well, officer, we
are patients at this hospital and we are trying to get back in.'
'Oh,' he said, as if this was the most natural thing in the world,
'we'd better help you.'

So then we had the unlikely sight of two young officers
sprawled across the gates with a couple of policemen trying to
haul us up. There was so much noise that the wardens came
out. They took a dim view. Roehampton was a military hospital.
We were in trouble. They opened the gates and we shot back to
Ward B.

The next morning we were summoned to see the general in charge of the hospital. He told us that it had been an absolute disgrace and a bad example to the men but we could see his heart wasn't in it. He gave us a rocket. We apologized profusely. The next day the ward door opened and in came the same general giving Field Marshal Lord Wavell, the Viceroy of India, a hospital tour. John and I had adjoining beds and the general, who could have chosen any two patients, stopped by us and said, 'Field Marshal, I can't introduce you to all these young officers, so I will introduce you to the two most insubordinate.' It turned out that John had served under Wavell in North Africa and had once shown him around their very exposed company position. Wavell remembered it perfectly and was delighted. It was amazing that, after so many campaigns, he could still fix his mind on one company position in North Africa and the subsequent battle. They had a happy reminiscence. We had met a great man and so emerged rather well from the gate affair.

There were other companions on my excursions to London, notably Timothy Jones. The son of the novelist Enid Bagnold, he had been in the next bed to me when we were in the ranks, at OCTU, and we shared a room at Windsor when we were commissioned. He went abroad before me and I didn't see him again until he was carried into our ward at Roehampton over a year later with one leg amputated above the knee. So once again, we were alongside. He had a very unreliable car which we took out on VE night with two girls, with one of whom I fell in love. It was a wonderful moment – the cheering crowds, the royal family on the balcony at Buckingham Palace, the sense of everyone rejoicing in victory. Wild scenes. Unforgettable.

The day before, 6 May 1945, Princess Elizabeth, as she was then, disbanded the 5th/6th Battalion of the Grenadier Guards. She was colonel of the regiment. So we were all in London at Wellington Barracks. There is a photograph of Timothy, another wounded officer and me being presented. My mother had a copy of it on her bedside table but later it got lost. Years later, when the Queen opened the Guards' Museum in London and my wife was in attendance, there were photographs of this occasion in 1945. The curator kindly found the original and gave us a copy.

I had many visitors in hospital. The one I remember best was Philip Schlee with whom I had shared a study at Rugby. In 1941, we used to ignore the Blitz and go to the theatre in London, sometimes taking in two shows in a day (you could get a seat for three and six). Once we had joined the army, our paths separated – until he appeared at Roehampton carrying a suitcase. I was thrilled to see him. He said, 'Well, I heard you were here, Dukie, so I thought I'd pay you a visit.' Out of his suitcase he produced some very good red wine and a bottle of brandy.

'Good Lord,' I said, 'where did you get that?'

'Well,' he replied, 'I was in France ten days ago in the Vosges. We sort of liberated a French village. The Germans left these behind. I thought, "That's just what Dukie will need."'

He was dead right. Four or five weeks later he came back with another suitcase and produced some excellent German wine.

'Well actually, we dropped behind the Rhine a few days ago and much the same thing happened so I thought, "Dukie could do with a second helping."' I could. And I still see him. He built up a successful business in Hong Kong.

My family was at the hospital as much as possible. Despite my good spirits, they were still worried about me. My father, who had returned from his posting in Ethiopia when I was reported missing, had begun working in 1944 for the British Council as Director of its Middle East section. His knowledge of Arabic, picked up in the Sudan, helped enormously. Many years later when in Bahrain to negotiate a transmitter for the BBC World Service, I was looked after by a Bahraini government liaison officer who told me that it had been my father who had appointed her father to be Director of Education in Bahrain. That was in the days when the administration of much of the Middle East was largely carried out by British officials. My father also retained his links with church schools as a member of the Colonial Office's Advisory Committee on Education in the Colonies until 1947. And from 1940 he had been the Nigeria representative on the governing board of the School of Oriental and African Studies.

In many ways my spell in Roehampton was a carefree period.

The war was over, everyone was having fun, meeting girls, seeing life. There were dances and dinner parties. London and the whole country was celebrating peace. We should though have paused to remember the 14th Army who still had terrible battles ahead to defeat the Japanese in Burma in the lead-up to VJ day in August.

For me one big problem remained. While the treatment and physiotherapy for my leg went well, the real issue was the wound to my back. My regiment looked after their own and found something for me to do – helping Nigel Nicolson write the history of the Grenadiers in Africa and Italy. So I was posted to assist him at Victoria Barracks in Chelsea where I could go to the sick bay every day for my dressings. It was a very relaxed Grenadier company. The company commander was Timmy Egerton, subsequently the distinguished chairman of Coutts Bank. The subalterns were Nigel Nicolson, Humphrey Lyttleton (who slipped off every night to play the trumpet in a nightclub) and myself. The men we commanded were mostly old, sick or awaiting demobilization.

I was there six months but I wanted the wound healed. So I went back to Roehampton and asked the surgeon, Mr Perkins, to have another crack. He was talented but tough. One day soon after my arrival he had stood by my bed and said in a matter-of-fact way, 'I hope you realize that the leg you have will be of less use to you than the one you've lost.' I suffer from drop foot so I cannot flex my left ankle and have to wear a caliper. He had then turned to Harry Grenfell: 'I can think of at least three reasons why I must amputate your other leg.' Poor Harry; he showed great courage and subsequently became one of the top directors of the British South Africa Company.

Perkins operated on me again, but still no success. I think, in retrospect, they just did it to keep me happy. He did not believe there was any chance of the wound healing and afterwards took me aside and said, 'Didn't you get a scholarship to Oxford?' When I said yes, he replied, 'Well, why don't you go back to your college? They'll take you back, I'm sure.' With hindsight, I think he believed, and indeed had implied to my parents, that the wound was mortal.

So I was welcomed back to Trinity after Easter in 1946. They gave me wonderful rooms on the ground floor. It was a fascinating period to be there with an odd but stimulating mixture of undergraduates. At one end were people like John Baring who at eighteen had come straight from school, at the other seasoned war heroes like Dick Wakeford VC, Tommy McPherson with three Military Crosses and Ozzie Newton Thompson, a distinguished South African who captained Oxford at rugby and was awarded the Distinguished Flying Cross. Many of them had stunning careers at Oxford, not least Anthony Rowe, a musician and a scholar who had used sherry for ballast in his wartime submarine 'to cheer up the troops'. He captained the Oxford boat and won the Diamond Sculls. A genuine eccentric. It was a very larky place.

Among other contemporaries were James Ramsden and Dick Hornby, both ministers in the Macmillan and Douglas Home governments, Robin Leigh Pemberton, future Governor of the Bank of England, and David Windlesham, a future Leader of the House of Lords. It may sound exclusive but they all went on into public service. I was elected president of the Junior Common Room in the Christmas term of 1947.

By this stage my parents had moved to a charming house outside Lindfield, near Haywards Heath, to which I used to go back as often as possible. It was there that I found all my team photographs from my prep school, Rugby and Oxford. That part of my life, I decided, was over. Finished. I didn't want sporting photographs as mementos. I burnt the lot. I regret it now, but at the time it was right. Psychologically, it had a therapeutic effect. No more games, period. I can honestly say that, although many of my friends were playing rugby, athletics and cricket for Oxford, I never had a twinge of regret. I was alive.

Back at Oxford there was the daily grind of going to the Radcliffe Infirmary to have my dressings changed. I rode there and back on a bicycle. I rather enjoyed that. I moved out of Trinity, into a house in Oriel Street which I shared with Ludovic Kennedy. John Grigg and Ian Gilmour were next door. I took my studies rather more seriously than during my wartime period in Oxford. There is even a letter I wrote to my parents where I talk about my hopes of getting a First.

I was certainly better off than I had ever been. I still had a £100 scholarship, but what was even better was that there was a long-term, badly wounded treatment rule in the army which guaranteed the cost of your treatment and full pay for up to three years after you arrived back in this country. I think I got £500 a year, tax free.

One vacation I went on holiday with Ro Wadham (who got a DFC in the Fleet Air Arm) and his aunt Dot, a tough and intelligent lady. We travelled by car to the South of France. There were very strict limits on taking money overseas but we got round it by stashing Ro's US dollars and £25 in my wooden leg, working on the assumption that no customs officer would be a big enough shit to ask me to take it to bits. The aunt was treated with exaggerated respect by French waiters and hotel staff. We were too innocent to know why, but she did. They thought these two great hulking youths were her lovers. It gave her great pleasure. She was actually a trained nurse who changed the dressings on my open wound each day. I wouldn't have been able to travel without her.

There was an interesting insight into the French psyche immediately after the war. Confronted by someone so young and lame, not once did anyone suggest that I might have been wounded in the war. They asked me often if I had had a skiing accident. It was, I suppose, the scar of their humiliating defeat.

That wound on my spine wasn't getting any better. It was still discharging large amounts of pus each day and the abscesses around it and inside my body were getting worse with the osteomyelitis. It came to a head when the sister in charge of casualty at the Radcliffe Infirmary said, 'Honestly Dukie, I can't go on. You are very seriously ill and I've got no authority to do your dressings.' She insisted that I find a doctor to supervise my treatment. I said, 'Funny you should say that because I met a very nice man recently at Vincent's Club who told me he was a doctor. We had a long talk about hospitals. His name was Girdleston. Do you think he would do?' It was another of those chance encounters. The sister nearly fainted as he was one of the most distinguished doctors in the United Kingdom and certainly the most famous in Oxford.

Undeterred, I chanced my arm and wrote to him, 'Dear Mr Girdleston, You may not remember meeting me, but we talked about hospital over lunch at Vincent's. I think you may have thought I was a medical student but I am not. I am a patient. As the result of a wound, I have to have dressings done daily. The casualty sister at the Radcliffe insists I report to a doctor to authorize the treatment. Would you mind very much giving me a note so I can keep getting my dressings done? Yours sincerely, Dukie Hussey.'

I got a charming letter back, saying, 'I remember you well, and of course I would be delighted to help you but I must examine you first. Can you please come to my surgery at the Wingfield-Morris Hospital in Headington?' I went to see him and, having had a look, he said that he wanted to have some X-rays taken. I was sitting on the side of the bed getting dressed when he came through, looking rather severe. I said, 'Please don't worry about this, Mr Girdleston. I am perfectly all right. All I want to do is to get back to Oxford and do my exams.' He replied, 'Young man! I don't think you realize how ill you are. You are dying. There are very few people in this country who could save your life and you are very fortunate that one of them is me.' I remember it well.

He wanted to admit me that day. 'Oh,' I said, 'I can't possibly do that – I've got to do my exams.' We made a deal. This meeting was in October 1947, just after the start of the Michaelmas term. If I agreed to give up alcohol and go to bed at 10 p.m. every night and live a very quiet life, he would admit me to hospital at the end of June the following year when the exams were over. Of course I had no intention whatsoever of keeping my side of the deal. Much later his registrar, Dr Taylor, said to me, 'I don't think you know how much you owe to Mr Girdleston. You were a hopeless case and very, very few people would have had the courage to take you on, at the end of a distinguished career, and leave themselves open to the charge of carrying on for too long. That is not the sort of man Girdleston is. He thinks only of the patient.'

I never got round to the exams. I collapsed one day at Trinity shortly after Easter 1948 and Johnny Lowther – who had spent some time there himself with an amputation – took me to Nani Ward (the officers' ward during the war) at the Wingfield. He said to his old ward sister, 'Anne, I have got a friend of mine here. He's a bit sick.' She took one look at me and said, 'He is not sick – he is very ill!' For the next two years I was more in hospital than out. There were occasional breaks. At one stage, it was suggested I might go to Ireland on holiday. They wanted to fatten me up for the next slaughter. I took the train to Preston, walking on two sticks. I was still very innocent at this time, not at all at home in chatting up women. Into my carriage came the most glorious girl. She sat next to me. I thought I must try and engineer a conversation. So I got my cigarette case out, dropped it, scrambled around her legs to pick it up, and finally said, 'Would you like one, after all that?' She generously accepted and we got talking.

It turned out she was the actress Valerie Hobson, later to marry Jack Profumo the future Secretary of State for War. I went off for a meal in the restaurant car and when I returned she had got off, but she'd left a big basket of fruit for me with a note saying have fun in Ireland. She was a great lady.

At the hospital Mr Girdleston first put me in a plaster bed which means literally what it says. You lie in plaster from your neck to your knees so you can move nothing except for your arms and legs. There was a hole at the back to dress the wound. It was while I was lying immobilized on the ward that the National Health Service was created. Around me in the ward were patients, most of them with infantile paralysis. Many came from poor homes. In those days serious illness was a financial disaster for most families. Some of these patients were in tears at the thought of free treatment at the point of delivery. It seemed a miracle. I have now been connected with the health service for a long time both as a patient, on the management committee of the King's Fund and as Chairman of the Royal

Marsden Hospital for fourteen years. I know the problems of the
NHS and will refer to them later. But don't let any of us ever
forget that, for all its difficulties, it is a wonderful service and
without a shadow of doubt better than what preceded it. It gave
hope as well as treatment to millions, many of whom without it
would have had neither.

Mr Girdleston had decided on a major operation. Sister Anne
took personal charge. She was a wonderful ward sister but didn't
usually attend individual patients – she had twenty-five in her
care – yet it was she who took me down to the operating theatre.
She was very worried, not just about the operation but the
immediate post-operative hour. I told her how I prepared myself
for operations by convincing myself that I would come through
them all right, that I would recover from the anaesthetic and
that I would not be sick. 'I know how to do this,' I said. She
didn't believe me. It turned out exactly as I had foretold. I came
back from the operating theatre and then came round. I wasn't
sick and I was in little pain. Nowadays they would say I psyched
myself up for the ordeal.

Faced by operation after operation first in Italy, then in
Germany and now in England, I had developed this technique
of preparing myself mentally and psychologically for operations
and to control the pain thereafter. I used to will myself into a
state of trance. It is about will, the will to come easily out of the
operation and the anaesthetic. I willed myself to come out of
it, not feel pain, and what pain I did feel, I would control. It
worked.

The technique has stayed with me always. About three years
ago, I was having trouble with my back and I went to see a
leading orthopaedic surgeon at St Thomas's Hospital in London.
He kept me waiting twenty-five minutes. When I got in to see
him, it turned out we had met before. I said, 'I've been a patient
for a long time and I've been a chairman of a hospital for ten
years. I know all the reasons why you have kept me waiting and
I quite understand but I now have only twenty-five minutes
before I leave for the first day of the Test Match at Lord's.'

He laughed and replied, 'I know all about you and your

medical experience, so you will understand when I say that we have mislaid your X-rays. But that doesn't matter. I have seen them. I'll just give you an examination.' He had a prod around. 'Many surgeons,' he said, 'of several different nationalities have used all their skill and experience to keep your spine working. Against all the odds they have succeeded. I have no intention of even touching your spine again or indeed of letting anyone else do so. It's working. God knows how, but it is. But I will give you something for the pain.'

'I don't need it, I don't like drugs,' I said. 'I can handle the pain.'

'But what do you do if it gets bad?'

'I have a very large glass of whisky.'

'Well, what do you do if that doesn't work?' he asked.

'I have another.'

'Probably the best you can do actually. It relaxes the mind, the muscles and the spirit.'

Back to Oxford. For ten days after the operation Sister Anne did all the dressings every day. If you have a long-standing problem, you get to know the parameters. Suddenly I felt it had gone wrong. The discharge had started. I asked for Sister Anne who took one look and immediately put back the drips and did another dressing. She didn't say anything. I didn't say anything. We both knew that the operation had failed.

On 20 July, Mr Girdleston had another shot, this time trying to get at my back through the stomach. My parents came to see me two days before the operation – lovely to see them, but ominous. That failed too. In September, he decided to risk everything on one last major operation. This was one of the great crises of my life although I didn't realize it at the time. Mr Girdleston came to see me and explained the operation. In his opinion there was no other option if the wound was ever going to close, but I might not survive it.

I have, from my parents' papers, the letter he wrote to them on 22 September 1948. It begins: 'This is sure to be a difficult letter and may be a long one.' It details the risks of the operation as 'uncontrollable haemorrhage, infection and damage of the nerve structures which might lead to residual weakness or pain'. In explaining his reasons for undertaking it, Mr Girdleston writes:

It is only Duke's very grave present condition and future prospect which make us willing to undertake and to subject him to so serious an operation with so doubtful and probably partial a result. There is no prospect of the deep and far-reaching abscesses healing with conservative treatment, even with the utmost aid from the latest chemical antiseptics. Furthermore, without repeated re-establishment of free drainage by enlargement of the long track into the pelvis, periods of fever with acute toxaemia and progressive poisoning will altogether spoil his life until it leads to lardaceous disease with progressive limitation of physical and mental function and ultimate death.

I'm only glad I didn't read it at the time.

When Mr Girdleston said to me, 'In view of the possible consequences I must formally ask you for your permission to do this operation, as you may not survive it,' I didn't hesitate. 'I won't survive without it, so let's go ahead. What's wrong with Tuesday?' This prompted him to question me again. I told him about the experience I had had in the convent in northern Italy, when I had kept myself awake because I knew that to sleep would be to die. 'Since then,' I said, 'I have never believed I would die from this wound.' He gave me a long look – he was a very religious man – and said: 'Well, Dukie, you are probably right.'

The following Saturday, I was allowed out and was sitting in the Trinity garden with Ro Wadham. It was a beautiful autumn day. Suddenly we saw two dons – Tony Crosland, the future Labour Foreign Secretary, and Mike Maclagan, the Dean, walking down the lawn. They were total opposites in every way and far from friends. They carried a silver salver and on it was a bottle of port and four glasses. 'Dukie, how lovely to see you,' said Mike. 'Tony and I just caught sight of you in the garden and thought it's such a lovely day we might celebrate with a drink.

So we've found a bottle of Taylor's 1920.' We sat down together, chatted and drank the bottle. I was very touched. Nobody said anything but we knew the score.

That Sunday I saw all the top men meeting when normally they would have been off duty. My room at the hospital happened to overlook the surgeons' coffee room and there were all the doctors who had a hand in my case. I couldn't help thinking that maybe they were talking about me and then, as if to confirm it, Mr Girdleston came to see me. He told me that they were going to postpone the operation. At first, I was disappointed. I had girded up my whole mind and body to face up to it. It was a let-down.

He said that they had a new plan. What he didn't tell me was that, instead of cutting all the bone away to root out the osteomyelitis, they were going to inject something into my wound which would attack the poison and hopefully defeat it. They stuffed this concoction up the wound twice a day. They did that every day for a week and nothing happened. I learnt afterwards that what they thought would happen was that the mixture would blow the whole wound up inside me like a bomb. Apparently, outside my room was piled every possible piece of equipment to deal with the anticipated crisis.

Nothing happened. They did it for another week. I didn't much enjoy it. Another week passed. They got worried and did an X-ray. They found that the poison, which was right across the whole of my back, had marginally diminished. So they went on with it. In the end, what was supposed to be a kill or cure in a week finally achieved the result after six months.

The position stabilized. The treatment was working but very very slowly. I still needed dressings every day, but simpler ones. I had started academic work again in January 1949 from the hospital, but soon afterwards decided to go back to Trinity, who generously gave me rooms, leaving me only to pay for my upkeep and work for a degree. There was no point in leaving Oxford without one. I had, of course, been reading history and, according to Trinity records, I had taken and passed (not quite sure how) those two exams in my first spell before going off to war.

Before I'd gone into the Wingfield, I was concentrating on American history. I found the whole concept of America fascinating: this huge continent which drew people of courage to face the Atlantic to escape from some form of persecution – political, religious, social or starvation. And when they arrived, if they didn't like what they saw they just went west until they did. I also believed that American historians wrote much better than their English equivalents (not a popular view I suspect). There was a less creditable motive. Not many people would make it a special subject so it would be easier to shine and, more deviously, there were so few pupils it was even odds your don would be setting the questions. It paid dividends. At the end of March 1949, I passed the final history paper I took with Distinction. The college is kind enough to record that this was a 'significant achievement' as I had started working in hospital. I tend to believe it was a charitable judgement by the examiners who couldn't read my handwriting. Anyway, I got a BA and an MA.

I stayed on in Oxford, latterly with Elise Northcote, a generous and hospitable lady who had a special feeling for the wounded. She had as lodgers me, Timothy Jones and Jimmy Stuart-Menteth who had lost both his legs with the Scots Guards about 300 yards from me at Anzio. In August 1949, my treatment took a dramatic turn. I used to go from Elise's house in North Oxford every morning to the Radcliffe where I came under a house surgeon, Ian Mackenzie, who had previously worked with Mr Girdleston and therefore knew all about my case. He was brilliant.

One day he said he was busy; could I come and see him later that night? So I drove round (my father had given me a Ford Prefect) after a very good dinner and was frankly rather sloshed. We were alone in the casualty ward. Ian put me on the operating table and gave me a local anaesthetic. He then cut a fresh major path through the flesh to the seat of the wound and stitched up the old channel. This allowed the pus to drain away without further infection. He had always believed that that was the only way the wound would heal. About an hour later, with the effects of alcohol and anaesthetic slowly diminishing in my system, he suddenly said, 'Okay, that's done. You can go home now.' So I got down from the operating table, climbed into my car, drove back to Elise Northcote's and went to bed.

It was unorthodox, it was contrary to medical etiquette and the treatment was not authorized. Yet Ian Mackenzie was right. It worked. And, indeed, it became increasingly obvious that it was working.

In July 1949 Mr Girdleston was again writing to my parents about 'the irrigation plan' and how it had been 'gloriously successful so far'. He added: 'Dukie has earned our admiration as a patient as well as our affection as a person.' On 9 November 1949 came the news that my wound had finally healed. 'My own feeling,' Mr Girdleston told my parents, 'is that if he keeps thoroughly fit, avoids over-strain, is well fed and keeps in good training with regard to alcohol and tobacco, there is every prospect of his having no further trouble at all.' The outcome, he added, in terms uncharacteristic for a man who took a measured approach to everything, 'has been exceedingly remarkable and one feels that our human efforts have been blessed.'

So many people had helped me – Ralph Smith and the doctors at Bad Soden (one a German); Mr Somerville-Large, who extracted the bullet; the nurses and surgeons at Roehampton; Mr Girdleston, who had taken on an apparently hopeless case of a young man who had not even officially been sent to him; the dons and undergraduates at Trinity who added so much to my enjoyment of life; the sisters and nurses at Headington; and lastly Ian Mackenzie who risked his reputation for me. I am deeply grateful to them all.

With all this behind me I thought it was time to look for a job. Trinity advised me to become a schoolteacher – the long holidays and absence of stress would suit my condition. So I opted for a life in newspapers.

Chapter Five

It was September 1949 and I was out of hospital at last but without any income as my army pay had ended. The army had been very generous in looking after me. I had proved a poor investment as a soldier: expensive training, huge hospital fees set against negligible damage to the enemy. That feeling has haunted me all my life even if logic tells me that you cannot do more than hazard it.

It would have been great to have spent a couple of months in the South of France enjoying the complete rest and sunshine the doctors had prescribed to get fully fit, but neither my parents nor I could afford that. Instead, David Henley Welsh and his wife asked me up to stay with them for a month on their farm in Lancashire. Wonderful country, and it certainly did me as much good, perhaps more, than the South of France.

I was excited at the prospect of getting a job, earning some money for the first time and planning my future. I had always wanted to go into the diplomatic service where I had several relations but they warned me that my health would not stand up to the life and climate changes a Foreign Office career imposed. In retrospect that was fortunate. Modern conditions and, above all, communications have radically circumscribed the responsibilities of ambassadors. I know of one who did not even know the British Foreign Secretary was in the country until told by his opposite number in that country's foreign office. It is not that ambassadors do not still have important positions but, just as Britain is less dominant in the world, so ambassadors are less influential.

So I went to the Oxford University Appointments' Board

which recommended two alternatives, ICI or the *Daily Mail*, each of which was looking for graduates as management trainees. I applied to both. ICI had a long waiting list but gave me accelerated entry to their exam because of my age and medical history. The *Daily Mail*, with what I was soon to learn was the customary speed of the newspaper industry, asked me to see their managing director three days later. Along I went, excited by the prospect, to meet Stuart McClean, the dynamic managing director who interviewed me for ten minutes and then said, 'All right, start on Monday at a salary of £5 4 shillings and 7 pence per week as a clerk in the advertisement department.' It was noticeably less than I had been enjoying as a graduate on long term military treatment. And incidentally this was before the five-day week came in: everyone worked an extra half day on Saturdays.

I was left with the problem of the ICI who had a much more formal approach, inviting you to stay for thirty-six hours at the Charing Cross Hotel in central London at an arranged date, two or three weeks ahead, with a group of candidates. That form of selection process was then quite common. The diplomatic service did it. You were given a range of activities – discussion groups, a debating session, general knowledge questions – on all of which you were carefully marked. It is difficult to do that sort of thing badly deliberately, so I thought my great chance to fail would come with the personal interview on the second day. Totally naive about the ways of industry it had seemed to me to be very bad mannered, after ICI had been so kind to push me through their waiting list, to ring up and say 'no thanks, I've already got another job'. I thought a more gracious way was to take the test and fail.

At the end of the first day, we had a formal dinner, each candidate sitting next to a senior member of the management. Pompous but agreeable. It was partly a check on table manners and social behaviour. My neighbour said, 'Well, tomorrow is the most important day of your life, you'd better have an early bed.' I thought this an excellent chance for a bad mark, so I rang up a couple of friends, went out with them and got back at half past one. This did not go unobserved as I realized the next day when, with a hangover, I was called for the great interview.

I sat down with brash over-confidence, almost impertinence. One of the panel asked me what I thought of discipline.

'I think it's a jolly good thing,' I replied bullishly.

'Well, what do you mean by discipline?'

'You tell someone to do something and they do it.' (In retrospect, not a bad definition.)

'What if that person doesn't do it?'

'Well, I'm afraid I've never thought of that.'

'But surely, Hussey, you've been in the army. What happened if your men didn't obey your orders?'

'Sir,' I replied pompously, 'I had the honour to serve in the Grenadier Guards and that was not a situation that ever arose.'

I left the room, confident that I had done more than enough to fail, only to be horror-struck when they called me back and told me that I had scored the best marks they had awarded for months. With great embarrassment, I then had to explain that I had taken another job. 'I can assure you if I had been trying to get this one I would certainly have failed,' I told them. They were charming and said if I got bored with the *Daily Mail* I could get in touch with them again.

So I joined the *Daily Mail* in December 1949. I began at the very bottom – as a copy clerk in the advertisement department, first entering the block and date of each advertisement as it arrived and then carrying it up to the printers on the due day. Not a great intellectual strain. From the very start though, I was intrigued by the process of making up the pages, preparing them for printing and then sending the product down to the presses. The smell of the ink, the immediacy and the whole ethos of working on something that not only changed every day, but several times during the night, was fascinating.

The life seemed faster and more exciting than the more normal alternatives. I have never wanted, for instance, to go into politics. For me, it is a riveting spectator sport – much better to be watching from the stands than playing on the pitch. I have never been a member of a political party and at various times have voted Conservative, Liberal or Labour, although most often Conservative. And I didn't want to go into the City. I thought the handling of money was boring and pedestrian (I couldn't have been more wrong).

Set against that I had no experience of commerce and nor had my immediate family. They all tended to be in government service of some sort. I have been told, I think correctly, that I am a corporate man, not an entrepreneur. I have never had the courage or the initiative to start anything on my own. In a conventional civil service way, I like a ladder to climb as fast as I can, not worrying too much on whom I step on the way up.

The *Daily Mail* was the principal title of Associated Newspapers, the publishing group presided over by the Rothermere family. Its other papers included the *Sunday Dispatch* and the London *Evening News*, and an extremely profitable local newspaper chain in Bristol, Leicester, Grimsby, Hull and Gloucester. The regionals produced the money to fund the nationals.

Esmond Rothermere had succeeded his father, Harold, in 1940, albeit with some reluctance. His two older brothers, earmarked from birth to carry on the business, had been killed in the first war and so the task had fallen to Esmond who was not a natural press baron, but he knew all about money. Family obligations overrode any other plans he had for his life. Harold, the first Viscount Rothermere, had taken over from his brother Alfred Harmsworth, Lord Northcliffe, the founder of the whole enterprise, on his death in 1922. So now it was Esmond's turn. During my time at the *Mail*, Esmond was somewhat haphazardly training his own son, Vere, to take over the reins, as he did in 1971.

Esmond was immensely rich and lived at Warwick House, one of the great London houses just off the Mall, in princely style (appropriately he had once been asked to be King of Hungary but politely declined on the reasonable grounds that there was a better future as an English peer than as a Balkan monarch). He had other homes in Monte Carlo and Daylesford in Gloucestershire, thought by some to be the most beautiful house in England. It had been built for Warren Hastings, who in 1774 became the first Governor-General of Bengal (comprising much of what was later British India). He had funded Daylesford from his ill-gotten gains. Esmond restored it completely. He had an automatic order with every antique dealer in this country and abroad that if ever an item came up once owned by Hastings, he bought it.

Years later when Sue and I went to stay there, Esmond took us round. He had managed to secure almost all Hastings' possessions – pictures, chandeliers, china, books, furniture and elephants (not live). It was an amazing achievement and he loved the Daylesford he had recreated. One day, he stumbled on an old map of the garden which showed a large lake. He put one back the next week.

Esmond entertained hugely in all his houses waited on by butlers and footmen. The first time I stayed there with Sue, though married, we were put in separate bedrooms as was the tactful custom in some great houses in those days. Sue ended up creeping down the corridor to my room with a pillow under her arm. Esmond very much liked Sue. On our first weekend, when we were obviously on approval, a subject came up about which there was some doubt. Esmond turned to Sue and said, 'You will know the truth of that, Susan.' 'Yes,' she replied, 'I do and I have no intention of telling you.' 'Quite right, quite right,' he barked.

Northcliffe House, just off Fleet Street, was an old-fashioned and formal place, with commissionaires in dark-blue uniforms and the proprietor presiding imperially over the business from his office suite on the second floor. Esmond was a much less flamboyant character than either his father or his great rival at the *Express*, Lord Beaverbrook. The general view of Esmond was that he was not a dominating press proprietor, didn't wholeheartedly want to be and therefore could be whimsical and confused instead of clear-sighted and determined. Francis Williams, the leading commentator on the media in the Sixties and Seventies, summed up the accepted wisdom on Associated Newspapers when he described it as suffering from 'amateurish ownership and wobbly management'. Arthur Brittenden, editor of the *Mail* in the late 1960s, adds to the charges against Esmond that, fundamentally, he did not like or trust journalists which made running a newspaper a somewhat inappropriate business for him to be in.

History has not been kind to Esmond. 'Raised by his father to be a gentleman of exemplary conduct,' his biographer S.J. Taylor has written, 'Esmond lacked the ruthlessness and confidence that was an integral part of being a successful newspaper magnate. He was shy and this made him seem a distant figure, difficult to talk to, difficult to approach. At one moment he was conciliatory and in this guise he was considered a patsy and at the next moment he was remote and in this, dictatorial guise, a threat.'

It is certainly true that the conflicts in Esmond's character did not naturally equip him for the dynamic and grasping attitude of most proprietors, totally absorbed in their products, but these views are on the whole an exaggerated portrait of both Esmond and his newspapers and ignore the successful provincial chain and newsprint companies. Moreover, they are examples of precisely the sort of criticism that Esmond took to heart, especially when it came from his exclusive social circle. Randolph Churchill (who once remarked 'poor Esmond? Oh no, not poor Esmond, very rich Esmond') criticized the *Sunday Dispatch* in the Fifties for serializing *Forever Amber*, a novel considered racy at the time but tame now. He labelled Esmond 'the nation's pornographer-in-chief' (a phrase pinched by Paul Johnson in the 1990s to damn Michael Grade at Channel 4). On Esmond's instructions the offending material was immediately dropped, even though it had boosted circulation considerably. A few years later he off-loaded the *Sunday Dispatch* to the *Sunday Express*, its great rival.

Esmond was certainly a great one for changing editors. In the twenty years I was there, we had Frank Owen, Guy Schofield, Arthur Wareham, Bill Hardcastle, Mike Randall and Arthur Brittenden. Looking back, the problem lay in Esmond's character. He was indecisive, prone to taking the advice of the last person who had spoken to him. There was never a settled editorial policy and no settled top team. At that time, newspaper proprietors were even more powerful than they are today. They had a major grip on public information since there was virtually no television and only radio. Standards were in the main much higher over what was considered fit to print and how politics should be handled.

Of course, Esmond, like his fellow proprietors, was very well informed, had high-level contacts and much enjoyed the political gossip to which they were party. Beaverbrook, Esmond's great rival, however, used that power in a quite different way. He had founded the *Express* and built up the empire himself, whereas Esmond had merely inherited his. Beaverbrook was a dominating, irascible, brilliant businessman, passionate about newspapers and fascinated by journalists, with an impish sense of humour, driven by ambition and not handicapped by scruples. He built around him a a close-knit team at the top – Arthur Christiansen and John Gordon as editors, Osbert Lancaster and Giles as cartoonists and Tom Blackburn as managing director.

Esmond was different. He had his coterie of social friends with whom he would discuss the political gossip and the fortunes of the newspaper – Noel Barber, Patrick Sergeant and Iris Ashley, the fashion editor – but as a rule he avoided the company of journalists. Instead he surrounded himself with layers of sycophantic managers who served to insulate him from his papers. These people were no competition for the long-running Beaverbrook team.

Esmond might have been weak but he was no fool. In September 1964, Hugh Cudlipp brought out the first edition of the *Sun* (it had been, as the *Daily Herald*, the Labour paper and was previously owned by the party before Hugh bought it for the Mirror Group). Esmond stayed in the office to see the first copy. I brought it in, adding with glee that they had a production problem and were losing copies. 'Make sure they solve it,' Esmond said to my surprise. 'The more people who see this paper the better as far as I'm concerned. It will never sell.' He was right. Within weeks its circulation halved and five years later Cudlipp sold it as an ailing paper to Rupert Murdoch who immediately and flagrantly imitated the *Daily Mirror*, with enormous success. Esmond enjoyed that. 'It is the only time in my life,' he chortled, 'that I have seen the victim sell his murderer the dagger that ends up in his back.'

And he could laugh at himself. The week after he had replaced Bill Hardcastle with Mike Randall, he passed me a letter and said, 'Read that.' 'Dear Lord Rothermere,' it began, 'I see you have fired another editor. I expect you are right. All these editors are pretty poor stuff but if you leave the stars out of the *Daily Mail* again, I will give it up after fifty faithful years.' Esmond roared with laughter, but the reader had a point. People like regular features in their newspapers, in the same place, every day.

But it was many years before I met Esmond, although I went up the company quickly, allegedly, my colleagues said, because I was connected to the Harmsworths by marriage. Not quite right. The connection was 'a man called Hussey' (no relation), cited in Esmond's first divorce.

After seven months carrying up the blocks, I was sent to the Manchester office to deal with public relations. The most testing task I had to do was running, with Eric Morley (later of Miss World fame), a bathing beauty competition at Morecambe for the *Sunday Dispatch*. In theory it was open to all comers, but it fell to me to persuade some girls to reconsider putting themselves forward. They would not – how can I put it kindly – appear at their best in a bathing costume. Some of them hadn't even shaved their armpits. A public parade could have only invited embarrassing ridicule. It was a great exercise in tact.

As a very junior figure in the world of newspapers I was immensely flattered to receive an invitation to attend a board lunch at WH Smith from one of my father's oldest friends, Arnold Power, a director there. I was, needless to say, nervous and anxious to acquit myself well, but just as we were sitting down to lunch one of the joints on my artificial leg gave way and my foot fell off. David Smith looked horrified. 'Can we get a doctor?' he asked. 'A blacksmith would be more use,' I replied.

It could have been worse. Years later I was invited to attend a very grand dinner at the German Embassy to mark the Queen's first visit to Germany since the end of the war. Just before I set off, my foot fell off again – it has only happened twice in fifty years. I couldn't find the spare and ended up cobbling the broken one together with sealing wax and bandages. I was frightfully late and it was very clear what the problem had been. Since the dinner was aimed at increasing goodwill between the two nations, it was unfortunate to say the least, but the German Ambassador, who had a distinguished record in the resistance to Hitler, was charm itself. The only sticky moment came when Christopher Soames took me to one side in great hilarity and said, rather too loudly, of the ambassador, 'Splendid, he was probably the bugger who shot your leg off in the first place.'

My attitude to my artificial leg has occasionally failed to impress my doctors. Once when I turned up at Roehampton so that the leg could have its annual service, the doctor asked me what I had been doing with it to get it in such a terrible state. 'Well, I've just been up in Scotland salmon fishing,' I replied. He took great offence. 'You have no right to maltreat government property like that,' he told me. My reply is not suitable for publication.

After six months, at the start of 1951, I was brought back to London to work in the *Daily Mail* circulation department as number three immediately under Mick Shields. The circulation manager was Joe Hull, a hard, old-fashioned professional. One day, I made an appalling and expensive mistake. As soon as Joe came back from his good lunch, I ruthlessly woke him from his customary sleep and said, 'I'm afraid, sir, I've made a frightful balls-up.' 'Well, well, Duke,' he replied, 'come and sit down and we'll work out how to put it right.' A lesson in good man-management never dates.

Mick Shields and I worked well together. Circulation departments were hard work, with several thousand wholesalers altering their supplies daily. These had to be recorded by hand and sent down to the publisher who, once the papers had been printed, had to allot them in the correct number to catch the correct train. That went on every night. And we were in charge. There was one famous occasion when the 1955 General Election and a railway strike followed on successive days. This roughly quadrupled the job and Mick and I worked in the office for two days without going home. As I was a bachelor I used some of my limited resources to buy sandwiches for us all. It did not go unnoticed by the circulation manager who told us we could each have a £2 bonus.

The *Mail* took over the *Daily Sketch* in 1952 and I was entrusted with making this low-brow publication a circulation success. Bert Gunn was the editor and David English the features editor. Our great triumph was running the 'win-a-pub' competition. We put on 100,000 copies in a month to reach 1.5 million. The prize was a pub in Devon. I travelled down with Vere Harmsworth, Esmond's son, and his future wife, Patricia, for the ceremonial handing-over of the keys. At some stage during the hilarious proceedings, Patricia (later known as Bubbles) suggested she would cook me a quiet dinner in her flat. Vere was not amused and I reluctantly put my long-term career before immediate adventure.

A few months later, in another managerial change, Vere and I were put together in the same office. It was an odd arrangement and I can only think, in retrospect, that Esmond had already some inkling that he was going to move me up the company and that I therefore should get to know his son and heir. Vere was then manager of the *Daily Sketch* and I was manager of the *Evening News*. We got on very well, shared views about the papers and frequently went out together in the evening. It was fun. One day in 1957 he arrived a little later than usual, at about eleven, looked across and said, 'Dukie, I hope you will come to my wedding.' I said, 'Of course, I'd absolutely love to, didn't realize you were engaged actually. When is it?' He looked at his watch, and said 'in half an hour'. It was a small ceremony at Caxton Hall of which I am the only surviving witness. Later it was celebrated by the immediate family in the Dorchester.

I was gradually oiling my way up the company. In 1958 I was promoted again – to Scotland as general manager of the *Daily Mail* north of the border. It was immediately obvious that the Scottish *Daily Mail* was no longer viable as an independent entity. Circulation was poor, much lower than the *Express* or *Record*, both printed in Glasgow. Edinburgh is a wonderful place in which to work, particularly if you were courting, as I was then. It was within easy reach of the most beautiful country and many hospitable houses. After eight months there, I was promoted again and moved back to London.

Later, when I became managing director, I closed the Scottish *Daily Mail*. It was a tough decision which I took and personally told the staff. We gave them and the unions three months' full notice and never lost a copy. It was an object lesson proving that if you are straight, trusting and frank about what is going to happen, you have a much better chance than if you dissimulate or dodge. Uncertainty is what damages staff and destroys confidence.

It was another good lesson – like the advice the then managing director, Bobby Redhead, an Old Etonian and the world's best Fives player, gave me in 1958 when he appointed me to Scotland. 'It's a big jump for you,' he said, 'but don't worry too much because in the context of a very large company, the Scottish *Daily Mail* is a very small operation. Even if you do make a bad mistake it's not going to be very damaging. Treat it as experience. Here's my private number. If you are in real trouble you can always ring.' Sending promising executives to run small areas is good training which I tried to carry out later in the BBC and it paid off. Bobby gave me another piece of advice that I have never forgotten. When you start a new job, don't think you've got to begin by having wonderful ideas, coming out with bold initiatives: just learn the job. Let the ideas come later.

It was hard work, with many late nights. Because I was doing well, my days grew longer but it didn't stop me having a good time in the evenings. I usually got away at 6.30 p.m. and I had a small car. There was no breathalyser – luckily. At weekends I normally went to see my parents at Cuckfield where they had a modern house with a wonderful view of the Downs just by a very attractive church. My father still worked in various educational ventures, going to Eritrea in 1953 to advise on schools, and was a fellow of the Woodward Foundation, but his health was deteriorating. I didn't like to miss too many weekends.

He died comparatively young, at seventy-two, in 1958. We had never been all that close, something I now regret enormously. Though I believed at the time we were different, I see now with the benefit of hindsight that in many ways we were similar. I inherited from him the desire and determination to innovate, to change things, persuade people to see beyond their usual prejudices and accepted ways of doing things. We both suffered some disdain for our efforts. And both went firmly ahead when more gentle diplomacy might have helped – or perhaps it might not.

There was one family with whom I did keep in touch and that was that of Hermione Hichens, from whom I rented a small London flat in Danvers Street. I stayed often at their home at North Aston Hall, near Banbury, once the English base of the Longford family. In 1951, Hermione's daughter Stella married a close friend of mine from Trinity, Dick Hornby, later a Conservative MP and minister. I was the best man. Among the bridesmaids was Susan Waldegrave, aged twelve, whose mother was Hermione's niece.

I didn't think much more about it. She was, after all, sixteen years younger than me but then much later, in 1958, we met again, at North Aston Hall. We were both there for the weekend. Sue was eighteen. I was thirty-four. We went with a party to the Grand Prix at Silverstone. Sue accompanied her two younger brothers.

I was bored stiff by motor racing, so after a good picnic I fell fast asleep on the grass and was woken by this young woman saying 'You may be very grand and grown up and bored by motor racing, but my brothers think it's marvellous, so you ought to take more interest.' I recognized the voice which was to rule my life thereafter.

It all happened very quickly. We fell in love. I went down to meet her father, Geoffrey Waldegrave, and her mother at their family home at Chewton Mendip in Somerset. To ease the introductions, they also asked my old hospital friend, Harry Grenfell (Sue's uncle). The Waldegraves were very welcoming. It was a large family – five girls and then two boys. They were kind and hospitable and we were distantly connected. Geoffrey Waldegrave was a man of great charm, clever, amusing, but something of a talker. He farmed with distinction and probably knew as much about agriculture and forestry as anyone in England. I was not a countryman and going round the farms with him was fascinating. His was an old family and the land in Somerset had been given to them by Queen Mary in the sixteenth century. It is a beautiful estate. They had inherited many of Horace Walpole's possessions which fascinated my future mother-in-law, an accomplished historian. There is a good family story of a large lunch party at Chewton House. One of the five daughters said the word 'fuck' very loudly. Her slip was followed by a terrible silence. Finally my ethereal and scholarly mother-in-law said, 'Do you know that George III always spelt it with a ph?'

We got engaged in November 1958 and married on 25 April 1959. The age gap should have worried us, I suppose, but it didn't seem to and hasn't since. I was, of course, in Scotland during our courtship and when our engagement was announced Bobby Redhead arranged for me to be posted back down to London to coincide with our wedding. That was thoughtful of him.

We were married in Bath Abbey, where, although I did not know it at the time, my great grandfather had also been married, having migrated from North Bradley in Wiltshire, twenty miles away, to become a master baker in Bath, 200 yards from the abbey.

We leased a flat in Carlisle Mansions in Chelsea overlooking the Thames and settled down to domestic life although, even then, my working hours were worse than most of my contemporaries. We didn't have a child immediately and Sue first took a job teaching at her old secretarial school; then, out of the blue, she was offered a job as a temporary assistant to the Queen's ladies-in-waiting who needed extra help to deal with the huge amount of mail received at the time of Prince Andrew's birth.

Then, at the end of that same year, there was a vacancy for a lady-in-waiting. My father-in-law had been associated with the court for many years through the Duchy of Cornwall and, to everyone's surprise, Sue was asked if she would like the job. It was a big decision. Lurking in the background was a potential conflict between a wife at the Palace and a husband in Fleet Street, but I am proud that right through to the end of my working life, except for the last months at the BBC, no one has ever suggested that this link has influenced me in my decisions. Out of respect for Sue, I was never asked about the royal family. Anyway, it was always better to know nothing.

In August 1961, our son James was born, followed in February 1964 by our daughter Katharine. With two children we then bought a house in Chelsea Park Gardens and lived there for more than twenty years, during which time we also bought the one next door and put them together. It had been owned by the Blacks, parents of a contemporary of mine from Rugby. He had been killed in the war and they had planted a mulberry tree in the garden in his memory. Part of the arrangement in selling us their house (at a price below the market rate) was that we would look after the tree. So we had a large house with a good garden, facing south. In due course, when the children grew up and wanted to share with their friends, we sold the house and with the proceeds I bought three flats – one for James, one for Katharine and one for us. I did not have much change, but had enough to make the flat, in which we are still living, comfortable.

Both James and Katharine have three children. And so, the six grandchildren, the two children and their mother have been and remain the centre of my life and a source of lasting happiness. It's a dreadful admission but I probably see more of my young grandchildren than I did of my own young children. They were very rough years in Fleet Street. I was constantly late home, sometimes very late and frequently received midnight telephone calls. It was always the same message – trouble at mill. In those days, such a working pattern was relatively rare, but nowadays of course, everyone works much harder. The late starts and the long, leisurely and far from alcohol-free lunches are a thing of the past. Moreover, in those days, people joined a firm in whatever business and expected to spend their lives there. To move was relatively rare. Now I am told it looks bad on your CV (I never even had one) if you don't change about once every five to ten years.

Back to Fleet Street. I returned to London in 1959 as assistant general manager under Bob Hammond, the general manager of Associated Newspapers. I was to handle the company's labour relations, a prospect I approached with deep gloom, although by

Fleet Street standards the Harmsworths' labour relations were extremely good. They had engineered and attained a real close feeling between family and staff and were among the first to introduce a non-contributory pension scheme. The Harmsworths were humane employers at least at the lower levels, but Esmond could also be tough with the unions.

He was chairman of the Newspaper Proprietors' Association and led them through the five-week electricians' stoppage in the mid 1950s. He was alleged to have resolved it. I don't know the history but I was present once when he humbled the union leader Dick Briginshaw at a critical moment in national negotiations. We thought we had an agreement. Briginshaw, alone of the unions, suddenly wavered and said he must consult his members. Esmond, tall, immensely good-looking and imperious, banged the table and said, 'I represent the newspapers, and I on behalf of my members have accepted this agreement. If you on behalf of your members are not in a position to accept it get out and send back someone who can.' It was difficult to work out who enjoyed it more – the other proprietors or the other union leaders.

Although an intensely competitive industry at every level, the big problem was labour. It originally stemmed from the undertakings the proprietors had given to their staff, at the outbreak of war in 1939, that they would take them all back in to their old jobs once the fighting was over. By 1945 the shortage of newsprint had reduced the populars to eight pages a day and the qualities to ten. As the old staff came back, the temporary staff were also kept on. Newspapers were vastly overmanned as a consequence.

In time, the papers gradually increased their pagination as prosperity, supplies of newsprint and advertising grew and the unions demanded more staff with every increase in size or indeed whenever any other change was made, however small. We struggled to bring out twelve-page papers using a larger staff than had printed twenty four-page papers before the war.

The problems were immeasurably increased by the competitive nature of the proprietors who were more frightened of their rivals than they were of the unions, who were slowly but steadily bankrupting them. It goes back to Esmond and the dagger. The unions posed a dagger threat to all newspapers. The problem was that no one newspaper was prepared to stand alone and resist outrageous claims. The proprietor practically always gave way. Of course, it was a deadly threat if a newspaper stopped publishing, for the costs remained and the competitors collared the sales. For that reason no one was willing to tackle the problem. The focus was on getting the paper out whatever the cost. The newspaper industry was akin to the airline industry. You had a product today which could only be used today. It had no value tomorrow, like airline seats. That industry also has suffered difficult labour relations.

The fifties philosophy of newspaper owners was dominated by what I called the four Ps – personal prestige, political power, propaganda and pleasure. It was only in 1966, with the spectacular growth of television and the advent of new figures on Fleet Street like Lord Thomson who bought the *Sunday Times* from the Kemsleys, that a fifth P was added – profit.

Broadcasting in particular caused changes. A good example was the classified editions of the evening newspapers on Saturday, brought out specially for the football results. The *Evening News*, when I was manager, brought in thirty-four machines to print 600,000 copies with the full football results in sixty minutes. It was a tremendous operation with journalists hanging on open lines to shout down the final score as the referee's whistle blew in the background. It was also hideously expensive, but basically, I thought, more about gambling than football. The readers wanted to check their pools' coupon. I was sceptical about the cost and was proved right when suddenly a bright spark in the BBC broadcast the results on radio. Within a few years the Saturday classified editions all over the country were killed stone dead. An ominous sign.

Redhead's advice to me in my new job was simple and straightforward. When they come to you with a claim for more money, just use your common sense. They will recognize that and in the *Mail* they usually did. But above all never, ever, get caught out telling a lie. The unions are casual with the truth – for them it is all part of the negotiating game – but the management must not be caught at it. You are the spokesman. You may consult professional advisers but you have to make the decision. The unions, although in theory united, come in as a group each vying with the other to impress their colleagues on their militant advocacy. Keep a cool head.

It was all about adopting the most effective strategy and sometimes a little cunning. When I wrote to a union official or someone else with whom I was having a dispute, I always bore in mind Redhead's advice that he or she might have to show the letter to other people and, certainly in union cases, read it out to the men involved. For this reason, I always softened the letter with phrases like 'I am sure you will understand that . . .', 'could we not agree that . . .', etc. It gave my opposite number room for manoeuvre and avoided driving him into a hole.

I was learning, but there were occasions where I had to resort to low cunning. I was facing a particularly tricky confrontation with J. V. Manning – a brilliant journalist but an aggressive and militant union official. So I greeted him with my leg off, on crutches. My secretary arranged the chairs in my office so that Manning and his delegation were sitting in the middle of the room, too far away from my desk to do any table-banging. And then she brought in tea. Their hands were tied by the cup and saucer. I won the argument.

In my belief, the trick is always be polite, always talk to as many people as you can wherever you are, whoever they are. I always did. In what was a revolutionary step at the *Mail*, I went down regularly to the press room, sitting down on the bench and talking to them. In other places I have always talked to those I share the lift with. It must have worked, because in the *Daily Mail*, and later at *Times* Newspapers and the BBC, the top executives complained about it.

Perhaps I could just nail a canard, that I interrupted a union meeting to announce the birth of Prince Edward as if I was some royal creep. The truth of this much repeated story is that we were planning a special edition of the *Evening News* in March 1964 to mark the birth of the Queen's fourth child. The unions wanted a bonus for the extra work (none!). Suddenly the telephone rang and Sue told me the baby had been born. I called the meeting to a halt and told them to get on and print the bloody thing, which they did.

Our game plan at the *Mail* throughout the 1960s was still to beat the *Express* at their own game. In 1960, Esmond absorbed the ailing *News Chronicle* which was then running at six figure losses on a circulation of 1.1 million. It became part of the *Daily Mail* in the hope that by adding its readership to ours – which had by then fallen to 1.5 million – we would achieve a combined figure to 2.6, a good deal closer to the *Express*. The scheme failed miserably. The *News Chronicle* had a mainly Liberal readership which deserted in droves faced by amalgamation with what was an overwhelmingly Tory paper. We were no better off than before.

In retrospect, it was a disgraceful as well as a profitless enterprise. The Cadburys who owned the *News Chronicle* (and the London-based *Star* which was absorbed into our *Evening News*) wanted out. I don't know how the deal was fixed because I was too junior at the time but used to attend all the planning meetings in Warwick House, mainly to take notes. In simple terms, Esmond bought both papers. The plan was negotiated and operated by Redhead and Hammond. I suppose they thought it would be a quick fix. It was more in the nature of a slow death for the *Daily Mail* and a fast one for the *Chronicle*. The unions at the *News Chronicle* were told at 8 o'clock that night that they were being shut down immediately. If they wanted to salvage any jobs, of which there were several hundred, they must cross over into our machine room at once and print the combined *News Chronicle* and *Mail* and the same with the *Star* and *Evening News* the next day. In retrospect it was a brutal and short-sighted policy. It seems almost unbelievable today that we could have done it.

It has remained ever since a debatable issue. But the *News Chronicle* was losing money. It would have required a very considerable philanthropist to keep it going. I don't think the *Star* had a chance but a really brilliant editor, if you could find him, with financial backing could have saved the *News Chronicle*. Newspapers go in waves. Up and down. The heights and the depths. They need firm, consistent policy backed by editorial genius and financial investment. If they lack any one of those three, they fail. The bottom line was that the Cadburys were no longer willing to support the paper with their money and no one else appeared willing to do so.

However, the *News Chronicle* debacle was, I suspect, an opportunity for me which, all unwittingly, I took. I seemed to have given the impression of sound common sense and good judgement (not all will agree). Anyway, from that moment onwards, I was clearly in Rothermere's good books, Redhead's and Hammond's. A nice hat-trick for promotion.

I became manager of the *Evening News* in 1962. Its strength lay in its total grip on a very rich London classified advertising market. It had a superb distribution system, not just throughout central London but within a range of seventy miles outside. Esmond told me once that every paper inevitably reflects the character of the editor, so when you choose an editor look at his character and that is what the paper will be like. The *Evening News* was a classic case. At the helm was Reg Willis, a simple, straightforward Devonian, keen on sport, very professional, with no pretensions to politics or society. Every headline had to have the name of a London district in it, and there was to be no sex. It offended the London stores. When I joined him as manager, he said, 'We don't want any bright ideas, lad, we just want the system to work. No need to be clever. This is a sausage machine from 8.10 in the morning until 4.50 at night, one page goes off the stone every ten minutes except between 12.30 and 1.10 when the comps have their lunch.'

Elsewhere, despite our various efforts, the *Mail* was, if anything, getting ever deeper into trouble. The money spent on the *Chronicle* would have been better invested in promoting the *Mail*, something Esmond was always reluctant to do. At the *Daily Mirror* his cousin, Cecil King, had boosted circulation to five million to sprint past the *Express* and *Mail*. King held some sort of personal grudge and contempt for Esmond. He felt that he had been frozen out of the Harmsworth empire but regarded himself as the real heir to Northcliffe. In the end, however, he so overstepped the mark that he ruined himself. In May 1968, he used the front page of the *Mirror* to launch a personal appeal to Harold Wilson to step down. His shareholders decided he had gone mad and booted him out.

At that time, it was a sensation. Cecil King ruled the newspaper world. He was chairman of the Newspaper Proprietors' Association and the confidant of prime ministers. In some ways he was the most powerful man in the United Kingdom. Hugh Cudlipp and Frank Rogers went down to see him one morning while he was shaving and said he had lost the confidence of the board who required his immediate resignation. It fell to me to ring Esmond and tell him. He was in tremendous form. 'There you are,' he shouted down the telephone, 'it's all arrogance. Cecil was arrogant. De Gaulle was arrogant, and they've fallen on the same day. Serves them right.'

Cecil had always been kind to me on the Newspaper Proprietors' Association so I wrote to say how sorry I was. He must have had a tremendous postbag but I got a letter by return, thanking me and adding, 'It was rather sad to be shot down like an eagle in full flight.'

In 1963, Redhead resigned, to be succeeded by Bob Hammond as managing director. He was a good man to work for, with a wide knowledge of the industry based on his origins in Northcliffe newspapers in the West Country. He was generally liked and trusted but, like many senior managers at the *Mail*, he had no sense of editorial values or indeed of newspapers other than from the production and labour side. So he didn't win the confidence either of his editors or his executives. There was potentially a vacancy.

I was unaware of this, although by that time I had been promoted as his deputy to look after the sales of the newspapers while Mick Shields was also a deputy looking after the advertising. We both reported to Hammond. Esmond, like many an insecure man, used the policy of divide and rule with his management team and so liked to set up people in competition with each other. Yet though we were rivals – Mick had been number two in the *Mail* circulation department when I was number three – we were also good friends and had joined the company at about the same time, though Mick was a shade older than me.

I don't think I was conscious of any looming crisis, although I noticed that Mick spent a lot of time with Hammond, but why shouldn't he? So did I. It came as a complete surprise in 1967 when I was summoned to see Esmond in his office and told that he had decided to make changes in the organization of his company. The national newspapers would be formed into a new company called Harmsworth Publications which would embrace only the *Daily Mail*, the *Daily Sketch*, the *Weekend Mail* (a not sleazy enough weekly) and the *Evening News*. He wished me to take over as managing director with Mick as my deputy. The provincials plus the various extra-curricular activities of Associated Newspapers – in short the ones that made a profit – would be dealt with separately.

I had no idea that this was coming, but I rapidly realized how bitterly disappointed Mick would be. Nor did he trouble to conceal it. It also became clear that I was not Vere's choice, or Hammond's, but that didn't matter. He was leaving.

The secret was my relationship with Esmond. He was not a man who trusted people easily, but he had grown to trust me over the years. Moreover, I think he felt more comfortable with me than Mick. Esmond imagined we moved in approximately the same social circles, whereas he regarded Mick as rather different. I also think that Esmond reacted better to my skills with the staff than to Mick's outstanding abilities as a financial planner. Arthur Brittenden, editor of the *Mail* in the period, tells me now that he believes Esmond appreciated my way of standing up to him, but doing so with deference and respect. Arthur calls it bravura.

I tried to ease Mick's disappointment by putting him in total charge of advertising and all the other bits that national newspapers had accumulated like National Opinion Polls which he had helped to found. I kept the editorial, circulation and newsprint side of the newspapers.

The new job was my first big challenge and made me in 1967, at the age of forty-four, a prominent figure in a national newspaper industry that was at a watershed in its history.

Chapter Six

My first date on being appointed managing director at the *Daily Mail* was lunch at the Savoy with the Rothermere family lawyer, Dennis Walsh. He was a wise old solicitor who looked after the affairs of the Harmsworths and the Londonderrys. That was enough to keep him in business. 'You are a very young man about to take over a big responsibility,' he said, 'and I want to tell you something about the Harmsworths.' The family firm – Associated Newspapers – was, he informed me, controlled absolutely by Esmond. 'What about the shareholders?' I asked naively. 'Shareholders?' he replied. 'What are they?' And he added: 'Esmond is very involved in the business but he is an extremely rich man with an empire that spreads a good deal wider than newspapers. He sees the managing director of his nationals in the same category as his head gardener at Daylesford.' That clarified the issue.

If my relationship with Esmond was straightforward, my promotion made things more difficult with Vere. We had been close friends but, as I became ever more Esmond's man, Vere and I inevitably saw less of each other. Esmond gave his son no role, nothing to do and excluded him from decision-making. Leaving him at the end of the corridor behind an empty desk was a peculiar way to treat your heir. It was an even odder way of training him to take over the family business. I must admit straight away that I wildly misjudged Vere. He was always clever with a subtle and serpentine mind. But of course he was put in an impossible position by his father. I don't think Esmond even talked to him very much. However, as we all know, where large possessions are concerned, difficult relations between father and

son are not unusual. I tried to keep close to Vere because I was
fond of him, but it was difficult to deal with both father and son
without playing them off against each other.

Vere always had a ready audience in Mick Shields who,
although disappointed by my promotion, was relieved to have
nothing to do with the newspaper side of the business. Mick
regarded newspapers as a spectacularly effective way of dissipat-
ing a fortune. And he didn't trust journalists. There are, of
course, good arguments for both propositions. He enjoyed being
given a free hand to develop what he was very good at – the
creation of money in many different areas from oil to National
Opinion Polls and newsprint. There was a computer software
company which reaped handsome profits when it was sold. And
then Mick spotted the potential in an idea brought to him by a
bright young graduate from Harvard Business School for a chain
of restaurants called Pizzaland. By the time it was sold on, this
venture had made Associated millions.

It is always difficult to speculate why one has been promoted,
particularly if it is a surprise. Perhaps it was because I got on
very well with the staff at all levels. I believe that the Chief
Executive must be widely accessible, easily recognizable (not
difficult in my circumstances), and must quickly earn the reputation for being absolutely straight and honest. I never hid my
views and I was always completely frank with everyone about
our prospects and my ideas and plans. Above all I have never
found it difficult to make decisions quickly. There are very few
issues where resolution is helped by a long period of contempla-
tion and doubt. Particularly in the media, fast decisions are
of the essence and I don't think you get a much higher ratio of
correct decisions by spending a long time debating the various
options. Staff respond to fast decisions from the top. I think that
attitude helped. Mick was very clever but not so at home with
our colleagues who summed up the difference between us by
saying that, if there was a problem, I called for the staff list
while Mick reached for his slide rule.

One of the advantages of the new set-up was that it allowed
me to be clear from the start about my objective – to bring
Harmsworth Publications, the national newspapers, back into

profit by 1970. When I took over in 1967, they had just recorded a sizeable deficit. I undertook to tackle it by what I hope can be described as a quiet revolution – confronting our problems by using my background with the unions to cut new productivity deals, rationalizing their hold on the printing rooms, maximizing the use of our presses, introducing more training. In addition, I was tough on costs and cut manning levels by 15 per cent at the *Mail* and 700 overall across the papers. In retrospect not a bad effort, especially since it came at a time when the unions were at the height of their powers.

Controlling costs is not enough if no new money is being put in at the other end to encourage and fund enterprise and activity. It risks becoming a downward spiral. Lack of investment was a continual problem. Any scheme to spend new money to generate circulation or profit was opposed instinctively by Esmond and the circle of executives working around him. Particularly important was John Thompson, managing director of Northcliffe Newspapers, Associated's provincial papers, a canny and able man whose division made all the money which mine then lost.

All provincial newspapers are run on a shoestring. They operate in a monopoly market both for advertising and sales. They play major roles in their local cities, have loyal staffs and equally loyal readers. No wonder they are so successful and so highly rated on the Stock Exchange. Their workforce had no time for their wealthy and unscrupulous trades union colleagues on the national newspapers. With low costs and captive markets, these papers coined the money. In fact Esmond told me once 'You would not believe how much money you can make from a small paper in Leicester.'

Naturally Thompson had access to Esmond and was always putting in digs at our losses and what he regarded as unnecessarily lavish expenditure. This was a thorn in our part of Esmond's flesh. He also fortified Esmond's obstinate refusal to spend money to publicize the paper. Esmond and Mary, his third wife, once took the editor of the *Mail*, Arthur Brittenden, and his wife to their villa in the South of France. Esmond had been set up by Mary who was backing Arthur's demand that money be spent on promoting the *Mail*. One day Esmond took

Arthur to the beach and, out of nowhere, said, 'So Arthur, I gather you want to spend my money.'

'Well, we are constantly told that the *Mail* is much better, but if you want to sell the paper, you must advertise it,' Arthur replied.

'So what will it cost me?'

'Well, if you set aside a million pounds for an advertising campaign . . .'

'A million pounds?' Esmond exploded. 'Are you mad? If the paper's any good, it will sell.'

And with that he disappeared into the Mediterranean. The subject was never raised again. It wasn't until Vere took over that the policy changed.

Esmond's marriage to Mary, like Vere's to Pat, was something of a surprise. In late 1966, I was in the office one morning at nine when Reg Willis, the editor of the *Evening News*, called to say 'What do I do? I've just received a photograph of the chairman's wedding at Caxton Hall this morning.' I replied: 'What you don't do is put it in the paper until I have checked it out.' At the age of sixty-eight, Esmond had eloped with Mary Ohrstrom, a girl thirty-five years younger than him with six sons. She made his closing years happy and in June 1967 produced another son – Esmond or 'Little Essie' as he was called, after his father.

His decision to marry again was all the more unlikely since he had been diagnosed five years earlier with Alzheimer's (at just the point that he resigned as chairman of the NPA on health grounds). I only discovered this when I read S. J. Taylor's 1998 biography of him. It was certainly not apparent to me, though I knew nothing about Alzheimer's until my sister, Helen, developed it. This condition may well have accounted for Esmond's sometimes irrational behaviour.

I was seriously contemplating closing the *Sketch*. It was hovering around 800,000, well down on its 1950s heyday and facing a new challenger. In January 1969, Rupert Murdoch had bought the *News of the World* from the Carr family after a protracted battle with Robert Maxwell. By the end of the year he had acquired the *Sun* as well. It was the start of the Fleet

Street career of an extraordinary man who changed and dominated the newspaper scene. And still does, except that he now
dominates television as well.

Rupert Murdoch's background was in newspapers. His
father, Sir Keith, ran an Australian newspaper group but died in
1952 when Rupert as still at Oxford. Part of his will was to hand
the baton on to Rupert and from the age of twenty-two he was
immersed in the business, aided initially by his mother, Dame
Elizabeth Murdoch, now in her nineties and a most distinguished
lady. She is a personality of immediately recognizable quality,
highly intelligent, well informed, humane with wit and charm.
She epitomizes the best of any civilized society.

With his acquisition of the *News of the World*, Rupert
transformed the newspaper industry in this country. *The News of
the World* was a legendary reporter of sexual scandal, primarily
court cases. I always understood that the paper had a deal with
the police. They would tip it off about any lubricious case of
incest, sodomy or bestiality, provided that the story in the paper
started with the sentence 'Alfred Brown of Manchester was
sentenced yesterday for five years [ten, fifteen] for . . .' and then
naming the offence. There was some point to this arrangement
because, when the *News of the World* started at the turn of the
century and travel between villages and towns was long and
difficult, a high percentage of the population did not even realize
that incest was illegal. The *News of the World* put that right in
no time.

In November 1969, Rupert took the ailing *Sun* off Hugh
Cudlipp's hands. His first edition showed where he planned to
take the paper; the word sensation in capitals on the front page
over a story on horse doping, a Swedish model – admittedly
fully-clothed – on page three, and an extract from racy novelist
Jacqueline Susann's latest outpouring, *The Love Machine*, inside.

As with most revolutionaries, Rupert would not have succeeded unless he was in tune with the times, but he saw before
most people that the days of the old-style proprietors were
coming to an end, that we were entering a new, more business-
orientated age where papers would stand or fall by their sales
and what most effectively generated those sales. He broke that

cosy but competitive circle of newspaper families with all the brashness of an Australian go-getter, albeit with three years at Worcester College, Oxford, to which he was much attached and to whose finances he generously contributed.

His timing was brilliant. The old guard was falling by the wayside. He had helped the Carrs on their way. The Hever branch of the Astor family had relinquished *The Times* in 1966 to Roy Thomson, a Canadian businessman, though David Astor, from the Cliveden branch, managed to retain the *Observer* until 1976 when he sold out to Atlantic Richfield. The Kemsleys, who owned the *Sunday Times* and *Graphic*, had earlier passed control to Roy Thomson in 1959. The Cadburys had bailed out at the *News Chronicle* in 1961 in favour of Esmond who was fast becoming a representative of an endangered species. Later the Aitkens sold the Express Group and the Berrys, cousins of the Kemsleys, the Telegraph Group. Even the Pearson family is a much reduced presence on the *Financial Times*. Today, only the Harmsworths with their majority holding in the *Daily Mail* remain.

The old generation of proprietors was shocked by the arrival of the parvenu Rupert. And they didn't like his methods. His flagrant display of sensation meant that Rupert himself was slighted in society, something he never forgot or forgave. To them the *Sun* smacked of the gutter. Rather hypocritical. The Carrs had run the *News of the World* as a scandal sheet for many years, yet had occupied an unblemished place in society. When Rupert took over and did much the same he was treated as if he had invented sensation. Though they might cut him socially, the other owners knew they had to compete. Few were up to the task, but the readers were lapping it up.

Rupert, I discovered as I got to know him, has great charm, a lively sense of humour and an amazing business head. He could give you the exact and up-to-date figures on any of his newspapers. Later he controlled absolutely three newspaper empires: in the UK, in Australia and in the United States (where a distinguished proprietor once told my wife 'Rupert despises the English and worships the Americans which is why his newspapers succeed in England and fail in the United States').

One of Rupert's many strengths is that, unlike his competitors, he knows the production of newspapers back to front. He could write and set any story. He could make up the pages, choose the photographs and produce the paper. He was as at home on the stone (the critical composing room area before the introduction of modern technology) as he was in the board room. He also had a superb intelligence system and an uncanny knack of knowing who were the best journalists. Witness his brilliant choice of editor for the *Sun*, Larry Lamb, who at the time of his appointment had been working for the *Daily Mail*.

Finally, he has an unerring political nose. He can sense the victors in any forthcoming election. How far that influences the editorial policies of his papers is an interesting speculation. But he certainly finds it useful to be on the winning side. With the *News of the World*, he thought he would change the Sunday paper market and did. With his purchase of the *Sun* he did the same to the dailies.

From the start, he had a realistic view of the unions. He had seen what had happened in Australia and he knew that unless they were checked they might wreck the industry. Always a realist, he understood that you could not fight every battle – only those where principle or expense was the overriding issue. Otherwise fight hard but settle for the best deal you can get. Again he came along at just the right moment. Simultaneously the power of organized labour was changing. Since Attlee's victory in the 1945 election, the power of the trades unions had been inevitably and rightly increased. Trades unions became a positive factor in the management of the nation's affairs. After all, they largely owned the Labour Party. Yet with that increased influence and power came a similarly increased aggression, culminating in the Winter of Discontent in 1978, public disillusionment, the collapse of Callaghan's government and the election of Margaret Thatcher, determined to restore industrial order.

Rupert's success came at a price. It was always the belief of John Reith, founder of the BBC, that if you lowered your standards you inevitably lowered standards everywhere else. Whatever the rights and wrongs of business ethics, Rupert started a steady decline in the public esteem for the newspaper

industry. Journalists are now ranked with politicians and estate
agents as the three least trusted professions. Rupert acknowl-
edged only one standard – would it sell more copies?

I was just as keen as Rupert to change the newspaper
industry, but not in this way. The Harmsworths stood for high
standards and so did their executives. A revived *Sun* meant that
the *Sketch* had a fight on its hands. To survive, we needed a new
vision for the paper which defined it in relation to the *Sun*.
Popular journalism with standards was the aim. 'I never thought
a man could put more sex into the *News of the World*,' I once
told a publishing dinner about Rupert, 'but he made it with
several orgies to spare and he is doing the same with the *Sun*.'
So the *Sketch* would conduct in-depth investigations – we had a
star reporter called Anthea Disney who won awards for her
undercover exposés – but would present the findings in an
acceptable way. She later went on to become a high flier in
Rupert Murdoch's News Corporation.

The *Sketch* was certainly affected by the *Sun* but it did not
take a battering like others. It lost 50,000 copies over a three-
month period when the *Sun* started up while the *Mirror* was
down a mighty 398,000. Nonetheless something had to be done.
In the rapidly expanding tabloid market, we all had to change. I
realized that it was not possible for Harmsworth Publications to
own two papers that were losing money. We couldn't fight on
two fronts. Moreover, the experienced editor of the *Sketch*,
Howard French – another who remained close to Vere – was a
kindly but rather pompous man with a toothbrush moustache.
No match for Rupert.

I told Esmond about the problems caused by the advent of
Rupert's *Sun*. He suggested we had lunch at the Connaught to
discuss them. I outlined my views and the threat posed to both
our titles: 'You are a rich man with a historic and widely
respected family tradition in the newspaper world. You cannot
close either paper without a fight and you mustn't close the
Mail. So you ought to keep the *Sketch* going for at least a year
and give the staff a fighting chance but not with Howard French
as editor. You need to get a new one.'

Esmond agreed. 'Who do we get to fight Rupert?'

'There is,' I said, 'only one man I can think of: David English, current deputy editor of the *Express*.'

'Go and get him.'

David, whom I'd known much earlier at the *Sketch*, was a brilliant young man of great promise and was known to Vere. So I invited him to lunch and put the prospect of editing the *Sketch* to him. In its current predicament it was a hard sell as David was expecting soon to be editor of the *Express*. We met again and he was not enthusiastic. It was then that I had one of the few brilliant ideas I have ever had. 'I can see you are doubtful,' I said. 'There is only one man who can change your mind. That is Esmond' – not that I called him Esmond in those days – 'whom I happen to know is spending a week in Paris at the Ritz. I suggest that you and your wife, Irene, fly out to Paris and stay at whatever hotel you like except the Ritz. I will tell Esmond you are coming and wish to discuss with him, as proprietor of the newspaper, your future and position at the *Sketch*. You are on a winner either way. You will either come back as one of us and join the fight, or you will come back as deputy editor of the *Daily Express* laughing your head off having spent the most luxurious weekend of your life at the expense of the *Daily Mail*.'

He bought it. I freely confess I am always willing to fire top executives who I think aren't up to their responsibilities, but I have also usually been able to identify talented successors. It was David who turned out to be the saviour of the *Mail* after he was appointed as editor in 1971. Much later, shortly before his death in 1998, David wrote to me to confirm that 'it was quite likely the weekend in Paris that did it. But I put that all down to Irene who hit it off so well with both Esmond and Mary. Anyway, as weekends go, it has turned out to be a pretty long one since I am still here.'

So that was the *Sketch* in safe hands for the moment. Over at the *Mail*, the drop in circulation slowed and the gap with the *Express* narrowed thanks to our new editor, Arthur Brittenden. He had joined in 1964 as number three under Mike Randall, then editor of the *Mail*. Arthur was at the time deputy editor of the *Sunday Express*, a journalist of exceptional charm and ability. He had been working for the *Express* both in this country and as their man in the United States. Solly Chandler, a senior ex-*Express* man, had telephoned me to say that Arthur had been virtually appointed editor of the *Sunday Express* in succession to John Junor who had resigned because he told Beaverbrook he could no longer support the government of Harold Macmillan. Junor was serving out his notice when Macmillan resigned as Prime Minister on the grounds of ill-health. Junor then asked Beaverbrook if he could stay on. Beaverbrook said yes, leaving Arthur as deputy and short-changed.

Solly suggested Arthur might welcome a change. We met in the usual discreet restaurant, liked each other, and I recommended him to Esmond and Mike Randall. They accepted him with alacrity. When Esmond decided in 1967 that Randall's somewhat quirky liberal instincts did not suit him or the paper, Arthur took over. And frankly, as a young managing director, I was delighted. He had to his finger tips one of the really important qualities in management. He knew when to be firm and when to give way. Many managers fail on one or the other of those two alternatives. Never Arthur. He also had a real feel for popular journalism, matched by higher standards than many of his contemporaries.

Though I had no money to initiate any new ones, I put zest into our existing promotions – the Ideal Home Exhibition, the International Caravan and Camping Exhibition, the British Grand Prix, a transatlantic air race. And I encouraged Arthur in his plans to update the paper with a new section for women, FeMail, to introduce colour printing for the first time in the national press, and to start a money digest called Money Mail. I funded the new ventures by keeping costs down. In 1969 I restricted them to a rise of just 1 per cent. For the first time in a long time, I persuaded the *Mail* and its editorial team to define their vision for the paper – 'a paper which tells you accurately what is going on all over the world not just in other people's bedrooms. Anyone can get circulation by lowering their standards but we feel confident that by producing this sort of paper we can send our circulation up without diving into the gutter.'

One extraordinary episode was when we got involved in a

criminal attempt to take over a public company. We ran an article in the paper – I nearly fainted when I saw it. By the time I reached the office, the writs were flooding in and I couldn't bear to think what the damages would be. I suddenly got a call from Sir Jack Waldren, head of the CID at Scotland Yard, who asked me to come and see him immediately.

'You've got to defend this case,' he said. 'The allegation is true.'

I said, 'How? We've no evidence. What do you expect me to do about it? Couldn't you help us?'

'I'll have to think about it,' he replied (i.e. take political advice).

Meanwhile, I got in touch with our lawyers and we went to see Jack Waldren together. He said in rather elliptical language that he might be able to help. I then bearded Esmond who was incandescent about the story but I managed to persuade him that his duty, as a public figure, was to sanction the money required to defend the case with some evidence, to be supplied to us by various sources, and thereby frustrate the criminals.

We had to use some fairly dicey informers, one of whom reported a violent conversation. At our next meeting with the lawyers, a secretary, a charming and innocent young lady, had to read it out. She looked somewhat embarrassed. 'Go on girl, read it out,' our lawyer said. 'Well, it's that man Hussey,' she read. 'You can tell him any more trouble from him and we'll cut his fucking balls off!'

I was apprehensive. We were holding secret meetings with strange people in my home at Chelsea Park Gardens. Next time I saw Jack Waldren I said rather haltingly: 'Well, I suppose this is all right isn't it?'

'What do you mean all right?'

'Well,' I said, a little embarrassed, 'I suppose I mean, well, you know – safe.'

He directed a fierce look at me. 'You were an officer in a good regiment? You know where your duty lies!'

I crept out, feeling very small. In the end, in 1971, we won it.

As I was now his managing director, Esmond tried to enlarge my horizons and also teach me more about politics. Three weeks after his election as President in 1968, Richard Nixon came over to London. Esmond was very well informed on American politics and handed on to me an invitation to a press conference which, as he put it, was being given by one of Nixon's aides. I duly turned up at Claridge's and asked for Suite 16 as instructed. I knew it wasn't quite as I had expected when a liveried footman showed me in to a smallish room filled with newspaper proprietors and ministers. I was by a mile the most junior man there. While I was still taking it in, the door opened and in stepped the President accompanied by an official from the US Embassy in London whom I knew. The official smiled and introduced me to the President.

It was – as Esmond had known it would be – an intimate, high-level briefing session. Nixon gave a brilliant address and finished with three predictions. First, there would be no war with the Soviet Union. There would be arguments, he said, but he had already in his short time in office spoken to the Soviet leader Nikita Khrushchev three times on the hot line. This was surprising but encouraging. Moreover, while he was President, there would be a detente between China and the United States This was a sensation since at the time the two seemed close to war. But he said the Middle East was the real danger spot and that is where the third world war would break out. He said that he did not have the faintest idea what to do about it and didn't know anyone else who had. His forecasts were and still are uncannily accurate. In what turned out to be an unfortunate postscript, he said that it was the responsibility of people in positions like his own to set an example to the young. He certainly goofed on that one.

My role as managing director was not to interfere in day-to-day editorial decisions. I agreed the parameters and kept a careful watch over the finances. I tried, in so far as I could, to encourage in what were often depressing times. If I had met someone who liked the paper or saw some statistic that showed we were doing better, I'd make sure to go into Arthur's office and tell him I was feeling bullish and inject him with a little optimism. That is what leadership is about – as every general knows – even if you are painting a more hopeful picture than reality. Cheer up the troops. Occasionally I was called in by Arthur to help out. We had a very bright reporter in East Anglia, Charlie Wilson, who later went on to edit *The Times*, but he was hopeless with his expenses. Arthur was at the end of his tether and asked me if I could sort it out. I made a note of the amount in question and called Charlie up to my office. He came in somewhat apprehensively. I said: 'Charlie, I'm not going to bugger about over this, you are in debt to the company. That is quite unacceptable for someone in your position. I'll make a deal. The company will pay half and you will pay the other half.' The interview lasted three minutes and worked like a treat. The cheque was on my desk within hours. A short, sharp decision.

Esmond, as proprietor, felt that he could intervene as and when he liked. It could lead to difficult situations that required some tact. Every day at 5 p.m. precisely, wherever he was, the editor was required to ring Esmond to discuss the proposed subject of the next day's leaders. Once Arthur had run a leader opposing capital punishment, then a burning political issue. In the House of Lords Esmond had voted in favour of Sydney Silverman's bill to abolish it, but three days later, he sat next to someone at dinner who had said that the pro-abolition leader was a great mistake and would cost the *Mail* readers. Esmond told Arthur to write a leader reversing the original position and backing capital punishment. Arthur came to see me in despair.

'Leave it to me', I said and went to have a general chat with Esmond in the middle of which I said that I thought his views over the retention of capital punishment were absolutely right for *Mail* readers, but perhaps we should wait a little before we changed our minds so publicly. That worked. Esmond was always vulnerable to accepting the opinion of the last person he had spoken to.

It was not only Esmond who put Arthur under pressure. Esmond's coterie of executive directors regarded access to the editor as a divine right. In Arthur's office, there was a dictograph on which all these self-appointed experts would ring in with their suggestions as to what should go into the paper. Vere, Arthur recalls, was one of the worst offenders, rambling on for twenty minutes, a sure sign that he was lonely. The classic, though, came from one man who told the machine that he had been very surprised that the rise in the price of sprouts, noted by his wife the previous day on Bromley High Street, had not merited an article in the *Mail*. It didn't make editing the paper easier.

As managing director I got ever more deeply involved with the Newspaper Proprietors' Association. I had first joined as the *Mail*'s junior representative in the mid-1960s. It was exactly what it says it was: the meeting of the proprietors or chairmen, usually accompanied by their managing director and a more junior executive. The big decisions were taken by and with the proprietors. Esmond had been chairman from 1934 to 1961 until he gave way – officially on health grounds – to Cecil King. Esmond was at his best chairing the NPA. He knew all his colleagues intimately and when necessary could command complete authority over them and the unions. The agenda was nearly always labour, labour, labour. Prices were not mentioned. We were not allowed to make agreements on prices. That would not have been apparent to the consumer.

When Cecil was unceremoniously heaved out of his position as Chairman of the Mirror Group in May 1968 he was succeeded at the NPA by Lord Drogheda – Garrett Drogheda, managing director of the *Financial Times* – who in January 1970 made me his Vice-Chairman in succession to Frank Rogers of the *Mirror*. It was an extraordinary appointment, putting me, as a relatively junior hired hand, not a proprietor, in a position where I might have to be spokesman for the entire industry. It was another sign that the newspaper world of the old proprietors was changing. Garrett (who combined his job at the *FT* with chairmanship of Covent Garden) and I – neither of us proprietors – got on well with the unions. I thought he and Rupert Murdoch were the two outstanding brains in the NPA. And of course, it was those two who fashioned perhaps, each in his own way, the two most distinctive and successful papers in Fleet Street: the *Financial Times* and the *Sun*.

My golden rules for all union negotiations were: (1) always be polite; (2) always be punctual; (3) never tell a lie (however much they might – that was part of normal union tactics); and (4) never lose your temper (unless it was an act).

There was a splendid moment once when a row broke out as it frequently did between the National Graphical Association (the aristocrats of the union world, representing the old compositors and the machine managers) and National Society of Print Assistants (regarded by the NGA as the dogsbodies who worked the machines). The two were forever falling out over differentials. None of the professionals could think of a way through it. It was going to blow up into a big Fleet Street crisis. Garrett and I had a talk together and I said, 'I think the only way to get round this is for you to ask the two general secretaries, Jack Bonfield of the NGA and Dick Briginshaw of NATSOPA, to a private lunch which I will lay on. They will love the idea.' They did. I booked a private room at Prunier's.

The conversation, as the wine began to flow, got increasingly easy until a fierce argument broke out. Briginshaw accused Bonfield of lying. Garrett leant forward with his rather feminine manner and voice and put his hand gently on Briginshaw's thigh, saying, 'But Dick, you do that to us the whole time.' Briginshaw was so overcome by the touch of an earl that we solved the dispute in five minutes.

In the summer of 1970, Garrett retired from the NPA. It was his hope, he later said, that I should succeed him, but I was still regarded by others as too much of a novice. They opted for Arnold Goodman, the arch fixer and a man of whom I grew to be immensely fond. Though not a proprietor, he was chairman of the trustees of the *Observer*. I know he had his critics, but I found him kind, funny, humane and very clever. He would always help anyone in trouble. He liked life at the top, being on good terms with all the right people, but that is not a unique failing. In private, he was clear-sighted about the proprietors. He told Donald Trelford: 'If I was to choose a cricket team of the most unreliable villains I've ever come across in my life, some newspaper owners would be there.' He described the NPA as the most impossible body of men that could be assembled outside the League of Nations. My own view evolved over the years. The NPA was a club held together by common interest and common enmity. And for sheer wilfulness, it would be hard to beat some of the proprietors – men like Lord Kemsley who ran the *Sunday Graphic* until 1959 on behalf of his rich wife. One Sunday morning, the first edition of their paper arrived at their home with a front-page picture of a bull that had just won first prize at Smithfield. Lady Kemsley was outraged because the reasons the bull had won were much in evidence. Her husband rang the editor and insisted that the offending articles be painted out. The owner of the beast then sued the *Sunday Graphic* – and won!

Arnold Goodman was a man of great good humour. He was always late but was by nature a conciliator and rarely got angry. Our first great drama came on the eve of the 1970 General Election when a newspaper strike was threatened. The newspaper proprietors and the unions were summoned to Downing Street by Harold Wilson. I had never been to Downing Street before, so it was an event for me. We sat round the cabinet table. The Prime Minister clearly wanted to mastermind a peace because of the forthcoming election. He needed to be seen to have ended the strike and so to be powerful and decisive in the eyes of the electors. A not unreasonable objective for a prime minister on the eve of an election. The unions didn't mind what happened as long as they got the money. The Conservative proprietors were torn between wanting to get their papers out and inflicting damage on a government that was not of their persuasion. It all got terribly bogged down so Arnold suggested an adjournment. These three competing elements made a settlement difficult.

I went down in the lift with Arnold and Max Aitken. They were going to the Savoy Grill for dinner. 'Why don't you join us?' Arnold suggested. We had an excellent meal but time was slipping past. Max was drinking whisky sours and Arnold lemonade. We were in the middle of our main course. I looked at my watch and said, 'Actually it's just after 9 p.m. now and we are supposed to be meeting the Prime Minister and the unions at 9.15 in Downing Street. Don't you think we'd better make a move?'

Arnold turned to me and said, 'Sir, I have had a very long, very tedious and very exhausting day. I'm expecting a far longer, infinitely more tedious, and inexpressibly more boring evening. I do not intend to face it without a pudding.' And promptly ordered a double helping of baked apples. When we finally got to Downing Street, everyone was waiting. If it had been anyone other than Arnold, the Prime Minister would have appeared, saying, 'Well, now all the employers have been good enough to turn up no doubt after their second glass of port . . .' and put us totally in the wrong. But, as it was Arnold, Wilson simply said, 'Are you all right, Arnold? Is there anything we can do to help?' Another two hours of discussion followed, with the unions tucking into the free drink, but somehow we managed an agreement. The newspapers rolled out and the election took place, with the proper coverage – a good example of the way Arnold could exploit his powerful connections.

Arnold Goodman and I used to breakfast at his flat at least once a week. It was a good breakfast too. He liked his food, and the telephone never stopped. At that time, among his many clients he numbered the leaders of three political parties. He was also chairman of the Arts Council. Once, after I listened to a whole series of to me, immensely confidential calls, he put his hand over the mouthpiece and said, 'My dear Duke, would you mind leaving the room? This is confidential.' I thought, well, it has to be the Queen or the Pope. We've had everybody else.

There were constant disputes and often I had to take the chair in Arnold's absence. The first time was terrifying. The proprietors all sat on one side of the table, the unions on the other. The etiquette was that I, as acting chairman, was the only one allowed to speak for the proprietors, while each union leader could speak for himself. So there was the NGA, NAT-SOPA, SOGAT, the electricians' union, the engineers' union and so on. And they would all – save for Jack Bonfield at the NGA who was a good Christian – be vying to outdo each other with the force and coarseness of their language. Each union was jealous of the next and no one wished to be isolated. The proprietors' spokesman – me – had to answer all the points from each union, without losing the confidence of his own side, or the argument.

The dispute in question was a threatened strike at the *Daily Mirror* (much enjoyed by all the other newspapers). It was, as always, about pay – the relative pay of the machine managers of the NGA to their NATSOPA assistants who were considered a lower order. I was dispatched to Congress House on behalf of the NPA to see if I could do a deal with Victor Feather whom I didn't then know. We met in a small room alongside his office and, much to my surprise, after half an hour we seemed to agree a formula which we felt would satisfy both sides.

'Well, Mr Feather,' I said, 'this seems okay, why don't you get your secretary to type it out and we can go downstairs?' The ground floor of Congress House was packed with journalists and reporters from radio and television, the first time I had ever encountered anything so public. 'Now, now, lad,' he said, 'you don't mind my saying this, but you're just a little wet behind the ears. It's no bloody good you and I going down after half an hour. My lads want us to have a bit of a ding-dong. Now, what's that they call you? Duke, isn't it? My name's Vic. Now look, Duke, you and I are going to see a lot of each other in the next few years [as we did], so let's get to know each other. There's three-quarters of a bottle of whisky in that cupboard, let's sit down and drink it. By the time we've got through it, it'll be about time to go down and see the boys.'

So this is what we did. We finished the bottle, and then his secretary was called in to type out the agreement. I suggested that Vic, as general secretary of the TUC, should read it out. We emerged from the lift. The cameras flashed. The journalists crowded round. There was a long silence. Vic looked exhausted. 'Lads,' he said, 'this has been one of the toughest afternoons of my life. This young bugger Duke, he may be young but by God he's tough. There have been times in the last three hours when

I didn't think we would make it. But we've just managed it.' I watched transfixed and could hardly believe my ears. The *Telegraph* the next day had a front-page headline – 'The Toughest Afternoon of Vic Feather's Life'.

It was the start of a good working relationship. There was another occasion when the NPA and the unions were at loggerheads. A strike had been going on at the *Mirror* for three days and Hugh Cudlipp was desperate to end it. It looked as if the other papers would be dragged in, and they shared his anxiety. Vic murmured to me that he needed to go to the Gents and suggested that perhaps I did too – a well-known expedient for a quick private conversation in a fix. Once there, Vic said, 'We're in deep trouble, lad. I think the only thing you can do is to invite all the unions to the NPA tomorrow when you will have ideas to put to them.'

'What on earth can I say then,' I protested, 'that I can't say now?'

'We'll worry about that tomorrow.'

We went back to the meeting room. 'Well lads, we seem to have had a draw at Congress House,' Vic announced, 'so let's follow Duke's advice, go to the NPA tomorrow and hope for an away win.' With some reluctance most of the unions agreed except Briginshaw who, using the most extreme words in the British language, accused me of dissembling and asked what on earth I would say tomorrow that I couldn't say now. Difficult, because neither Vic nor I had the faintest idea. In the face of this volley of expletives Vic patted me gently on the leg in case I was going to intervene – no way – and said to him: 'Now, now, Dick, I don't think it's a very constructive approach to the problem.'

Before I met the unions the next day, I consulted with the NPA. They told me to wave the white flag and settle for whatever I could get. The actual dispute was about the relative rates of the NGA and NATSOPA – again. The dispute was costing too much to let it drag on. So I went into my meeting with a heavy heart. We had to make a wage adjustment and leave it to them. It looked like a humiliating defeat. I could hardly get the words out and was waffling around not really

knowing quite what to say. Suddenly, Vic was speaking, blath-
ering on like me and I realized that he had also been told to get
a deal at whatever the cost. Bonfield then made their proposal,
saying as he did so that there came a moment in every general
secretary's life when he had to accept a deal that was not in the
best interests of his union with all the dignity of an honest man.

I returned to the proprietors to report the deal. They could
hardly believe their ears. Rupert Murdoch said: 'I haven't a clue
how you pulled it off, but well done.' Well the fact was, I didn't
know how I had done it. Except that I suppose, by rambling on,
I inadvertently forced the unions to speak first. I suppose they
thought it was a clever ploy. It wasn't.

I had learnt when I was with Nigel Nicolson, whom I was
helping (not much) to write the history of the Grenadiers in
Italy, that many battles turn on minutes. There is one battle
where troops attack a hill-top position, suffer heavy casualties
and fall back. There is another, where troops on the hill top see
the advancing troops, believe they are all going to get killed and
so surrender or retreat. The difference between the two scenarios
is sometimes just a matter of a few minutes or even seconds.
The victor is the one who holds his nerve.

It was a difficult time. The problem lay in aggressive trades
unions, short-sighted proprietors and the vulnerability of newspapers to industrial action. Any threat to production or any stop
in production was hugely expensive. If a newspaper ended two
or three hundred thousand copies short that was sales lost for
the day. This could happen in any event because printing papers
was a difficult and chancy production process. Machines could
have a fault and stop. The paper could break – putting one of
the machines out for an hour. This was one of the reasons why
the newspapers all had a much greater machine capacity than
the strict size of their print run required. The advantage of this,
incidentally, was that in an emergency – a late news story, for
instance – they could increase their print volume to cater for the
extra demand, by 15 or 20 per cent with no difficulty and at no
cost.

That was the plus side. The minus side was that the fragility
of this process made the newspapers critically vulnerable to

industrial sabotage. It only needed a hand movement to break the paper. The union leaders were, on the whole, decent men who understood the problems of the proprietors, but of course were only representing their members. In the end, their power to negotiate depended on the consent of those they represented. The leaders cared about the industry and were intelligent enough to see that, unless there were changes, there would in the end be an explosion.

The members were not so clear-sighted. It varied according to the union and according to the power of the top man. The two most difficult unions were the electricians and the engineers, both communist-led and therefore both extreme in their views but highly disciplined in their behaviour. The Fleet Street leader of the engineers was a delightful man called Reg Birch. He was the leading Maoist in this country. He would have strung any of us up at the drop of a hat, but he was very good to deal with. When you had made an agreement with him, it stuck. He and I got on extremely well for that reason. There was a famous occasion when the NPA got into a dispute with the AEW and Arnold was told to go and talk to Mr Birch. As he lumbered out, Arnold said to me: 'The usual sort of fellow, Duke?' 'Not quite,' I replied, but didn't have a chance to warn him. He was only in the meeting room about five minutes before he re-emerged white as a sheet. Asked what happened, he replied: 'Well, I went in and said, "Mr Birch, we have not met before, but I don't think you realize that the conduct of you and your members might bring a great national industry and major national companies to their feet with disastrous consequences to the industry and the companies concerned." "Yes," was the reply. "And I wish there were a few more that I could wreck so easily!"'

Pitchforked into this position at the NPA, I was widely pictured as an arrogant, ex-Guards officer who had no idea about how union negotiations should be conducted. I don't think this was the view of my colleagues in the NPA or indeed the top officials at the TUC and the various print unions. My crime – if crime it was – was to tell the truth about what was going on in the newspaper industry and suggest how it could be put right. It was not just newspapers the union members were damaging. They were wrecking the whole economy of the country and bringing increased unemployment and a rising level of poverty in their wake. That is not to ignore, of course, the fact that much of this was the responsibility of the employers who, had they taken the long view and in some cases been less greedy, could have averted many of the problems. But I think, looking back on it all, that we in the newspaper industry had got ourselves into an insoluble fix. We were an old-fashioned industry using old-fashioned equipment, when highly economic and efficient alternatives were available and used all over the rest of the world. But that is for the next chapter.

Back at the *Mail*, I kept out of day-to-day editorial policy-making, but I couldn't entirely keep out of the perennial debate about the future of Fleet Street which still goes on today. Much to my surprise, I made the front page of *The Times* by forecasting an inevitable increase in cover prices. I also had a public argument with Roy Thomson, the proprietor of *The Times* and *Sunday Times*. Speaking to a gathering of Young Conservatives, he cheerfully revealed that *The Times* was losing a million pounds a year. He did not see any point in running newspapers if they weren't making any money. With all his crafty simplicity, he suggested that the newspaper situation would be much improved if the *Mail*, the *Sketch*, the *Guardian* and the *Sun*, which Rupert was at that stage subsidizing heavily, closed down. I pointed out by way of response that nine national newspaper titles were serving fifteen million readers. If four closed down, millions would be deprived of the paper they enjoyed. Of course, it would make life much easier for the survivors.

Too few people in this country realize that our distribution system, particularly by rail and now by aeroplane and road too, is so fast that the national newspapers can all be printed in London and regional centres and still be available all over the British Isles in time for breakfast. This is a unique system. In every other country the papers are based on large capital or provincial cities. In the United States it is the *New York Times*, the *Boston Globe*, the *San Francisco Chronicle*, the *Los Angeles Times*. Only *The Wall Street Journal* has a national circulation by printing in several different cities. It is the same in Italy with *Corriera della Serra* in Milan and *La Stampa* in Turin.

However, that historic scene is now changing with newspapers going on the net. It won't replace papers, but there will undoubtedly be a certain number of people who would rather get their news that way. Newspapers have survived many crises, like the advent of radio and television, and they will survive this one.

My favoured approach to the problems of Fleet Street was not to close the unprofitable newspapers but to make them efficient so that they could survive and provide a proper range of choice. Which brings me back to the unions – the major obstacle to profitability. Union relations, like so many in life, are about power. The proprietors owning these vast enterprises had the power to demand greater efficiency but not the collective will to use it. The unions had the power to demand more money, not just for little work, but often for people who weren't even on the premises. They did have the will to use it. Something was bound to break.

My own analysis in the late 1960s was twofold – first, that London could only support one evening newspaper which would have a monopoly of advertising revenues, and second that with very strong development at the bottom end of the market, sparked by Rupert Murdoch's purchase of the *Sun* in 1969, the day was not far off when there would be room for only one middle-of-the-road newspaper – either the *Express* or the *Mail*. If we merged the two – and also merged our London *Evening News* with their London *Evening Standard* – we would, I was sure, create two newspapers that were strong, profitable on account of their stranglehold on middle-market advertising, and powerful enough to face down the unions. We'd dominate the middle and evening market and leave the tabloid press to Rupert.

Looking back I was clearly right about the evening newspapers – the two titles eventually merged in 1980. I haven't been proved right yet about the middle of the market, although with the *Express* now so weak and the *Mail* so powerful, I think I might soon be.

My thinking was reinforced by a report that we com-

missioned in the autumn of 1970 from the American management consultants, McKinsey. They concluded that if the last five
years were anything to go on, the Mail Group of papers would
lose £14 million in the forthcoming year. If we took just the last
three years, then that loss would go up to £32 million. Something had to be done.

My solution was to seek a merger between the Express
Group and the Mail Group. In my years in the business and at
the NPA I got to know my opposite number at the *Express* very
well. Johnny Coote was a dashing wartime submarine commander who subsequently went sailing regularly with Max Aitken. So we got together. Since the death of Beaverbrook in
1964, things had been changing at the *Express* too. It was on a
downward slide under Max with their *Evening Standard* in
particular losing money. The meetings were meant to be private,
but Fleet Street was a gossipy place and eventually news leaked
out. I didn't let that put me off. Johnny and I were progressing
things nicely and I managed to win Esmond round to the idea,
though Vere and Mick Shields remained opposed. The vital
point was that the *Express* was looking vulnerable.

Esmond summoned Barings, his bankers, to discuss it with
him, Vere and me. Their chairman, Lord Cromer, was his son-
in-law. He asked Esmond who would be the Chairman and who
would be the Chief Executive of the new company. 'Well, it's
obvious,' said Esmond. 'I'll be the Chairman, Hussey will be the
Chief Executive.' 'That,' replied Rowley Cromer, 'is the issue
upon which most putative mergers break down.' And he was
right, though they were later resumed after I left the *Mail*.

I had sensed a change of atmosphere. The 1970 figures were
not as good as I had hoped. We had had some successes – one
major advance was to set up a printing consortium on our presses
in Manchester with the *Guardian* and the Manchester *Evening
News*, a first joint venture in an industry where rivals were
notoriously suspicious of working together – but despite all my
efforts we remained in the red, though to a much smaller extent
than before. The deficit was mainly caused by a 15 per cent rise
in the cost of newsprint. I began to feel my position was getting
exposed.

I had always tried to foster better links between the senior managers, founding an informal club where we would all meet and have a drink on Friday evenings. Most of the time I was the conciliator, smoothing things over between Esmond and Vere, Esmond and Arthur, Arthur and Vere. But the position changes in all companies and the balance of power shifts. I was Esmond's man, but Esmond was moving towards retirement. Mick Shields had made a great success of the non-newspaper side of Associated's business. His achievements had attracted the attention of other proprietors, not least Lord Thomson at *The Times* who offered him a job. Vere was determined to keep him and so persuaded his father to sanction a Rolls-Royce for Mick.

I cared nothing for the car, but I knew how it would be seen at the papers – as a direct criticism of me, a downgrading and the cause of speculation about the likelihood of my retaining my job. I had seen it happen so often on Fleet Street, and I could now see it happening to me. Whether I had been good, or whether I had been bad, I would carry the can – just like so many editors at the *Daily Mail* had before me.

I am not one for sitting about, so obviously the time had come to look elsewhere. The logical place was Times Newspapers and the job Shields had turned down. So I rang Gordon Brunton, Thomson's number two. In no time the deal was done. I was leaving to be Chief Executive and managing director of Times Newspapers. I ran through the new job with Arnold Goodman and mentioned my difficulty in knowing what to say to Esmond. When I touched on my relationship with Vere, Arnold suddenly perked up. 'That's it. Tell him you can't work with the son.'

I did, and, as Arnold had predicted, it worked. 'Quite right, quite right,' Esmond said, 'neither could I. I understand.' He treated me very well and sent Sue and me off to the United States on the newish *QEII* to mark my departure. So I left the *Daily Mail* in the autumn of 1970 after almost twenty-two years. I thoroughly enjoyed my life there and I was very fond of many of the people. It had its ups and downs, and particularly, in the last two or three years, the strain of industrial relations put an equal strain on family life. Of course, nowadays that is not unusual. Executives in the City work probably double the number of hours during the week, if not more, than they used to during the 1950s. There are compensations: salaries are enormous, not least the big bonuses. When I left the *Daily Mail* my salary was £10,000 per year and I think the editor got £11,000. Inflation has changed the value but nevertheless it cannot be considered a generous reward for the work.

I left the *Mail* with regret and feeling to a certain extent I had failed. I had tried and I think succeeded in developing a more coherent and organized company, able to compete more effectively in a fast-changing scene. I suppose I must have been judged to have been good at it to have been given sometimes terrifying responsibilities at the NPA. If my merger plan had gone ahead things would have been very different. Still during my years as managing director we had no stoppages and virtually no disruption. All the difficulties – and there were plenty – we settled by negotiation. In part this was due to the good management of my predecessors who had built up a real spirit of loyalty in what was essentially a family company.

After I left, the *Express/Mail* merger plan was resurrected, although I of course was not privy to the discussions. In January 1971 Esmond and Max Aitken met at Warwick House, to discuss the merger. Vere, who was adamantly opposed, was there too. I am told that the meeting was interrupted by a power cut and that most of it was carried out by the light of candelabra. The plan to merge the *Mail* and *Express* and *Standard* and *Evening News* and set up a jointly owned company was debated. Reluctantly Esmond agreed but at the last moment he announced that he wanted to keep the *Evening News*. It was, he explained, more a part of his family's history than even the *Mail*. It had been through the *Evening News* that his father and uncle had first made their mark on the newspaper world. He might have added that the *Evening News* was the most profitable part of Harmsworth Publications.

Max Aitken was willing to agree but Arnold Goodman, there as his legal adviser, put his foot down. To exclude the *Evening News* made the deal unviable. Esmond refused to budge. The whole thing collapsed. The very next day, 18 January, Esmond resigned and handed over as Chairman to Vere. At least that is what I have been told, and it has the ring of truth.

I have to admit that from the day I left the *Mail* its fortunes rose almost daily. I like to think this is more a tribute to the virility of the new management than to the impotence of their predecessors. From the start Vere showed great courage, foresight and powers of decision. He had at his side three very able lieutenants – David English, Mick Shields and John Winnington-Ingram. This created for the Harmsworth family the top quality team equal to that which under Beaverbrook had been at the heart of the *Express*'s success. Vere immediately made the *Mail* tabloid – a recommendation of the McKinsey report and something I have to admit I would probably have resisted, wrongly. Starved of funds for so long, the *Mail* needed a dramatic change. It had always been haunted by the unhappy flirtation of Esmond's father, the first Lord Rothermere, with the fascist blackshirts of Oswald Mosley. The new *Mail* – it had to be seen to be different. Vere supported it with huge funds to be spent both on promotion and on hiring top quality staff. The funds had always been there, but in the bank. The team worked closely together to overhaul the *Express* and turned the *Mail* into a huge success.

Mick's attitude to newspapers was unchanged. He had nothing to do with them. 'It's Vere's box of trains,' he said to me, once. 'It's his money, he can do what he likes with it. And I will try and make certain that there's plenty for him.' To which he added with a customary gleam in his eye, 'and for me too'. They were a formidable and successful duo.

The casualty was Arthur Brittenden, who lost his editorship although he continued a distinguished career writing the leaders for the *Sun* which Margaret Thatcher thought a vital factor in her election victories.

Arthur's final Harmsworth meeting was not uncharacteristic. Vere, somewhat embarrassed, asked him to lunch – the traditional way of sealing the exit with a cheque. It was some time before he got round to it, and then said: 'My father wants you to be treated very well and has written me a letter telling me what I should offer you.' He produced it, looked at it, puzzled for a few minutes and finally said, 'I can't read his handwriting, can you?' 'Well,' said Arthur, taking the note from him, 'it says here three years' salary' – which was actually pretty generous although in his place I would have been tempted to say four. There was always a charming touch of the bizarre about the Harmsworths!

Relations also changed with Vere – particularly later after I became Chairman of the BBC. He asked me to lunch to discuss the future of radio and television, told me his plans and asked me for my advice. We had a very enjoyable conversation, and each with I think total sincerity congratulated the other on what had happened to us and what we had achieved.

Chance is unpredictable and can be cruel. By the end of 1999, Vere, Mick and David had all died and there was I, seventy-six, having spent the best part of five years in and out of hospital, still active, and so far, touch wood, fit. It was sad and moving to attend the memorial services of those three, all of whom I had known well and, apart from occasional misadventures, much liked and admired. It didn't seem quite right.

My last memory of Vere is an especially happy one. We were at a memorial service for Eric Cheadle, a long-time servant of the Kemsleys. Vere and I were placed in a position in church which appeared to make us the two most important members of the congregation outside the family and the firm. We walked down the aisle together, I said, 'Vere I'm really enjoying this. Listen to the whispers.' He replied, 'So am I. Let's do it more often.' I think that was the last time I saw him.

My last words with Esmond were also memorable. We met occasionally at parties in London, and I think we stayed at Daylesford for a weekend after I left. Mary had discovered that Warren Hastings had a llama so she bought a couple and hoped that they would breed. They didn't, but nevertheless tending them gave Esmond great pleasure. The last time we met was at a cocktail party in 1978 not long before his death. Sue had been chatting to him and came across and said, 'You must go and talk to Esmond: he has something he very much wants to say to you.' I opened the conversation. 'Well, I'm surprised to see you here, Esmond.'

'Why?' he asked.

'Well, it's a lovely June evening, you're a fine tennis player and a member of Wimbledon. That's where I thought you'd be.'

'Quite right, quite right,' he said. 'But I wanted to say something to you. I wanted to thank you on behalf of my whole family for getting David English to join my company. It has changed the whole fortunes of the *Daily Mail* and the Harmsworth family.'

And then he leant forward, poking me in the chest with his forefinger, and shouted in a voice audible all over the room: 'It was the weekend in Paris that did it! The weekend in Paris.' For all his faults, I was very fond of him.

Chapter Seven

When Roy Thomson died in August 1976, I wrote to his son, Kenneth, to express my sorrow. I still have a copy of the letter. 'I did not know Roy for long,' I said, 'but it is hardly an exaggeration to say that I loved him. I have never worked for anyone who was so frank, so honest, so encouraging and so helpful. The five and a half years I have spent in his company have been the best of my working life and I am proud to have been one of his employees.'

That was no flannel. Those first years at Times Newspapers from 1971 were exhilarating and challenging. Finally out from under the shadow of Esmond and the complex rivalry at his court, I was blessed with the support of a clear-headed and decisive proprietor who shared my vision of modernizing Fleet Street by evolution not revolution. Roy had worked his way up from nothing, building a chain of local radio stations and newspapers in Canada before coming to Scotland in 1953 to buy the *Scotsman*. Three years later the British government was seeking applicants to run the newly established ITV franchise north of the border. There were none. Roy, however, heard about this, put his name forward and was given the nod. This was to lead to the most famous and characteristic of his many indiscretions. It was, he said, a licence to print money. Later he moved on to London and purchased Kemsley Newspapers, owners of the *Sunday Times* and many local titles. Later still, Roy also got involved in oil.

We got on well and both found it easy to make decisions. He gave me a very warm welcome to his company. Neither of us cared too much about what other people thought. Roy was folksy, laid back and relaxed where Esmond had been, for all his charm, formal and surprisingly insecure. Roy and I shared a sense of humour. He had a limitless fund of jokes. Some of them weren't that funny and virtually all were extremely coarse, but his delight in telling them never failed to win over his audience. He particularly enjoyed explaining to me the logistics of his first-ever radio station, run on a shoestring at a place called Timmins in Ontario, Canada, a small town which could be regarded as the birthplace of the Thomson Organization. He only started the station because he had been selling a job lot of radios but the lucky purchasers had nothing to hear on them. He lacked a weather forecast but that would have cost him five dollars a week which he couldn't afford. 'So each morning, Duke, I'd go out, lick my finger and stick it in the air. That was my weather forecast and it was just as good as anyone else's and cheaper!' Typical Roy.

Above all, it was a real thrill for me to be Chief Executive of *The Times* and *Sunday Times*, two of the world's great newspapers. I was proud to work for such titles and to be in the company of so many distinguished journalists. When I joined, Roy was based at the *Sunday Times* building on Gray's Inn Road while I was installed at Printing House Square, the historic home of *The Times* between St Paul's Cathedral and the Thames. However, I often had to go up and see Roy. He liked to discuss with me all the intimate details of the paper, particularly the advertisement revenue and what costs could be cut. When he was flying up to Scotland to visit the *Scotsman*, he always cancelled his evening paper because there was a free one on the plane. One occasion was unforgettable. Soon after I left the *Mail*, its star columnist, Bernard Levin, also joined *The Times* – though that had nothing to do with me. Bernard had grown increasingly disaffected by Esmond's autocratic style and solid Conservative support. Much to the proprietor's fury, he had used the *Mail* to urge readers to vote Labour in the General Elections of 1964 and 1970. I had hardly settled into my new role at *The Times* when Bernard, in March 1971 in his column in *The Times*, mounted a scathing attack on the Rothermere family, who had just announced that the *Daily Sketch* was to be merged with the *Mail*, describing them as arrogant, secretive and irresponsible. 'I will say this much for the Rothermeres,' Bernard wrote. 'They remain in character, even at time of crisis. The staff of the *Daily Mail* and *Daily Sketch* only discovered that the papers were to be merged when the *Mail*'s Geneva correspondent telephoned to sympathize.' Bernard went on to criticize Esmond for leaving the country for South Africa, home of apartheid, while the *Sketch* staff were being made redundant.

It was an appalling article. My heart sank when I read it. It sank further when Gordon Brunton, the Chief Executive of the Thomson Organization, rang me to tell me to come across and brief Roy about it. This, of course, should have been done either by Brunton or the editor-in-chief, Denis Hamilton. They funked it and sent me in to do their work. Nothing ventured, I went in, chatted for a few minutes and asked Roy if he had read the paper that day. 'Well, I saw we had two full-page ads and eight columns of classified.' He paused, always quick to sense an atmosphere and said, 'Well, should I have done?'

'Well, Bernard Levin,' I replied, 'has written an article attacking Esmond and Vere. On page eight.'

'Oh Jeez,' said Roy, whose eyesight was terrible, pulling the paper up to within three inches of his face. 'Hell, I can't read the goddamn thing. Is it actionable?'

Rather cautiously I replied, 'Well, it might be.'

'Oh Jeez, Duke. Well, read out the expensive bits.'

This presented me with something of a selection problem, so I decided to read out any sentence that might cost £20,000 or more – like the suggestion that Lord Rothermere had chosen to put a few hundred employees out of work while he was staying in a South Africa riddled with apartheid.

'Oh Jeez, Duke, he shouldn't have said that about Esmond. Anything else?'

'Well,' I went on, 'Bernard says that Esmond left the business in the hands of his son Vere, "known universally as Mere".'

'Oh Jeez, Duke, he really shouldn't have said that about Vere. Anything else?'

Summoning my courage, I continued that Bernard said Esmond had allowed his newspaper to be used by his wife Bubbles (Patricia) to promote her social-climbing activities.

Long pause. 'Oh Jeez, Duke, we really shouldn't have said that.'

Even longer pause. 'Say, give me that bit about Pat again!'

I did.

'Oh dear, oh dear, you'd better sort it out somehow.'

That was Roy. He understood the business and there was never a word of blame. William Rees-Mogg, the editor of *The Times*, subsequently used a little-known by-law to give evidence in the ensuing libel action for a second time in order to counter the suggestion made by the *Daily Mail* that I was behind the article as a way of getting my own back on the Harmsworths. They had tried to paint me as the Judas Iscariot of Fleet Street. This, of course, was totally untrue and William confirmed that I knew nothing about the article. In the end, the libel case was heard three times and ultimately settled out of court, much to Bernard's disgust, but with no blame attached to William. My reputation was cleared.

Roy presided in person over his empire. 'I make so little over here,' he once told me. 'Jeez Duke, it's bird shit. I make ten times as much in Canada.' So he teamed up with Paul Getty to prospect North Sea oil. Being Roy, he hit it and the profits gushed, like the oil. In addition, the travel side of his business turned in £4 million a year, and the regional papers £10 million. Times Newspapers – comprising *The Times*, *Sunday Times*, *Literary* and *Educational Supplements* (to which we added the *Higher Education Supplement*) – was a small part of the big picture, but Roy was extraordinarily proud of it. A hick Canadian selling radios in Timmins had ended up owning the most famous newspaper in the world. Yet whatever the prestige of ownership, it irked Roy that Times Newspapers lost money. He couldn't see the point of owning anything that lost money.

The *Sunday Times*, of course, did make money – plenty. The *Educational Supplement* did well financially (it had a tremendous and very loyal market in the whole of the education field). But those gains were more than accounted for by the other titles, especially *The Times* itself. My job was to get the whole unit, especially *The Times*, into profit, reversing a £1.4 million deficit. In that I obviously had Roy's wholehearted support. There were, however, problems.

Under Roy, the management structure was complex and often confusing. Brunton was the Chief Executive of the Thomson Organization. At Times Newspapers, he was a member of the main board on which I sat alongside representatives of the Astor family, who still had a 15 per cent stake in *The Times*, and some distinguished public figures whose role was to protect the national interest in such a respected and important newspaper. The main board was chaired by Hamilton, who as editor-in-chief was technically under Brunton and on a par with me. Then there was an executive board which I chaired and which was made up of the two editors – William Rees-Mogg and Harold Evans of the *Sunday Times* – plus key executives responsible for advertising, marketing, production and finance. Hamilton was no longer on this board. This was Brunton's decision. He told me that, whatever his qualities, Hamilton had no capacity for management – and he was right. But it took Brunton two days to persuade Hamilton to accept this.

It was brave and correct of Brunton to make the change, but heightened the antagonism between the two which was awkward for me because I had to deal with both. Hamilton resented anyone being his boss and would criticize Brunton as a newcomer in political and sophisticated London circles. Brunton, on the other hand, had no regard for Hamilton as a manager, but it seemed to me he had an exaggerated respect for his contacts in high places. I surmised that he realized that Hamilton had played a major part in securing *The Times* for Roy – against opposition within the Establishment. And Brunton therefore believed that Hamilton could pull strings to get him a knighthood. Hamilton was a founder member of the networking club. He never stopped. I have never networked, regarding it as demeaning and stemming from a sense of inferiority.

While Roy was alive, these various overlaps and personality clashes didn't seem that important. If a decision needed making, he was there to do it in person. Without him at the helm, and

with Kenneth remaining based in Toronto, there was a weakened
management structure with much characteristic Fleet Street in-
fighting and back-stabbing. Brunton liked to control all access to
Kenneth and his aides in Toronto, and saw any attempt to speak
to them independently as tantamount to treason. (I was certainly
treasonable but must say in my defence that I was encouraged
by Canada to keep in close contact with them.)

My first impression of the executives at Times Newspapers
was that, apart from a brilliant finance director, Michael Brown,
they were not very impressive. They were long on management
theory and short on management practice. For instance, I discovered that there was a long-term strategy group, which had
long lunch-time meetings every month, waited on by a butler. I
called them in and put a stop to it. Without a successful short-
term strategy, I pointed out, there wouldn't be time for a long
one. Ultimately I fired most of them.

The management, however, was not my most immediate
problem. I had realized in taking the job that there was a much
tougher union problem at Times Newspapers than I had encountered at the *Daily Mail*, but, despite all my experience of the
excesses of the print unions at the NPA, nothing had quite
prepared me for what I discovered when I got there.

The *Sunday Times* union chapels were a byword in Fleet
Street for ill-discipline and disruption. There were, between the
various titles, eight unions and sixty-five chapels representing
the 4,250 staff. It made negotiating a nightmare and gave rise to
many petty rivalries and jealousies. Into this delicately poised
situation I made a characteristically bold but chancy entrance. I
decided in my first month to address all the chapels of *The Times*
and *Sunday Times* in two separate meetings, telling them that I
was proud to be joining them but that I knew something of the
very serious problem both titles had to face. It went very well
with *The Times* staff. The *Sunday Times* lot, however, had the
reputation of being the most rebellious bunch on Fleet Street. I
expressed to them my pride in joining them and was carefully
pitching my story to the composing room – the most loyal group
there. Aim at the moderates, never attack the villains was my
invariable strategy. I outlined my views. Someone suggested I

wasn't telling the truth. I replied pompously: 'I have dealt in one way and another with your general secretaries, your branch secretaries and with your chapels. No one has ever accused me of lying. I resent that.' Then I added, in a moment of mind-blowing over-confidence: 'Aaagh, I see my old friend Samson from the *Daily Sketch* at the back there. He will vouch for what I am saying to you.' He leapt to his feet. 'No I won't!' he said. 'You were a bloody liar then, and you are a bloody liar now!' All I could do was laugh out loud, which won most of them on to my side straight away.

I'm afraid my sense of humour could sometimes backfire with my management colleagues. Roy Thomson had a Christmas dinner every year. Ken took over the custom and in his first year there was a disaster when the turkeys passed on salmonella poisoning. About a hundred people fell ill – some very badly – and had to be taken into hospital. At the next board meeting, this became a major item and was taken seriously. But after an hour and a half of pompous platitudes, I'd had enough. Brunton said, 'We have not heard from you, Duke, on this subject: what's your view?' I replied: 'The main problem is our recruiting policy. If you consider people like William Rees-Mogg – Charterhouse; Charlie Douglas Home – Eton; Frank Giles – Wellington; Mike Mander – Tonbridge; you, Gordon – Canford; and myself – Rugby, none of us, accustomed to public school food, has been affected. There should be more of us.' That contribution was not a success.

The Times's production staff had the reputation for being honest, decent, six-day-a-week workers with great loyalty to their paper. The *Sunday Times*'s, by contrast, was by repute dishonest, uncaring, greedy and corrupt freelancers. They had other jobs on Fleet Street during the week and the *Sunday Times* was their Saturday night job and the strawberry jam. They were hugely overpaid but still constantly disrupted the printing process on the flimsiest of excuses, costing us thousands of copies, a fortune in advertisement revenue and, in the process, fuelling their own demands for overtime to get the print run back on time. So constant was the disruption that the paper gradually became known as the *Sunday SomeTimes*.

The whole situation had arisen when Roy bought the *Sunday Times* in 1959. It was printed on the *Telegraph* presses. So Roy, ever the opportunist, invaded Michael Hartwell's office at the *Telegraph* and told him with his characteristic bonhomie that, as Michael was making no money, he, Roy, would buy the *Telegraph* and turn it round. This approach did not endear him to Michael, a man of great distinction who personally edited and controlled his own newspaper of which he was justly proud. As soon as Roy had left the room, his offer firmly rejected, Michael called in his executives and told them first to give the fastest possible notice to the *Sunday Times* to leave his press room and then to prepare to launch a Sunday *Telegraph*. This was the start of a paper recently quoted as the best in the country. It left Roy to buy a massive line of presses and find the staff to print the *Sunday Times*.

This he did and set them up at Gray's Inn Road. At short notice, he had to recruit a Saturday-night-only staff. He got the dregs of Fleet Street – and some were dregs. Even when he bought *The Times* in 1966, things did not improve because *The Times*'s presses at Printing House Square and their staffs were contracted out to the *Observer* on Saturday nights in a very successful and economic arrangement.

That contract was near to expiring when I arrived. Brunton and Hamilton cooked up a scheme which may have looked good on paper, but which, in the light of current newspaper practice, was idiotic. They had agreed to sell Printing House Square to the *Observer* – for what Arnold Goodman told me was a bargain price – and move *The Times* into a new building which was to be built next door to the *Sunday Times* so that they could print on the same presses. In staff terms, it was picking a bunch of good apples and pouring it into a barrel crammed with bad apples.

Brunton and Hamilton explained all this to me. I asked them, 'Why on earth are we doing it?'

'The great saving in staff,' they replied.

'What savings?' I asked. *The Times*, I pointed out, had a full complement, to cover production seven days a week, and the *Sunday Times* a full complement of journalists, but only a composing room to set the pages. The rest of the staff, the foundry, the machine room, the publishing room, were Saturday-night-only workers. 'So what savings will there be?' I asked again. One of them rather weakly replied, 'Lift men.'

Since neither building required lift men, I suddenly realized with deep apprehension that they had totally misjudged the position. On top of that there was a very complicated financial deal about the new building in Gray's Inn Road which was not to be owned by the Thomson Organization, but leased by us.

Moving the two papers side by side was a fundamental mistake which wrecked any chances we had of modernizing them. In his history of The Times, John Grigg describes it as a 'damnosa hereditas for which Hussey was in no way responsible but which was to poison and prejudice his task in the years ahead'. It would have been a very different story if they had left The Times printing as it was alongside the Observer with loyal, regular staff.

Moreover, physical proximity contributed to the temptation among some of my senior colleagues – though not Roy – to blur the difference between the two papers. Hamilton was a brilliant editor who had created the modern Sunday Times and set a benchmark for all Sunday newspaper journalism, but I don't think he ever understood The Times. It is a unique newspaper with a unique history and record, based on high journalistic principles (although, like all principles, sometimes disregarded). By trying to make it more like the Sunday Times, which was Hamilton's policy, we were driving away its natural readers. Hamilton was mesmerized by the success of the Sunday Times but could not see that what was, as Arnold Goodman once put it, a brilliant collection of detective stories might do well on a Sunday but would fall flat on its face during the week.

The Times was a journal of record. It was published according to a very strict allocation of editorial. So many columns each day for home news, political news and foreign news, so much for features and editorials, so many for sport and so many for the odd quirks like the crossword puzzle. The readers knew what they were going to get and where it was. It was a creature of habit. Times readers did not want surprises. They knew what they liked and expected to get it. It had a steady sale and a small but devoted readership. The task that I inherited and the colleagues I collected had a straightforward and simple objective: make *The Times* profitable.

The decision to move away from Printing House Square to Gray's Inn Road had been taken in 1969. I had to carry it out – or to be more accurate, I handed it to the man I brought in as general manager, Harvey Thompson, the erstwhile managing director of the Manchester *Guardian*. He was an enormous catch, a man with a profound knowledge of the newspaper industry, its workings and its customers. He was held in high regard both by the unions and by all his colleagues in Fleet Street and had a pleasant, dry sense of humour. Roy brought over some of his tough Canadian directors to lunch at *The Times*. Harvey sat next to the toughest. 'Do you spell your name with or without a P?' the visitor asked. 'With,' Harvey said. 'Bad luck!' Harvey loved that story. In his capacity as general manager, he immediately upgraded radically the quality of the management to which I referred earlier.

It was Harvey's job to move *The Times* from Printing House Square to the new building in Gray's Inn Road, in just thirteen hours. It was thought impossible. We employed all the usual wheezes like setting as many pages and articles as possible in advance and transferring the matrixes up to Gray's Inn Road. The operation started at 5 a.m. on Sunday morning when the *Sunday Times* edition stopped printing and had to be completed by Sunday at 6 p.m. when the Monday *Times* edition started printing. To everyone's amazement we did this without losing a single copy. It was a tremendous tribute to Harvey and his team but also to the loyalty and dedicated support of *The Times* staff. Tragically, it was the last time they operated independently.

When he bought his first Fleet Street paper, I don't think Roy understood how the unions operated there. In Scotland and Canada, it had been a less confrontational relationship with management. The London papers were clustered within a hundred yards of each other in Fleet Street in what was a hothouse, with everyone gossiping endlessly about who was doing what and where and for how much. The regime was based on an uneasy compromise between companies, unions and chapels in order to get the papers out and sell more than their rivals. By the time I arrived at Times Newspapers, however, Roy had certainly got the measure of the people he was dealing with. The situation was brought home to him violently on the first night the *Sunday Times* was to be printed on his very costly brand-new presses. At the last minute the NATSOPA members refused to work unless they got an extra payment for doing what they had already agreed to do. Roy had to give way or risk losing the whole run. He was a pragmatist. He knew when to submit.

Yet his fundamental concern was that we were virtually the only country in the world not to take advantage of the new technology that was available to our industry. And the reason why we weren't was because the unions – and principally the NGA – saw it as the end of their stranglehold on power. Which it would be. The NGA members were the aristocracy of print, highly skilled, highly paid operators. They weren't going to relinquish that gold mine in favour of computer terminals operated by journalists and tele-ad girls. Their union had got for them an unbelievable deal. They were paid by the size of every piece of type which went into the paper whether they had worked it or not. All the display advertisements came in preprepared blocks. Whatever the size, the NGA charged the top rate as if they had done the setting although they hadn't even touched it. It was just one of a range of outrageous scams that proprietors up and down Fleet Street had tolerated for years.

At the *Sunday Times*, because of the casual terms on which most of the production staff were employed for only one night a week, we never had working more than a third of those we were paying. The Inland Revenue, having gone through our books, concluded that at least half of the names given by these freelancers were false. Among them were several Marmaduke Husseys and even more Mickey Mouses. It was a corrupt system, apparently orchestrated by NATSOPA union officials (another profitable scam), but the culture was such that the management had felt obliged to live with it. Yet even turning a blind eye was not working. We were constantly losing production. They would deliberately sabotage the presses. A paper break shut down the presses for forty minutes. So then we had to pay overtime. I was appalled. We had a valuable and important newspaper at the *Sunday Times* but no loyalty from a one-night-a-week staff who just took us for a ride week after week after week.

Roy and I both believed that this anarchy could no longer be sustained either on principle or if Times Newspapers was to become self-financing and not dependent on the Thomson oil revenues. The way forward was obvious – to increase productivity and reliability and to cut costs by installing new technology. To that end, Roy had approved the purchase for £9 million of a computer-based composing system which was put in on the third floor of *The Times* building in 1976. It was a new system his Canadian colleagues had installed at Santa Monica in California where he owned the local paper. It worked wonders. He planned to phase it in with the *Times Literary Supplement* in 1979 and thereafter with the other titles.

Harvey and I went to Santa Monica to meet the paper's managing director. 'It's a great honour to have the Chief Executive of Times Newspapers here today,' he greeted us. 'It so happens to be our bi-monthly Rotary meeting. We've cancelled photographs of Brother Jake's visit to Italy and instead we'd like you to give a talk to the members.' Thanks a bundle, I thought. It got worse. 'Our members are pretty highfalutin fellers – no fools – so pitch it good and high,' he told me. 'We – you – start in ten minutes. We're greatly looking forward to it.'

My heart sank and I rapidly started thinking of the new technology and what to say. I was about to go on a quick visit to the Gents with Harvey to sketch out a few major points. Suddenly, in a moment of inspired caution, I asked, 'Incidentally how have you billed my talk?' 'Duke,' came the reply, 'a man of your importance and experience needs a broad canvas so we just labelled it "The problems of the world".' 'Boy, am I looking forward to this,' I heard Harvey mutter.

The Americans appeared to have an exaggerated respect for anything to do with *The Times*. On another trip, to the Virgin Islands, organized by the advertisement department in an effort to drum up revenue from American states, I was accompanied by Sue. They found the combination of my job, my Christian name and her title confusing. We were met by a splendid black chauffeur who said, 'We'll put the Duke in the front and Duchess in the back!' At the hotel, I was asked to give another talk to all the staff on what it was like to be an English Duke. I thought what the hell, no one will ever know. Sue was appalled. 'But if it gives them pleasure why not?' I said.

Roy had been ill for some time but his death, from a stroke at the age of eighty-one, in the summer of 1976 threw the plans for new technology into confusion. A few days before his death, he rang to make me promise to get the new technology in. 'We've got it in Canada. It'll save the papers over here, so go for it, Duke.' These were his last words to me and left me with a sense of a mission. I think he called Hamilton with the same message. In my opinion if Roy had been fit and well, we would never have run into the problems that we encountered later. He would have simply called the unions together over the new technology and said, 'Unless you buggers get together, and put it in, I'll close the papers. I own them and I'll do it.' And he would have done.

Without Roy, the mixed abilities and ambitions of those around me and the barriers to communication became more apparent. Ken Thomson was strongly in favour of forcing the unions' hand on technology as was his chief adviser, John Tory. But they were on the other side of the Atlantic and didn't understand English problems. Much was delegated to Brunton. My relationship with him was not easy. Both he and Hamilton, for example, resented my position as vice-chairman of the NPA. When Arnold Goodman stood down in 1977, there were moves to make me chairman. Garrett Drogheda wrote in his autobiography, *Double Harness*: 'In the eyes of many, Duke was considered to be an excellent choice . . . but his colleagues at *The Times* would not agree that he should become chairman whilst also running *The Times*, although their attitude was hard to understand for they had allowed him to carry on as the NPA deputy chairman and also to act as co-chairman of the joint board for the re-equipping of the industry.' As Garrett realized, Brunton's objection was nonsense. The top Thomson executives paid scant regard to what I achieved at the NPA and particularly

to my experience of joint negotiations with the unions both at
the *Daily Mail* and at *The Times*. The authority that the post of
chairman of the NPA would have carried might indeed have
helped us in the dispute ahead, especially when other papers
sought to profit from our problems. Only my own company
voted against me. Not a heart-warming vote of confidence.

Brunton was an able negotiator, a good bluffer, an inspired
and fortunate gambler and a good judge of a bargain. He had
presence and charm. From the moment I first met him, he
wanted to fight the unions (unlike Hamilton who told Cecil
King, when the three of us had lunch together in 1971, that he
did not believe there needed to be a confrontation with the
unions over their behaviour on Fleet Street. I, King recorded,
disagreed). Brunton liked the thought of being a big man taking
a tough line. Unfortunately he did not understand the parameters. He believed we saw things the same way. Perhaps that is
why he hired me. But he had got me wrong. We were very
different. There was, for instance, an odd attitude to money in
the Thomson Organization which I priggishly did not share. I
was told once that my expenses were too low and that that was
embarrassing the other directors. I replied that I put in what I
spent.

I did not want a flat-out fight with the unions. I wanted
negotiations. My instinct, shared by Roy, was to avoid any big
bang. Roy, like Rupert Murdoch after him, loathed the unions
for the damage they were doing but saw clearly that you had to
give way on the minor issues and fight on the big ones. In the
meantime I believed it was possible to negotiate our way through
the impasse in which the proprietors and unions had found
themselves.

The proprietors, whatever the show of togetherness they put
on at the NPA, were competitors and were jealous of each
others' success. For that reason we could never get together
except under very dire threats when the principle became if one
shuts down, we all shut down. In 1974, however, Sir Don Ryder,
head of the Mirror Group, pulled out of the NPA because he
wasn't willing to halt production if another title was in trouble.
Arnold Goodman, as chairman, tried to bring the Mirror back

into the fold with a new approach. If one paper was forced to close down, then the others would keep printing but would pay compensation to their wounded brothers out of the profits they made from lapping up its circulation. The Mirror resisted even this concession and for the other papers the problem with the new system was that as disruption at the *Sunday Times* became ever more frequent, we were putting in claims almost every week and they were getting heartily sick of paying out for them. Things were approaching breaking point.

The extent of the proprietors' disunity was exposed by Victor Matthews, an unprincipled entrepreneur who in 1977 bought the Express Group from Max Aitken. He made it clear from the start that another newspaper's problem with their unions was not his problem but his opportunity. When, ironically, the *Mirror* had a dispute, Victor announced that he was putting out another two million copies to take up the surplus. The *Mirror* took him to court to try and stop him but failed. This played into the hands of the chapels. They knew that any show of solidarity by the owners was a bluff. We had no safety net now.

My instinct, even in such unhappy times, remained to work towards the reform. That, everyone knew in their hearts, was necessary. Not least the union leadership. I am no opponent of trades unions. I recognize their benefits for members, particularly in a complicated industrial process. I simply wanted them to act reasonably in joining with us in changing out-of-date production methods and bringing in – much to the advantage of their members – the new. Therefore my relationships with the leaders of the various print unions were good. They knew the score as well as I did. The people in charge were fundamentally decent – for instance, Bill Keys at SOGAT and Joe Wade at the NGA. The problem was that they could neither persuade nor control their members.

In the summer of 1973, Garrett Drogheda, as managing director of the *Financial Times*, opened discussions with me to take collective action to break the hold of the union members. His idea was for the broadsheet papers to recognize their common interest – as distinct from the tabloids – and act together.

They were totally different products. The broadsheets (what Rupert called the unpopulars) needed large composing rooms for big papers, but small machine rooms for small print runs. With the populars, the position was reversed. They had few pages but many copies. The presses Roy had installed at the *Sunday Times* had more than enough capacity to print all the broadsheets – *Telegraph, Times, Guardian, Observer* and *Financial Times*. If we put all of them together we could have brought in the best – the least militant and most loyal – production staff, offering them generous seven-day working. We could then dispense with the disreputable Saturday-night-only staffs.

Garrett's enthusiasm was matched by that of his successor, Alan Hare. Garrett had originally wanted to confine the deal to the *Financial Times* and *The Times* but Hare wanted to include all the broadsheets. I saw that as desirable, but believed *The Times* and *Financial Times* could potentially have made it work on our own. Certainly by December 1974 we had moved far enough forward to draft a joint announcement. The proposal was to leave the various titles completely independent editorially and commercially, but to establish a jointly owned production company which would use new technology to take on the massive job of setting all the pages and our presses to print the papers. We estimated that it could make at least 3,000 jobs redundant and shave £10 million off the wages bill.

What became known as 'The Project' stumbled, however, because of the reluctance of the *Guardian* and the *Telegraph* to join. I handled the *Guardian* badly. It was my error. I was offhand and arrogant with their managing director, Peter Gibbings. One of my worst mistakes. He was and is a very able man and clear thinker. I mucked it up and the *Guardian* didn't join. What really broke it though was that Michael Hartwell, the proprietor at the *Telegraph*, couldn't get his mind round the situation that if we were all printing on the same presses, the other papers wouldn't pinch his best stories. Alan had been talking to him but after much dithering, in March 1975, Michael demurred. 'The disadvantage,' he wrote to Alan at the *Financial Times*, 'is that we should put ourselves at risk in facing the possibility of a long shutdown together with yourselves and *The Times*, while the rest

of Fleet Street printed.' He also wanted the *Daily Mail* brought
into the equation, which would have been a nonsense because it
was, by that time, a tabloid.

The Drogheda plan was brilliant. It recognized the total
dissimilarity between broadsheets and populars. I think we could
have worked it. But not without the *Telegraph*. We could jointly
have brought in the new technology, with union consent,
because they could not have played one paper off against
another. I shared with my colleagues on the *Financial Times* a
belief that if a shutdown did occur as a result – and we judged it
unlikely – we would only be talking about a few highly paid
union members. In which case the politicians and the industrialists would be able to force a settlement. That vision became a
constant theme in the various speeches I gave at industry functions. In July 1975, for example, I was on the podium at the
Printing World Conference developing my theme of the problems of over-manning and the promise of new technology.

I had begun by then to negotiate with the various print
unions, at the instigation of Arnold Goodman and on behalf of
the NPA, a comprehensive agreement on the introduction of the
new printing methods. My key ally was Bill Keys of SOGAT,
who chaired the printing industry group at the TUC and who
was nominated by the print unions to speak for them in the
negotiations. Len Murray, general secretary of the TUC, who
had succeeded Vic Feather in 1973, was right behind us. Funnily
enough, some of the strongest – although obviously not always
the most vocal – support for modernizing came from the TUC
where both Murray and Feather had been appalled by the
damage the newspaper unions inflicted on the reputation of the
trades union movement.

By October 1976 we had negotiated a total agreement
between the NPA and the unions and published our document,
'Programme for Action', with the full support of the union
leaderships, the TUC and the NPA. Alf Robens, the former
Labour minister and chairman of the Coal Board, then a director
of *The Times*, congratulated me on the best argued industrial
document he had ever read. The points of the agreement were
broadly that all matters – pensions, decasualization, redundan-

cies, new technology and disputes procedures – should be discussed at each paper by a joint house committee made up of
seven members of the management and two representatives from
each union, except NATSOPA which would have three, because
they also included the clerks. The union leaderships were solidly
behind the plan. 'If . . . the provisional agreements are rejected,'
they warned, 'there will be no agreed overall framework through
which the problems facing the industry can be tackled and the
consequences could well, in our view, be extremely grave. This
would have a serious effect on the viability of some titles in the
industry, the maintenance of employment, and the continuation
of a strong and effective trade union organization.' Prophetic
words but eight years early.

There were very many others who realized that a major clash
was coming. Lord McGregor, who was then heading a Royal
Commission on the Press which reported in 1977, wrote of the
behaviour of the chapels in the *Telegraph* at the time: 'If this
suicidal behaviour persists, it is a safe prediction that Fleet Street
will experience the fate of New York where five newspapers
were killed in the decade before 1975.' He went on to warn that
sooner rather than later 'a strong organization would set out to
break the mould of anarchy and establish the orderly production
which exists in that other great printing centre, Manchester'.

Confronted with such siren voices, we were all hopeful that
the union members would listen and see sense. Their verdict, in
January 1977, was a bitter blow. The NGA overwhelmingly
rejected the proposals, as did SOGAT. There was a narrow
majority again at NATSOPA. I was told the result could have
turned on one or two chapels.

Given this head-in-the-sand attitude by the rank and file, the
prospect of the all-out confrontation of which their leaders had
warned seemed ever more likely. My next effort to avoid it was
to work with the same union leaders to do an individual deal
along the same lines as proposed in 'Programme for Action' with
the staff at Times Newspapers whose papers were suffering
sorely from the current industrial climate. In 1977 I began
negotiating with the NGA. In private, the leaders recognized the

position and the advantages of new technology. We made some progress, agreeing in principle that the new computers could be used to compose pages by NGA members. This alone could have reduced the NGA staff by 45 per cent without compulsory redundancy but the concession was lost as we were swept into a wider confrontation.

I liked Joe Wade of the NGA. We got on well together. We had a dinner once where Joe summed up the issue of new technology in a simple sentence. 'The basic problem is, Duke, you are paid to bring it in and I'm paid to keep it out.'

On the other front, we had made progress. Our financial position was steadily improving, and, but for the sudden slump of 1973, both Times Newspapers and *The Times* itself would have been in profit by that year. Soaring newsprint prices postponed the happy day until 1975. Our success was in part due to keeping a careful eye on costs. The *Sunday Times* in particular had a habit of exceeding its budget. But Harry Evans, for all his mercurial brilliance, understood the basics. If he broke his budget in any one month, I told him and he guaranteed to restore the position in the next. And he always did. At that time, the *Sunday Times* was making £1.9 million per annum.

The *Sunday Times* was mercurial, like its editor – firing off whizz-bangs in all directions, leading debates on every issue, uncovering extraordinary scoops. It was a campaigning paper. The attack on Distillers over thalidomide was a classic and honourable example. Every week Harry would tell me how he was covering this very public campaign. When it was all over, I heard Harry interviewed on the radio or television (he was seldom off it).

'Is it true, Harry, that that campaign cost you many thousands of pounds in Distillers' advertising revenue?'

'Yes.'

'What did the Chief Executive say about that?'

Pause. 'He never told me.'

And indeed I didn't. I admired what he was doing, thought it was absolutely right and that Harry should not be concerned with the finances. (On the final week in which we trumpeted our thalidomide victory, the machine-room staff disrupted production and cost us 560,000 copies – a third of our sale. They probably did it on purpose. Typical.)

More significant to our profitability though was a reversal of the course on which Roy and Hamilton had set *The Times* since 1966. Both had wanted it to become more popular. Roy's experience, it should be remembered, was largely in local papers where he enjoyed a monopoly. He was a prisoner of his own experience. He saw things in simple terms – the more copies you sold, the more profit you made. But this didn't work at *The Times*. By moving the paper downmarket into the *Daily Telegraph* area, Roy and Hamilton alienated advertisers. Why should they pay premium rates for a slot in *The Times* when they could reach a bigger but similar audience for less in the *Telegraph*?

This dash for growth was, I believed when I arrived, putting up our costs – in terms of printing extra copies which were not always sold – and diminishing our advertising revenue. It had to stop. I believed *The Times* could be profitable if we kept to its traditional upmarket format, appealed to a smaller readership of A1s and were thereby able to offer a unique product to advertisers. In the end this strategy proved successful and brought us back into the black.

The achievement of 1975 was short-lived. By 1977 we were in the red again, but this time it was our own production staff who were destroying the hard work of everyone else to make the paper pay. In that year we lost 7.3 million copies, with a resulting loss in profit of £1.13 million and almost another £1 million in advertising revenue. The result was that Times Newspapers ended up £60,000 in deficit. But for the unofficial action by our own staff, it would have made a substantial profit.

Basically I saw my job as Chief Executive as looking after the finances and production of the newspaper. Editorial was a matter for the editor. It only became a matter for the management if the editorial either in general or in particular was likely to affect the commercial state of the newspaper. We used to discuss it, of course, and sometimes the editors would ask me for an opinion on current general or political issues. But I never gave one otherwise.

There were occasional disagreements. With an eye to a more profitable classified section in *The Times*, I was opposed to William Rees-Mogg's insistence on the paper having a 'fixed centre', made up of the leaders, comment articles and letters. His view was that it was what our readers expected and turned to first. He may have been right but it meant breaking up the classified section, reducing the revenue it yielded and adversely affecting profitability. We never resolved it but agreed to differ, although later, when Rupert Murdoch bought the paper, I pointed out that abandoning the fixed centre was one way in which he could increase revenue at once. He did it the next day.

William and I were close friends – and remain so. He has a house in Somerset near mine and my wife is godmother to one of his children. He has a great intellect and possesses a rare, eclectic and iconoclastic turn of mind. As a writer he finds it impossible to compose a sentence that is anything other than eminently readable. Even when he makes one of his wild, beguiling misjudgements, they are exquisitely expressed. A Catholic and a man of high principle, he writes like an angel. He was also very good on money; invaluable though rare in the editorial chair.

We didn't always agree. The *Sunday Times* once ran a mischievous story about the number of 'escort agencies' that advertised in the classified columns of *The Times*. I was appalled and ordered that they should be removed. William asked to see me. It was always that way round. I never went to his office. It might have looked to his editorial colleagues like managerial interference. He was not happy with this decision, pointing out that the ads in question raised £250,000 each year that we could ill afford to lose. I was adamant that *The Times* was the wrong place for such material. There was a long pause.

'I do not think,' he said, 'it is unreasonable for *The Times* to advertise one "escort agency" in any one issue.' I can spot a compromise when it comes, so I agreed, but added as an afterthought, 'Incidentally I do not think it is right for *The Times* to go down the path of reporting who is sleeping with whom.' Another long pause. 'Unless,' said William, 'the wife of the Foreign Secretary is sleeping with the Russian ambassador in which case it becomes a matter of public interest.' I settled for that. A typical exchange.

I was invaluably supported by the marketing director, Mike Mander. Mike had worked with me at the *Mail* but had steadily grown disillusioned with the new regime under Vere. Like me, he underestimated Vere and was nervous of the efforts of Pat to interfere in management. So he applied to join *The Times*. I was delighted. He was very able, dedicated and worked exceptionally hard, prompting great admiration and devotion among his colleagues. He had soon pushed up our advertisement revenue significantly. Jokingly one night over a drink Harvey Thompson, Mike and myself had speculated as to which one of us leaving would cause the most damage. We decided it was Harvey. I still believe with his genius for dealing with the unions he might have made a breakthrough.

On the morning of 1 January 1978, his wife called me to say that Harvey had died of a heart attack at the age of just forty-seven. We were staying in Somerset. I went for a long walk over the Mendips. It was a personal tragedy. He had a dear wife and small children. But it was also a massive blow to the fortunes of Times Newspapers. If anyone could have persuaded the unions to find a way of introducing the new technology without confrontation it would have been Harvey. Admiration for him and his powerful skills reached right down to the shop floor. His insistence that every agreement should be, in his words, 'clean' – that is, expressed in a way that meant the same to both sides of the dispute, rare in those days on Fleet Street – won him universal respect.

I gave the address at his memorial service. It was very, very well attended not just by Fleet Street but by all ranks of all the unions. I was apprehensive. Mike gave me some good advice. 'Don't think about Harvey, don't look at Eileen [his widow] and the children, stand up and will yourself that you are an actor giving a performance. Otherwise you won't get through it without breaking down.' He was right.

We replaced Harvey with Dugal Nesbit-Smith, a tall New Zealander who had worked for the Mirror Group in Scotland and who had succeeded in introducing technology and colour web-offset into the *Daily Record* and *Sunday Mail* up there. This, I believed wrongly, was a great advantage, but it made the unions hostile to him from the start. With great persistence and force, he had had it installed in Scotland, but no way were they going to let him do it in London. He was a man of enormous energy, courage and enthusiasm. I'm afraid I landed him in a real pit but he never complained or faltered.

At this moment, following the tragic death of Harvey, I needed to strengthen the management, especially with new blood from outside Fleet Street so as to bring in fresh perspectives. I brought in, on the advice of a friend of mine who was a top man at McKinsey, one of their brightest prospects, Don Cruickshank. He is not necessarily an easy and gregarious character, but he has an exceptional analytical mind, is very good on figures and possesses an inexhaustible capacity for work. In the months ahead, he was an invaluable support.

The latter part of 1977 was a sad time for my family. My mother died in the October. She had borne for some time, with great courage, arthritis in her hips. The doctors said she ought to have a double hip operation. I was worried about this as she was in her eighties and asked whether she really thought it was wise. She replied firmly, 'Yes, I can understand why you query it but you haven't got my hips.' I came to see her the day after the operation and it was immediately obvious that the anaesthetic had affected her brain. She was eighty-five and the decline thereafter was rapid and peaceful. It was senile dementia which is a terrible thing to witness in someone one loves. I saw her for the last time three days before she died. It wasn't the mother I remembered, the mother who had done so much to set me on my way in life, but she did just remember me with a slight pressure of her hands on my arm. Of all the memories, I prefer to think of her last prescient comment to a doctor at the home in which she was. He remarked: 'I see, Mrs Hussey, you are wearing two hats this morning.' To which she firmly replied, 'And can you, young man, see any reason why I should not, if I want to?'

Jim Callaghan's Labour government, with a knife's edge majority in the House of Commons and an economy that had only recently been bailed out by the International Monetary Fund, began 1978 determined to stand firm on an incomes policy that limited pay rises to 10 per cent. The unions were equally determined to get more and it led to many confrontations. Some employers, including all our rivals in Fleet Street, gave way, but we refused to budge. Because of the Thomson Organization's expanding interests in oil, we had to be seen to toe the government line. Brunton believed that we would not get the lucrative licences to explore the North Sea unless we were seen to abide by the 10 per cent. As our wage levels began to fall way behind the rest of Fleet Street, having previously been up there with the best, the hand of the chapel fathers in their militant and instinctive opposition to any management proposals was immeasurably strengthened.

To me this was hopeless policy. I didn't believe that falling in with characteristic Fleet Street pliability would cost us oil licences. Governments don't work that way. They are pragmatists. At Times Newspapers the capping of pay increases was a disaster. The build-up to the shutdown, whether we realized it or not, had begun. In the minutes of the executive board for 16 March 1978, we concluded that it was 'more than likely we would be faced with confrontation'. I should add, however, that at this stage we were anticipating that the *Financial Times* would be the first to take on the unions over new technology. We would be in the trench with them, but would watch as they went over the top. In the event, however, the *Financial Times* pulled back, saw us take the lead and then later followed, only to face a crippling strike.

Industrial relations deteriorated still further and faster as a result of the tough stance on wages. In the first three months of 1978, we lost £2 million in revenue because of unofficial union action. There were twenty-one failures to complete *The Times*, nine on the *Sunday Times*, and seven on the *TES*. We lost 20 per cent of our total output and were in danger of losing our readers as a result. Advertisers also were beginning to threaten that revenue. Saatchi and Saatchi formally told us that they were reconsidering placing their advertisements in our papers as a result of the poor industrial record. I was under pressure from all sides to do something about it. Moreover, the new technology installed by Roy in 1976 was lying idle still.

One afternoon Brunton told me that he wanted action and he wanted it now. 'It must be stopped!' he said. Even now, it is hard to see what alternative strategies were open to us. We could have continued down the path of negotiation, but as the collapse of the 'Programme for Action' had demonstrated, the prospect of success was slight unless we gave in wholesale to the activists' demands. We could have tried to work together more effectively with other titles, but for all my efforts that had come to nothing. The NPA was in a state of terminal decline and a new breeze was blowing down Fleet Street. We might have sat back, taken the damage the unions were handing out to us, and waited for another paper to take on the unions and then brought in reform in the slipstream of such a dispute. Yet the number of papers being lost at Times Newspapers was far greater than anywhere else. We were in the front line, like it or not.

Another course might have been simply to accept the union disruption as a fact of life, but the Thomson Organization had made it clear that they would not subsidize the anarchy any longer. Finally, there was the hope that a future government might tackle union militancy with the law, but this was 1978. The Labour government had a tiny majority and even Margaret Thatcher didn't face up to this problem until after her second election victory when she took on the miners.

I have been criticized for not splitting the question of wages and general working practices from that of the new technology – specifically that I should have tackled the wages first and then the technology. It was a fall-back position that was urged on us often during the shutdown. I may have been wrong in setting too wide an objective, but I did not think that separating them was practicable. The only way of handling the general working practices and wages on their own was to give the staff more money in the hope of bribing them into peace. And incidentally, why should we give higher pay to a staff who were constantly wrecking our papers and refusing to use the machinery we had purchased? It was outrageous. Moreover, that would have been a massive encouragement to those unions who did not want new technology introduced. They would play the same game over and over again. That could have closed the newspapers on its own. Basically if we were going to have a row we might as well have a bloody big row and throw in the kitchen sink. Ultimately, the real battle was technology. The instructions to observe the 10 per cent pay ceiling and to find a policy to handle the disruption were mutually conflicting. Uniquely observing the 10 per cent made disruption far worse and, as the losses mounted, forced us towards the shutdown. There were three insoluble factors in our dilemma: (1) the absolute refusal to introduce new working methods and technology which all the union general secretaries had advocated; (2) the total ill-discipline of NAT-SOPA and SOGAT staffs which resulted in the heavy losses of production; (3) the militant effect on all our unions of the instruction to obey the 10 per cent ceiling.

The only option left to us, the executive board unanimously agreed, was to set a deadline for a wholesale renegotiation of terms with the unions in order to achieve the key aims of uninterrupted production and the introduction of new technology. And if the deadline expired, we would close down the papers until the issues were settled. It was brave talk which went against all my instincts but I accepted the policy because I could see no other route to go. I never believed it would come to that final moment.

It was a collective decision. I chaired the meeting but Harry Evans, William Rees-Mogg, Donald Cruickshank, Mike Mander and Dugal Nesbit-Smith were all present. Later the strategy was described as mine and mine alone but that was a mistaken impression. I led, yes. I did feel a sense of mission in attacking what I saw as the canker of irresponsible trades union activity at the heart of the industry and, indeed, the country. It was, as William said, a moral issue. I took responsibility as was right given my position as Chief Executive. But we all agreed the approach. I went back to Brunton and told him what we had decided. He was absolutely delighted.

Many successful businessmen are bluffers. They build their success on playing the cards in their hands beyond their worth.

Most of the time they don't get called and so they get away with it and prosper. Now I realize that was what Brunton was hoping – that the unions would not call our bluff. Until they did, he was behind us. At the time, however, I took him at his word.

On 10 April 1978, I wrote a letter to all staff at the papers detailing the worsening situation during the first three months of 1978. 'No newspaper, even one as strong as the *Sunday Times*, can withstand such financial losses. Nor can we continue to put at risk the loyalty of our readers and the support of our advertisers.' I stated that the time had come for us to reach agreement on five key points – continuity of production; a fast and effective disputes procedure; restructuring based on new technology; efficient manning; and efficient redundancies, though none would be compulsory. I asked that all negotiations be concluded by 30 November. If they weren't, I warned in a subsequent letter sent out a few weeks later, 'publication of all our newspapers will be suspended. Suspension will last until we are wholly satisfied that publication can be restarted on a basis of reasonable staffing, efficient working and uninterrupted production. We earnestly hope that you can join with us in a final endeavour to avoid this inevitably painful measure.'

This letter was leaked to the newspapers and widely circulated. It had, in fact, been written after close consultation with the general secretary of the TUC and indeed the general secretaries of all the print unions. When the shutdown was in operation I was asked to meet the Labour Party Industrial Committee. One MP, Max Madden, who was sponsored by NATSOPA, attacked me violently for this letter. No one who had the faintest understanding of industrial relations could have written such an arrogant, stupid and irresponsible document, he said. He then read out one particularly strong sentence about the need to restore industrial discipline. With exquisite powers of selection, he chose a sentence that had actually been composed by Owen O'Brien, general secretary of NATSOPA.

What could I do except privately enjoy the irony of this bizarre intervention?

Chapter Eight

The *Times* shutdown was a most traumatic experience. It lasted for a year, became a major public issue and ended in a defeat. For me it was something of a crusade. The unions at that time were embarked on a disruptive policy which was destined not only to unseat me but, at a level far higher, the Prime Minister. The militancy in the newspaper industry was mirrored across the country in the Winter of Discontent. I always had at the back of my mind Roy Thomson's last words to me, extracting a promise to bring in the new technology.

I do not intend to go right through the various ups and downs of the struggle – well covered in specific histories of the dispute and none better than Eric Jacobs's *Stop Press* – but to outline the main principles and my own contribution and feelings at the time.

The burden of the constant negotiations, the continued pressure, the distractions, the late nights fell on everyone, but primarily on me and my family who were naturally upset at the personal attacks on me in the press and also no doubt wondered whether, in view of all the criticism, I was right. I myself was haunted by wondering whether an alternative policy would have been more successful. I am haunted by those doubts still.

In retrospect and, indeed, at the time, it was worse than my long period in hospital partly because during those five years I was strengthened by the efforts of everyone around me. Whether it was the German nuns or the nurses and doctors in the various hospitals in which I was treated in England, they were all trying to help. On *The Times* the people on whom I depended – with some very conspicuous exceptions – were not all trying to help.

During the long hospital years when the pain was difficult, I taught myself to regard it as a period of time which would inevitably pass and cling to that. 'For all the happiness mankind can gain is not in pleasure but in rest from pain.' It would, as Dryden predicted, end sometime, somehow.

What I have always wondered is how I would have stood up to pain inflicted deliberately on me. Not very well, I suspect. I am honoured to have sat next to Odette Hallowes three times. She had been taken prisoner and tortured repeatedly by the Germans while working for the British behind the lines. On the third occasion I asked her how she stood the pain. She turned to me, bared her mouth so I could see her teeth and said through them, 'I got so angry.' I have never forgotten that. No wonder she was an outstanding recipient of the George Cross.

The shutdown at *The Times* was my fourth attempt to handle union disruption problems in the newspaper industry. The first was with Garrett Drogheda to set up a printing consortium for the qualities. The second had been the 'Programme for Action', jointly negotiated with the general secretaries of the print unions. The third was a similar effort directed only at Times Newspapers and not the entire industry.

My own analysis of the situation at *The Times* was that, in the end, the unions would give in – provided we stood firm. That was the flaw. The management at the Thomson Organization and Times Newspapers were never totally united. Ken Thomson and his chief executive in Canada, John Tory, were strongly in favour of any action that might introduce the new technology that operated so successfully in their Canadian newspapers. That was their priority. The top management in England, led by Gordon Brunton, was also behind us, though from the start some were, if not hostile, at best equivocal. Denis Hamilton, in particular, while never voicing open criticism, made it plain he was against us. I would have respected him more if he had been honest about his views, but I suspect he feared that if he revealed them on the Thomson board he would be asked to resign and he had no intention of doing that.

In any battle, a united front on the main policy is absolutely critical. Some rejoiced in the fight, but flinched as the battle hardened. At Times Newspapers, the advertisement and sales staffs who were responsible for the revenue, the lifeblood of the newspapers, were wholly supportive. Their livelihoods and those of the papers were entirely dependent on the success of their efforts. Having seen his work damaged by union action, Mike Mander, our marketing chief, was, if anything, more hawkish than me. He had grown heartily sick of writing to advertisers and wholesalers week after week apologizing for our failure to produce the newspapers for which they were paying.

Equally supportive, at least on *The Times*, were the journalists. William Rees-Mogg was another who took an even firmer stance than me. He carried most of his staff with him. The same was true for some of the *Sunday Times* journalists, although the majority reflected Harry Evans's more ambivalent position and were less concerned about the issues. They wanted a compromise so they could continue to expose malpractice in every industry other than their own. Even among the production staffs there was a sizeable minority who believed we were right yet they were too fearful to say so.

In the end, as in any campaign, the answer lies in who can exert the maximum power at the point of conflict. We thought we had the edge, but when the time came internal divisions destroyed us. The newspaper proprietors as a group certainly had the power but were never willing, collectively, to challenge the unions. I am not suggesting they should all have shut down on our behalf, but at least they might have abstained from action that was positively hostile (i.e. helping the very unions who were damaging them also) while verbally expressing their support and delight that someone was at last challenging trades union power.

The general secretaries of the print unions had the authority but, as was demonstrated when their recommendations to support 'Programme for Action' were rejected, could not deliver. The TUC was constantly helpful and sympathetic, but they could only advise and prompt. The government, whether Labour until they lost the election in June 1979, or Conservative thereafter, was sympathetic but wisely did not rush to take sides in the dispute. In the end, the real power lay with the chapels who used it to grab as much as they could for their members without thought to the medium- and long-term implications of what was happening. They were happy to march their men over the cliff as long as their pockets were full. And in the end, they did, but that is another story.

Events began promisingly after my initial letter to staff which ended the last chapter. On 13 April Dugal, Mike and I, with the two editors, met the various print union leaders in Birmingham. I believed that we had a common approach – the anarchy had to stop. I remained convinced that we had the union leaders behind us when our group reconvened in London on 24 April. The atmosphere remained good, but there was some talk of letting chapels negotiate for themselves. I had known all along that we would have to carry the chapels with us – as we had failed to do in 1976 over the 'Programme for Action' – but I hoped that the union leadership would take a tough line this time. With hindsight, I realize that I placed too much faith in those printing princes.

The hammer blow came on 19 July. Joe Wade of the NGA wrote to me out of the blue to terminate discussions. On behalf of the NGA council members he said that 'the imposition of a deadline could only serve to exacerbate a deteriorating industrial relations position and they deplore and resent the confrontation mentality contained in the threat'. There could be, he said, no further talks about changes and new technology until the threat of a deadline had been removed. Since we could hardly back-track so spectacularly without losing credibility, there was an impasse. We were not to meet formally with the NGA again until 18 September, a critical delay since the issue of who operated the computers – what became known as key stroking – lay at the very heart of the dispute. When I got Wade's letter, I knew that the chances of a shutdown, which I had up to now dismissed, had suddenly grown very real. My response was to write to every member of staff, at their home addresses, setting out the damage being done to the papers and asking them to be reasonable.

Even before Wade's letter, some chapel officials at Times Newspapers had already made it clear that they would relish the chance of a long-drawn-out confrontation. In early May, Reg Brady, father of chapel for NATSOPA members in the machine room at the *Sunday Times*, wrote objecting in the strongest possible terms to the threat of a lockout – a threat incidentally that we never made – and demanding that the management negotiate not with the NATSOPA leadership, under Owen O'Brien, but with him. I found Brady to be an ambitious and flamboyant character, with a great gift of the gab. I also thought him totally unscrupulous and felt he rejoiced in his power to disrupt and destroy.

The other NATSOPA obstacle was Barry Fitzpatrick – clever, tortuous, though I felt him to be equally unscrupulous. He was FoC (father of the chapel) of the clerical branch. To my amazement, I discovered when I joined Times Newspapers that the management allowed him not just an office but also a secretary, for whom we paid. From this base he caused no end of trouble. The *Sunday Times* depended hugely on classified revenue. The copy had to be carried up to the composing room for setting. This was the responsibility of one man. Fitzpatrick's favourite trick was to withdraw that man by claiming he was sick or hadn't turned up. He would then refuse to allow anyone else to take the copy up to the composing room. Grotesque; you could hardly believe it. This cost us hundreds of thousands of pounds, while Fitzpatrick blithely claimed it was impossible for anyone but the nominated man to do this job. He would drag out the simplest negotiation for several hours by debating every nuance of every word.

I had always realized that a two-prong strategy was necessary – to carry along the union leaders in our efforts to win round the chapels – but now Brady was saying that he and his members would take no notice of what their leaders did or said. He confirmed the impression when in July he wrote again, along with eleven other NATSOPA fathers, demanding exclusive negotiating rights and stating that, until the threat of a shutdown was removed, there could be no talks at all. It was not an option.

In the background, given the worsening prospects, we had been working out the finer details of the various agreements we wanted approved by the staff. On 24 July we circulated details

of the new disputes procedure. It stated simply that if a chapel
stopped production then all its members would remain unpaid
until the dispute ended. It did not seem to me an unreasonable
proposition. Nevertheless, we should have got out those proposals more quickly. That was an error. The principal difficulty was
that all our managerial staff were working long hours dealing
with minuscule problems, deliberately made unnecessarily difficult by the chapel officials.

Brady stepped up the campaign by imposing a ban on
overtime which effectively meant that we lost copies every
Sunday until November. If we had hoped that the deadline
would concentrate minds on the union side over what was a
very real threat to the papers, it seemed to have the opposite
effect. Between early June and the middle of August SOGAT
members refused to complete the *Sunday Times* print order on
overtime and so we lost 1.3 million copies. Throughout October
and November Brady's overtime ban cost us four million copies.
It was madness. Between 1 January and 30 November 1978 we
lost a staggering thirteen million copies in total across our titles,
or £2.9 million in revenue, all due to unofficial wildcat strikes.

The situation at the three supplements, particularly the
vitally important *Educational Supplement* with its concentrated
and dependent market, had got so bad that by 5 October Dugal
was suggesting transferring publication out of London at once to
break the grip of our unions who seemed unable to see that the
papers and hence their members were living on credit – the
profits made by other parts of the Thomson Organization.
Dugal's instincts were right. Printing the supplements outside
London would have been the answer, but that might totally
have shut down our newspapers.

The clock was now ticking ever louder. Those summer
months were gruelling. One day ran into another and the toll on
my family was already getting to me. Sue, for instance, never
knew when or even if I was going to get home. It was the most
painful period. Sleep was difficult and, though physically
exhausted, I had continually to display confidence and good
cheer to the staff. Mike Mander told me that one of his memories of the dispute was walking past my office and hearing me

roaring with laughter. It may have been on hearing a good joke, but usually such good humour was my way of trying to dispel the anxiety felt by so many of the loyal employees.

I worried, above all, about my family. Sue, who meets many politicians, was frequently asked, not least by Conservatives, 'Why is Dukie being so hard? He ought to soften and negotiate' (they changed their minds pretty quickly when they ran into the miners' strike). But I was touched when my daughter, aged thirteen, sent me a book as a present with the inscription 'I am so proud of you, Daddy'.

It seemed absurd in this run-up to the deadline that the unions would not even talk to us and that all my efforts had to go into just bringing them to the table. I tried each and every way to put over our case and persuade anyone with influence to use it on our behalf. I was in touch with the Labour Secretary of State for Employment, Albert Booth. He was a decent, good minister who tried to get things going but failed. On several occasions I spoke to groups of MPs who had become involved in the issue. My abiding impression was that – save for a few mavericks like Tony Benn, then Secretary of State for Energy, who wanted *The Times* merged with the BBC as some form of public asset (ironic, in view of what happened to me later) – the politicians wouldn't touch us with a barge pole. Why should they?

Once during the dispute, I met the Prime Minister, Jim Callaghan. He said to me, 'Len Murray tells me you are doing an extremely good job. Keep it up.' Delighted, I naively suggested he might say so in public. He looked at me as if I was mad. In the years ahead, I got to know him well – a lovely man.

Everywhere I went, at all levels, people slapped me on the back saying, 'We're on your side, well done, fight to the end.' But they would not lift a finger in public to support us. There was universal hostility to the unions in 1978 and universal apprehension.

Cracks were beginning to appear on our side as the deadline drew closer. In particular, even though technology had been included in our original five-point agenda, Brunton and Hamilton began suggesting that it had never been intended that it should be part of the package of reforms we advocated. This spread such confusion that, on 29 August, even Mike Mander began to doubt and sent me a memo asking, 'Is new technology included in 30 November or not?'

Fleet Street was alive with rumours that we were about to cave in. Hamilton was reportedly urging caution in private but Brunton – whatever he may later have suggested – was hawkish, as I detailed in a memo of 9 June: 'Throughout the whole of the autumn of 1978, Gordon Brunton kept saying, "You mustn't give in; you must not alter, Duke. You aren't weakening, are you?"' Mike Mander reinforces my memory. 'I remember very clearly at a board meeting before the stoppage, Gordon Brunton told us, "In this enterprise anyone can make a mistake and they will be forgiven. But if they give in on an issue of principle, then they will never, ever, be forgiven."' I took him at his word.

We were by now actively thinking the unthinkable – that we would have to shut down the papers. My instinct was to dismiss everyone who had not by 30 November agreed terms with the company. To deprive them of their wages was the only way to force them to confront the consequences of their actions. But Brunton and the Thomson Organization management were nervous. They feared a repeat of the scenes witnessed recently outside the Grunwick photo processing company in north London. When strikers were fired, a massive, hostile picket was established that even attracted cabinet ministers like Shirley Williams. So it was decided to give notice on the deadline to those who had not reached agreement – thereby to keep paying some for one month and others for three. Only the casual workers would face immediate dismissal and they all had other jobs anyway.

Brunton feared sacking the staff would bring out all the Thomson regional newspapers. I told him it was rubbish, that the regional papers would never come out to support the London unions whom they regarded as overpaid, idle crooks. They would never sacrifice their good wages to help such rogues. He didn't listen to me. I don't think that there has ever been any occasion when provincial newspaper staffs took action to help their union colleagues in London.

We had our proposals for the future now, but what we hadn't got was the chapels to discuss them with. A meeting with NATSOPA arranged on 26 September was postponed until 20 October. With NATSOPA clerical, they refused to meet until November. If anyone was delaying, it was certainly not the management.

At least the NGA had now begun to talk to us. We made a concession – that the principle of new technology be on the agenda, but not the question of its immediate implementation. This was rejected out of hand. On 13 November we tried again. Even if key stroking was eventually done by journalists, we suggested, we would keep on any displaced NGA members for five years. I was prepared to make it ten if it would provide us with a breakthrough. But again we were met with a blank refusal. Wade wrote in the union journal: 'The outcome of the war over new technology will now be determined by the battle at *The Times* . . . there is no going back. We fight until we have won.' In the end, of course, though much later, they fought until they had lost, everything – including their existence as a separate union.

The deadline did focus a few minds. On 28 November the *Sunday Times* journalists' chapel accepted the new agreements, one of only two chapels to do so by the stated date (the other was the newspaper circulation reps). Despite a flurry of activity and our offer to extend the deadline for acceptance of our proposals – though not on the shutdown of the papers – 30 November came and went, with no agreement (though two more groups did sign up). We were faced with a strike that silenced our papers. People kept asking me when I thought it would be resolved. I wouldn't name a date, but I remained publicly upbeat. Yet in the back of my mind was a conversation I had had with Reg Birch of the Engineers' Union, who asked to have a private lunch with me early in November. A Maoist in public, he was a good friend behind the scenes. 'You are on a loser, Duke,' he told me. 'They [the unions] will fight and fight and fight. It's their jobs at stake and they will never give way. In the end you will be beaten and you will be let down by everyone who supports you.'

On the day after the shutdown, 1 December, William Rees-Mogg dropped into Mike Mander's office. Surveying the silent press rooms, William remarked, 'One thing's certain, we've met our Waterloo.' Then he paused before adding: 'What's uncertain is whether we are Napoleon or Wellington.' On paper, we were well placed to end up as Wellington. In 1978 the Thomson Organization worldwide had made £146 million in profits. Its North Sea oilfields were coming on stream. It was a potential war chest that dwarfed anything the unions could muster. Yet we could never make that advantage pay. Any pressure that the prospect of losing their wages might exert on our staff was removed by the other Fleet Street papers who promptly took them on their books officially to help print extra copies to lap up our readers once we had shut down, but in reality to placate the unions. All newspapers had grossly inflated staffs, particularly in the machine room and publishing room, and they could easily have printed more copies without employing additional men. Their action was not helpful, or indeed, in my view, honourable. The old etiquette of the NPA – however hypocritical it had often been – had entirely disappeared. We were on our own.

The shock of closure was mitigated by the Christmas and New Year period – in those days usually a quiet time for newspapers anyway. Come January, the cold reality struck us all the more forcibly. We were not publishing. We were still spending a fortune, and making little progress towards a restart date. What discussions were taking place tended to be about a timetable for talks. Talks about talks. The unions' position was that they wanted everyone reinstated before they would even begin negotiating on our proposals. Ours was that we could not take people back until we had some sign that the anarchy of the past would be replaced by a new climate of industrial relations.

Despite my public reputation as the face of management intransigence, the reality was somewhat different. The media were getting hostile. My colleagues tried to shield me by taking the stand in my place, but it was me the papers wanted to hear from. Rightly or wrongly this was seen as my fight. If it failed, I knew I would be the fall guy. I still have a long list, compiled by a colleague, of some of the adjectives used to describe me at the time – from arrogant, austere, autocratic, cunning, diabolical, evil, foolish, incompetent, out of touch, pathetic, thick through to very physical ones like bloody-minded, pig-headed, stiff-necked, two-faced and weak-kneed. Not bad! I enjoyed that.

Len Murray at the TUC, who certainly did not appear to share this view, was doing his best to break the deadlock. For all the rhetoric, he and I cooperated closely to bring the dispute to an end. He had engineered a potential deal with the NGA and asked me round to his office at 11 o'clock at night, alone, to discuss it. No one was to know I was there except Len and his secretary. There is a back entrance at the TUC building for such meetings. I went up, waited for a few minutes and then Len came in, deeply embarrassed. I thought he was ratting on the deal.

'I don't know how to say this to you, Duke.'

I said, 'Come on, Len, no one knows I'm here, we can say anything to each other.'

'Well,' he said, 'I've got this union in that room, another union in that room, and a third union waiting to see me.' (This was the Winter of Discontent and rubbish was piling up in the streets.)

He took a deep breath. 'I've got no one to watch my private telephone. Do you think you could possibly sit by it in my office and take a note of any urgent calls that come through?'

I said, 'Of course. No problem.'

I sat there on the far side of the desk, so no one could think I was looking at the papers on it and thought, if I was a villain, I could get the whole lot out now. Rather to my regret, no one rang. It's a rum world. No one would have believed that someone widely featured as the leading opponent of the unions would be happy to sit and mind the telephone of the general secretary of the TUC.

Throughout January Len was working on a scheme to introduce some form of experimental keystroking with the journalists and tele-sales girls. It was just an experiment but could ease our way towards the principle. He had discussed it at great length with Wade and Dixon of the NGA and we were all optimistic.

Two days later copies of the provisional proposals littered the *Sunday Times* composing room. That could only have come from the top NGA. I rang Len to tell him. He was absolutely furious. He had been totally let down. And, of course, that was the end of that proposal.

On 17 January Hamilton sent me a memo with the news that he had been appointed chairman of the news agency, Reuters. He planned to carry on as editor-in-chief at Times Newspapers and warned in his note that no one should misinterpret the move. 'I am totally behind Duke ... I shall do everything in my power to assist Duke in achieving a sensible settlement at the earliest responsible opportunity.' He was maintaining the public charade.

Meanwhile, Albert Booth was plugging away in the background on the basis that we put the new technology on the back burner and set a date for publication. It was a device to get the negotiations going, sliding past the union demand for reinstatement before talks. I thought there was enough goodwill to give it a go. We all met in Booth's offices and I took Mike Mander with me. There was an air of optimism. He sent his driver out to buy a massive amount of fish and chips. Good cheer was flowing, so well that Mike was approached by one of the union delegation who asked if he could borrow £20 to get a woman. With the negotiation promising and delicately poised, Mike decided to lend him the money though wondered how he would justify it in his expense account. The union negotiators were enjoying themselves. It was a game at someone else's expense.

This April optimism was misplaced. While the NGA had been talking to us – and Len Murray – they had forced the *Glasgow Herald* to drop its plans to let the journalists work key stroking. The *Observer* and *Express* loudly trumpeted deals on the new technology, leaving it forever in the hands of the NGA. We were the only ones taking a stand on the crucial issue – the ability of journalists and tele-ad girls to input their own copy via computers more quickly, more accurately and much more cheaply than the traditional methods we were using.

The Booth initiative was doomed. Our minds moved on to other possibilities. Mike Mander had been working for some time on a plan to print a weekly overseas edition of *The Times*. It made sense from his point of view since 36 per cent of our advertising revenue came from abroad. And it would have a symbolic importance for the unions – to show them that we could manage without them. William was right behind Mike; the prospect of a platform from which to comment on the forthcoming General Election was irresistible. Harry was initially opposed, though when details started to fall into place changed his tune and asked why it couldn't be the *Sunday Times*. Brunton supported us and Hamilton was okay until Mike decided on printing in Germany rather than the United States, either Miami or Washington. Under German law the name of the publisher had to appear on any paper and he or she had to be present for the printing of the first edition of that paper. As chairman of the Times Newspapers Ltd board, that should obviously be Hamilton, but as soon as he heard he had to be present in Germany he distanced himself from the project.

The final plan we all agreed on – and Hamilton and Brunton were a party to this whatever they later said, though William and I did decide, given their lack of resolve, not to give them precise detail – was to produce 80,000 copies of a sixteen-page *Times* in Frankfurt on Saturday 30 April. The printing would be done by the local subsidiary of the Istanbul daily *Tercuman*. It had the capacity because it produced 65,000 copies for Turks living in Germany. The typesetter was to be Otto Gutfreund and Son at nearby Darmstadt (funnily enough, very near my prison camp). It used new technology, operated by non-union women, many from their homes.

On 19 April the board decided to go ahead on the basis that it would be one issue per week. The next day, the *Times* journalists were told about the plans, but not where the printing would be done. The whole thing was cloaked in secrecy. At once the NGA announced a picket on Gray's Inn Road. We had them rattled.

The paper was to be datelined the first Monday in May. Slowly the details leaked out and the NGA did a good job lining up their German colleagues – and every extremist in Frankfurt – outside the *Tercuman* plant for the Saturday. Things were becoming dangerous. A German-speaking *Times* employee, Karin Dahmen, was attacked with a knife at Frankfurt airport. Since there was no robbery, local police assumed the incident related to our plans. When the *Tercuman* staff were preparing to set the presses rolling, technicians spotted an effort to sabotage the whole plant by placing petrol-soaked blankets against the external pit containing the compressor. If undetected, this sabotage might have blown the whole plant and everyone in it sky high.

Police numbers were reinforced and printing delayed. The German authorities were by now getting very nervous. William, his deputy Louis Heren and Mike Mander were all there. They advised the situation was now critical. Lives were endangered. We had to abandon the attempt – but managed to print 30,000 copies. The police later discovered there were more bombs at the factory.

In the aftermath of the Frankfurt episode, Brunton ordered us to abandon any plans to print overseas again, not just in Germany but also in the United States. His decision effectively robbed us of what was our strongest card – the threat that we could bypass the unions. That was the moment during the shutdown when we were at our strongest. I knew that from the number of conciliatory calls I suddenly received from Keys and Wade, saying that we must sit down and talk, urgently – the only time that suggestion was made by the unions (other than Len Murray).

We proved that we could print without the British unions. By running scared, we threw away the advantage. In effect Brunton saw the picketing at Frankfurt and read it as his bluff being called. To my mind he believed, wrongly, we were in an unsustainable position and that it was therefore time to backtrack. If conflict had not worked as a weapon, he was now going to try buying off the unions. I could not endorse such slippery tactical moves. As far as I was concerned we had embarked on a war and there was no substitute for victory.

Granted we made a critical mistake timing the Frankfurt experiment over the May Day Bank Holiday. During a normal working weekend it would not have been so easy to mount literally deadly threats. But other aspects were fascinating. Three German housewives sitting at computer terminals had set the whole paper in a foreign language in half the time it would have taken the NGA in London and at about a third of the cost. This alone was enough to get the unions rattled. But Frankfurt showed also that we could print the paper outside London. If we could have printed say 60,000 copies a night, people would have fought for them in the streets. We could have broken the strike. As it was the copies we did print became collectors' pieces.

On 30 April, Alf Robens reported a conversation that he had had with Ken Thomson. Ken had told Alf that he was sending 'a clear message' to the *Times* management that he was 'not prepared to foot the bill any longer' (was that suggested to him?). And as our owner began to shift position, so my own colleagues showed their true colours. I was so distressed that on 2 May I drafted a letter to John Tory, Ken Thomson's right-hand man in Toronto. If I sent it I would be committing the cardinal sin of bypassing Brunton, but I was so dismayed that I contemplated just such a step. 'The European issue which we have been ordered to abandon,' I wrote, 'has to my mind already yielded results . . . I think we would be making a terrible tactical error if we abandoned all thoughts of republishing a European edition . . . I cannot understand the sudden shift in policy now coming over so many of my colleagues just as we had started to worry them [the unions].' And I wasn't the only one. In the end I didn't send the letter, but it showed my true feelings at this juncture.

At this dark moment, inspiration came from an unusual quarter. My secretary rang to say that in my office was Sir William Haley, the austere and distinguished ex-editor of *The Times*, and ex-Director-General of the BBC. He was a patriarchal figure with strong views on declining standards and moral issues. I was somewhat apprehensive about his visit, believing that he would be dismayed at the non-appearance of *The Times*, but immediately asked him in for a cup of coffee.

'Sir William,' I started, 'I must apologize to you for being one of the prime reasons why *The Times* is not publishing.'

'No, no, that's why I have come to see you. I want to tell you that in my view you are absolutely right. You have my full support. We have got to get this new technology in.'

He told me that he had been in the States at an international conference on the future of newspapers and had met there a characteristically flamboyant Texan who was boasting to a group of Ghanaians about his new technology in such a way as to make plain that he believed they could not understand what he was talking about. He rounded off, Sir William told me, with, 'I'd like to help you people. I'll send all my old Linotype machines to Ghana and what is more I will even pay for the carriage.'

'No, no, that's most kind of you,' came the reply, 'most kind of you, but you see, we in Ghana, we have already had your new technology for five years and, what's more, we black buggers know how to work it!' I could hardly believe my ears. At that moment, Sir William's visit was like manna from heaven.

June brought a new government under Margaret Thatcher who had made plain her distaste for unions. Jim Prior replaced Albert Booth. He was determinedly non-interventionist. In desperation, I decided that we should try to use Ken Thomson to break the deadlock. I had written a memo in May to this effect, '. . . an initiative would now have to be on a different basis. Do they want the papers to survive? Put the onus on them. I think it should also be started with different personnel. It ought to be done at the highest possible level – i.e. owners not managers. There needs to be a considerable drama about it: "a last effort".' I also conceded that we had to place greater emphasis on the shop floor and less on the union leadership. And I even went so far as to suggest that key stroking – if not new technology in its entirety – might potentially be put to one side as long as we could cut a deal that was seen to be better than those reached by the NGA with the *Observer* and *Express*. It was a question of saving face. This was the strategy that in the end settled matters. It was music to the ears of Brunton and Hamilton.

Brunton told me to go and talk to Rupert Murdoch whom he had met at lunch and who, he said, had good advice for me. Here are the notes I wrote immediately after the meeting with Rupert:

'I don't think you will get the technology,' he said, 'but you must get everything else. It is perfectly obvious what is happening to you. GCB [Brunton] has sent Denis in to wave the white flag and he is waving it in all directions. This could be very damaging for your company. If this attitude goes on, the management will lose all credibility. Your chances of getting . . . a commercially viable newspaper company are negligible. There are only two people who have the authority to make a surrender or a compromise proposal, and they are Ken Thomson and GCB. If GCB is sending Denis in to do it for him, he is making your position absolutely impossible. He [Brunton] started you off on this road in the first place . . . and now if Denis waves the white flag, he is absolutely slaughtering you . . . You have sacrificed your working credibility and your neck, and he should give you £200,000 a year and tell you to run an oil well. On the other hand, if you can salvage a good compromise on technology, it is absolutely vital that you get the manning and continuous production.' Rupert told me that he had seen Brunton at lunch and Brunton had spoken of giving the strikers £1 million for their hardship. 'I knew then,' Rupert went on, 'that the balloon was going to go up and everything was lost. Gordon and Denis must be stopped from giving this surrender atmosphere to everyone.'

It was a sobering meeting, and a signal warning. On 27 June Ken Thomson came over for the AGM of the Thomson Organization. He knew he was walking into an industrial stand-off and took advice. I managed to persuade him to tone down a threat to sell the papers if there was not a settlement soon and instead to use his good offices to bring the sides together. By 29 June, Ken met with the NGA, NUJ and NATSOPA representatives and agreed publicly to what we had realized for some time was the only viable position – to postpone any talk of key stroking until after the restart. Then it was to be done by consent. We were pleased that at least it was agreed that it would be a joint decision.

During Ken's visit, Hamilton had finally got his way and on

12 June and again on 4 July met with all the FoCs. However, the FoCs could hardly claim to speak for all their members as a sheaf of documents in our possession showed. As early as 6 December, members of NATSOPA at Times Newspapers had written to their union general secretary, Owen O'Brien, to stress that they were 'in favour of the [management's] new proposals but hesitant to express our opinion openly'. In another memo sent to us on 5 January, members of the Rirma (Revisers, Ink and Roller Makers' Auxiliaries) branch of NATSOPA were virulent in their criticism of their own FoCs. Then later thirty-six members of NATSOPA disowned Reg Brady. 'It is obvious he is not trying to negotiate,' they wrote. 'He wants to get us the sack and he wants to close the papers down. He's power mad and thinks he's the Godfather.'

Yet these were the people that Hamilton wanted to placate. His approach on 12 June was heavy on chummy rhetoric and sounded to his audience as if we were beating the retreat. He gave the impression of capitulation, as he surely meant to. Then he said that he wasn't there to negotiate 'but to use myself as a catalyst to help get talks going'. Having pulled the rug from under our feet, he then announced that Dugal and I would meet with the FoCs effectively to dot the i's and cross the t's. Hugh Trevor-Roper, a director of The Times, was once asked by a colleague how Hamilton had got so far. It was down to his unique capacity for sitting on an ever rising fence, he replied.

Keys was absolutely furious. 'Just as we are beginning to get control of the chapels,' he told me, 'Hamilton is giving it all over to the FoCs. Where will that get us?'

Dugal and I still insisted, despite Hamilton, on a set of nine 'minimum practical conditions' for restart. We would not, we said, hire any staff until the points had been agreed but if they were then we would aim for a rapid return to production at old wages plus 20 per cent. The FoCs refused to negotiate with me. They insisted it had to be Hamilton or Brunton, already identified as soft touches. I was being marginalized, a fact that was not lost on observers of the battle. The Economist, in August, ran a splendid article saying Brunton and Hamilton were pulling the rug out from under my feet and that I had legitimate reason to

Uganda 1927, with my father, mother, nanny and the four 'boys' who looked after us all with care and affection.

1931, aged eight, at Pinewood – better with the ball than the bat as it turned out.

Bathing at Brockdale, the home of Arnold Power, a great patron of my father – Uncle Tam (father of Robin Ferrers), my mother and I. The house was subsequently bought by Peter Goodchild, a distinguished BBC producer, who found this photograph in an album that had belonged to Arnold Power.

June 1943, just commissioned as a second lieutenant in the Grenadier Guards a week earlier; taken by my mother in the garden of our house at Littlehampton – my father abroad in Abyssinia.

Geoff. Bedding

- Presents -

"WE'RE ALWAYS ON THE INSIDE"

A Non-Stop Intimate Revue

Produced by Jack Diamond & Ken Mountcastle

P R O G R A M M E

26th August, 1944

Bad Soden   Salmunster

Fourteen months later, on 26 August 1944. The enterprising prisoners of Stalag 9B gave an hilarious and irreverent concert which I watched from my stretcher – I gave a large barrel of beer. At the end, Major Charters, the senior British officer, announced that three prisoners, of which I was one, would leave the next day for repatriation.

After the war and with no barbed wire, the hospital and buildings at Bad Soden.

My visit to Bad Soden in 1980, taken by Sue. The nun on my right is the one who saved my life in 1944 and on my left is the Mother Superior who took us to the Hospital Chapel.

Two days before VE Day, Princess Elizabeth, in her capacity as Colonel of the Grenadier Guards, stood the 5th Battalion down and Timothy Jones and I were presented to her. (*Guards Museum*)

Esmond, Lord Rothermere, the merchant prince – more at home among his magnificent possessions than conducting his disparate newspaper empire. Seen here at Warwick House. (*Hulton Getty*)

Roy Thomson, the best of proprietors, adventurous, shrewd and understanding, with a great sense of humour. (*Hulton-Deutsch collection/Corbis*)

William Rees Mogg, close friend and neighbour, a man of high principle and wide interests who is unable to write a sentence that is not beguilingly readable. (*Hulton-Deutsch collection/Corbis*)

With two good friends at the Finnish Embassy in London in 2001– Ken Thomson (son of Roy), and Jalle Kohler, KBE. The Finns supplied all the newsprint for Times Newspapers and were loyal and generous colleagues – Sue and I often visited that beautiful country, where we have made many good friends – the chief of whom were Jalle and his wife, Jeanne.

"MR. HUSSEY? — WITH THE PRIME MINISTER'S COMPLIMENTS, SIR..."

From the *Daily Telegraph*: a telling comment on my appointment.

With Mike Checkland and me, the complete Board of Governors and Board of Management, comprising a bewitching medley of competing talents, views and objectives. (*BBC*)

With my family at my BBC
farewell dinner: daughter
Katharine with her husband
Francis Brooke, Sue, son James
and his wife Emma.

Captain Jonathan Savill MC; commissioned, like me, in June 1943, but he
went abroad a few months earlier. After the war he became a landscape and
portrait painter and is a good friend. This portrait was commissioned by Sue
and delivered to us in August 1999 at a party we gave for him. He told us
that I had taken his place on the boat to Anzio, as he had been told to
scrounge some food for his company. He turned to me and said, 'I've never
had the nerve to tell you that.' I said 'Jonathan, it was over fifty years ago and
here we both are drinking champagne. Who cares?'

complain since I was now being asked to negotiate a deal 'with persistent sniping from the Thomson board room'. The extent of our disunity was well known.

With our two leaders in full retreat, a restart date of 2 September was agreed by Brunton, but even with the management conceding on most of the points, NATSOPA still made trouble. A 20 per cent rise across the board was not enough. They wanted to negotiate in detail for their members before any return to work. Brunton again conceded. In a memo of 4 September, he told me to reach a deal with Brady at all costs. 'If the best you can do is unacceptable to your colleagues, I shall make the deal.'

Fitzpatrick and Brady were in their element. The whole settlement now hinged on them. They dragged it out, it seemed to me, to assert their own power and the weakness of their union leadership. Brady once tried to walk out of a crucial negotiation because the lunch menu was not up to scratch. It took until the start of October to pin the two of them down. On 4 October, Brady lorded it around the *Times* boardroom which he had demanded to announce an agreement. But by then the NGA was jealous of the concessions NATSOPA had gained. So they now insisted on negotiating a final and detailed deal before republishing. Their chapel members were up in arms about that age-old bugbear – differentials. It was inevitable and the fatal flaw in negotiating primarily with NATSOPA.

I began to doubt that we would ever find our way through the maze and, despite my weakened hand, warned publicly more than once about the continuing threat of a total shutdown. William Rees-Mogg used a particularly apt analogy for describing our predicament. Imagine, he said, a line of one-armed bandits at the end of a pier in winter. There are twelve machines. By an amazing coincidence we managed to get three cherries showing on four of the machines, but we needed them on all twelve. Some machines weren't working properly and the twelfth was sitting on a wonky floorboard. As we tried gently to nudge it towards three cherries it started to wobble which had a knock-on effect further down the line, displacing the cherries on the earlier machines so that we had to start again.

The final negotiations were due to start at the end of October. Dugal was going to conduct them. But after two hours he told me it was hopeless. The FoCs and their colleagues had brought in bottles of drink and were incoherent and incapable. I rang up Len Murray and told him we would have to abort the negotiations and why. He was naturally unhappy, so I suggested he rang them up himself. Which he did. He rang me back within ten minutes to say, 'Abort them.' We then discussed the matter an hour or so later and hatched out a wheeze. He would ring me in two days' time and suggest that we had one last shot which he would publicly support and he would get the unions there – early. This was between us two.

He was as good as his word and I rang in great excitement to tell Brunton that Len had made this proposal and we must agree. We did. We got all the unions in by 6 p.m. and I had made careful preparations to provide pea soup, fresh bread and cheese, but no drink. You can't get drunk on that. It worked well.

Dugal started the crucial marathon negotiating session. Brunton was on hand, along with James Evans, whom he was later to install as my successor at Times Newspapers. Agreement depended on two things – hammering out terms with the NGA on money and the refusal of certain chapels to budge on job losses. Brunton gave Dugal the responsibility to head the negotiations over my head. He even arranged for me to be taken out for a very long dinner by James Evans so that I could not influence the surrender. By 4 p.m. on the Sunday a hotchpotch of a final agreement had been completed.

Percy Roberts, managing director of Daily Mirror Newspapers, told me later that he knew there would be a settlement because the union leaders had rung him up to say that they had been told by Brunton that I would not be allowed to enter into the negotiations and if they had any problems with me, they were to ring him up and he would deal with it.

So Dugal brilliantly completed it. It brought out all the best in him – massive energy, mastery of detail and determination. I certainly couldn't have done it half as well. But I had one final involvement. The NGA tried to expel from the membership of their union all our loyal overseers who had stayed on throughout the dispute. Many of their members regarded them as scabs. To expel them from the union meant permanent unemployment because Fleet Street was a closed shop. I rang Wade and told him that this was the final breach of all our agreements and if he persisted in that attitude, I would shut the papers again. I saw it as a point of principle that all the staff who had stood loyally by us throughout the strike – the finance, marketing and circulation workers as well as the production team – should not suffer for their actions. Within twenty-four hours, Wade called back to say the union had changed their mind. For a modest payment of £70 they would be reinstated. When I told Alf Robens this, he said, 'That was brilliant, how on earth did you get away with it?' I said, 'Hamilton and Brunton were abroad!' He said, 'Ah, that explains it.'

Overall though we were defeated. I was defeated. I ended in a state of total exhaustion. Sue and I took a holiday in Marrakesh. I think we hated every minute.

The shutdown cost us £46 million – £33.4 million in wages and lost advertising revenue, £3.5 million for the back-to-work settlement, £1 million for advertisements to herald the relaunch and £8.1 million for lost advertising revenue in the last months of 1979 when the papers were finding their feet. I tried, initially but half-heartedly, to be bullish about our success. Actually, the agreements were good and I sent out, to many people – ministers, senior civil servants and so on – our internal breakdown of what had been achieved. 'The benefits are very substantial and my main worry is that in getting new technology in at lower rates than is currently paid for old technology we may still have wage differential problems. The whole secret lies in whether or not the continuous production is honoured. If it is, this will turn out to be an extremely good settlement.'

Denis Healey (always a supporter, a realist and a great admirer of Sue's) simply said: 'It's a waste of time, the unions won't keep them. As soon as they're printing, they'll break them all again.' I knew what he said was true but did not have the heart to think about it.

On 12 November, *The Times* returned. On the 18th, the *Sunday Times* joined it, although not without a last-minute dispute between the NGA and NATSOPA over who should press buttons on new computerized counter-stackers – not a good omen, but in the spirit of letting bygones be bygones we tried to overlook it.

The *Daily Telegraph* had always been sympathetic and supportive. They only started to print extra copies, with my agreement, when they were the only newspaper which wasn't doing so, having, on Lord Hartwell's instructions, explained the position to me first. The day *The Times* came back Michael Hartwell and his editor Bill Deedes asked me round for a drink to celebrate. They were not the only people to be generous. To my immense surprise Joe Wade and Bill Keys invited me out to a tremendously expensive and drunken lunch at a smart restaurant in Covent Garden. It was their way of saying, 'Sorry, you've been stuffed and probably lost your job but actually you were right.' In a way it was rather touching.

By March 1980, the papers had recovered and exceeded their pre-shutdown circulation. By 1981 the *Sunday Times* had reached 1.4 million, a figure not matched again until 2000. That was the good news. But the *Sunday Times* had completed its run only ten times out of seventeen. Anarchy and wage claims were breaking out all over. By the summer of 1980 my hour of reckoning had come. I had known there would be a fall guy and that it would be me. I was summoned back from a holiday by Brunton who told me James Evans was to take my place as Chief Executive and Dugal Nesbit-Smith as managing director. Mike was sent to run the Thomson magazines. I was given the non-job of vice-chairman of Times Newspapers Ltd under Hamilton and stripped of all executive responsibility. The *Telegraph* reported that after all my valiant efforts, I was 'being put out to grass like a tired and useless old warhorse'.

I contemplated resigning but Arnold Goodman took me to lunch at the Athenaeum. His advice was characteristic. 'Take the money' – to sugar the pill I had been given an increase of £5,000 a year – 'lie low and look around. Something will happen. You could do with a rest.' Bobby Henderson, chairman of Kleinwort Benson, also asked me round to see him. 'I think one or two of our companies would welcome you on their board.' I wondered out loud whether that was now the case. 'Nonsense,' he replied, 'you fought a good fight on an issue of great public importance with huge public support and got beaten. There's no shame in that. It happens to all of us at some time. The point is to fight on the right principles and you did that. That is what will be remembered. I'll be in touch.'

Around the same time, at an embassy dinner, Christopher Soames remarked to Sue, I think after someone had bemoaned what a rough deal I had had: 'Tell Dukie from me, there is an old Chinese proverb which runs as follows – "if the wall falls down, and the brick is good, there is always another wall to build".' Kind, sensitive and, as it turned out, prophetic.

So it was a bad patch. But a short one. I woke up suddenly one morning and thought, 'Why am I so miserable? Sod it. It's a setback. All right, I'm in a bit of a jam now but everything is relative. It's nothing like falling over three yards in front of a German with a loaded machine gun and spending, one way or another, the next five years recovering from his ministrations. I am alive and fit. I've got a lovely family, two splendid children and am lucky enough to have many kind friends. I'm only fifty-eight. There are plenty of things I could do. So let's go for it and see what happens.'

Some weeks after my demotion, the weakness of the final settlement was exposed. In the autumn the journalists went on strike – a personal affront to Hamilton. Ken Thomson had had enough. He put the papers up for sale.

Looking back with the benefit of hindsight, I still cannot see what course we could have taken other than a shutdown. Any negotiation would have resulted in a further costly capitulation. In the end force had to be met with force. And in the end, of course, it was.

One of the most fascinating documents I unearthed while going through my papers relating to *The Times* is a memo about a conversation with the electricians' union during the shutdown. They made it plain that they could see the writing on the wall for the old-style print unions and would be willing to take the opportunity of new technology to extend their influence over the whole industry, even if it meant usurping their fellow unions.

They cleverly saw that the new composing-room technology was in their bailiwick. They could do it, demand higher wages for high skills and hugely increase the size and importance of their membership.

They put out a feeler to us, but I dismissed it at the time. It would have alienated the TUC and the Thomson Organization would never have had the guts to take up the electricians' offer and shut out the other unions permanently. But it was precisely this tactic that was the fundamental plank in Rupert Murdoch's strategy to break the hold of the unions on Times Newspapers – and indeed on Fleet Street – when he bought the titles. In alliance with the electricians' leader, Eric Hammond, having cleverly got NATSOPA and NGA out on strike, he moved to Wapping with its state-of-the-art technology and braved the pickets, the boycotts and the threats of the old print unions. I can't say I shed any tears.

This alternative printing strategy required a man of Murdoch's guts, command of the printing process and political nous to succeed. It also had to be prepared for in great secrecy. The Thomson Organization could not have qualified under any category. It was a large, inchoate company which leaked like a sieve. In the end, the Thomson strategy failed because it was neither clearly agreed between Toronto and London, nor even in London itself. There were too many discordant voices. Above all the Thomson people lacked the determination to win.

When he took over, Rupert once told me, 'You gave me some of the best advice I have ever had. You told me that once I had printed the copies, got them through the pickets to the outside world, I couldn't be beaten. I had it in my mind all that historic first day at Wapping.' Where I tried unsuccessfully, Rupert later marched to victory. On another occasion, he said, 'If you hadn't tried and failed to do it the honourable and orthodox way, Dukie, I would never have got away with doing it so brutally.' As William Rees-Mogg once put it, my effort was the Dunkirk to Rupert's D-Day.

And thanks to Rupert, the whole landscape not just of Fleet Street but of industrial relations in this country has now changed beyond recognition. Twenty years on, what has happened to the contestants? Times Newspapers, as we have seen, has put in all their new technology under a dominating and decisive Australian proprietor. Other papers poured through the gap Rupert Murdoch blew in union lines. There are now more daily papers in the United Kingdom than there were before and they all have the freedom to increase their size, increase their print runs and send out pre-printed supplements. The readers and the advertisers have replaced the unions as king. The *Times*'s sale is now far higher than it was at over 700,000 a day. It has dumbed down, but so has everything else. The *Sunday Times* too is still forging ahead with larger and larger papers, more pages, more presets and colour printing bringing it ever-increasing circulation.

The NPA is a distant memory, while the print unions have shrivelled in size and now operate in a much scaled-down form as one union, the Graphical, Paper and Media Union, out of what was once the headquarters of the all-powerful NGA. So in the end, the narrow-mindedness and greed of their members led the various unions to ignominious defeat.

We in this country are lucky to have lived in a relatively stable and civilized society, not least over the last century. We have, for instance, not been invaded – literally – for a thousand years, though there have been occasions, not many, when some ambitious element or group has sought to become more powerful than the whole. First it was the Church and then the barons. Each, in turn (tall poppies, as the Australians call them), was cut down by the legal authority of the state – at that time, the monarchy. In the fifty-five years since the war another force grew up, the Trades Union Movement, which, in the 1960s and 1970s, appeared to challenge the basic balance within our society. The unions' origins were in essence, honourable and worthy. The industrialization of the nineteenth century – and the industrialists themselves – made necessary the birth of a trades union movement to protect their members, the employees, from exploitation. And it says something, but not much, for our society that it accepted that. But the unions were not content with that and lost sight of their essential purpose. Another tall poppy required pruning and got it.

These major shifts or adjustments in society are not achieved without changing the attitudes of the ordinary men and women in it. Perhaps the shutdown at *The Times* contributed – and no more than that – to such a change in attitude.

Like Roy Thomson and Hamilton, the union leaders, O'Brien, Wade and Dixon have left us. Len Murray is a much respected member of the House of Lords and the TUC is ably led by John Monks who was a junior but very helpful participant in all our struggles.

On the other side, Brunton parted rich from the Thomson Organization and owns a small but successful racing stud with which he won the Gold Cup. And our team? Mike Mander, the staunchest of the staunch, went on to be chairman and vice-president of the Institute of Directors and chairman or director of many companies in the media field. Dugal Nesbit-Smith was for fourteen years an outstanding director-general of the Newspaper Society. Donald Cruickshank became chairman of the Stock Exchange and Harry Evans the most sought after publisher in New York.

And what of the two chief hawks? William Rees-Mogg retired from the editorship of *The Times* when Rupert took over, but remains its chief columnist, a man of great influence and wisdom. He is now in the House of Lords. With me. In 1984 I became chairman of the Royal Marsden Hospital, and in 1986 of the BBC. In the end, it seems, Bobby Henderson was right.

Chapter Nine

The period between my demotion at Times Newspapers in 1980 and my appointment as Chairman of the Governors of the BBC in 1986 was an obvious opportunity to relax, recoup and look around. I was fifty-eight, not too old to be active (not too active!). Since I emerged from hospital, my life hitherto had been fairly hectic and a period of rest, though not for too long, seemed a heaven-sent opportunity. I spent much more time at Waldegrave House, the house in Sue's home village in Somerset which we had bought from her brother in 1975. Whenever possible I was in the swimming pool there which I keep at 82°. I saw much more of my family, especially the grandchildren who had started to arrive, and we went abroad to Portugal to a villa Mike Mander owned. Events at *The Times* rapidly dimmed in my mind.

Other opportunities of varying size arose quickly. Bobby Henderson was as good as his word and I joined the British board of Colonial Mutual Insurance and of MK Electric who made plugs – much to the amusement of my family who knew that I couldn't even change one. As it turned out, I was able to play a part in both companies. Dick Troughton (whom I had known for ages both as chairman of WH Smith and of the British Council) once told me that the great advantage of a non-executive director is that he or she is not dependent on the chief executive for mortgages or school fees so they are free to say what they like when they like. This I did. And it's surprising how often you hit a coconut.

I also joined the board of the British Council in 1982 and in 1985 of William Collins Publishers. The British Council post was particularly important since it enabled me, in some small way, to follow in my father's footsteps. It always amazes me that, while successive governments pay verbal tribute to the work of the British Council, they never supply it with the resources it deserves. The staff is devoted, hard working and poorly paid. Many ambassadors have told me that the Council's various activities – the libraries, the exchange visits to Britain, the concerts, the plays that they promote – do in many cases at least as much good as the more formal entertainments of our embassies. The British Council libraries, especially behind the Iron Curtain, were always packed. Imagine in Poland being able to walk into a place where you could freely read uncensored material, published in Britain, criticizing the regime in your country.

At Times Newspapers, from the vantage point of my non-job, I watched with interest as the strike of the journalists on *The Times* led to the sale of the titles. It was clear to me from the outset that Rupert Murdoch was going to get them, but I had no involvement. Nor did I particularly want any. (The only impact of the sale was that Brunton insisted I cancel a trip that I had planned for Sue and me to go to America on the grounds that I might contact the Thomson family in Canada. He was quite wrong, incidentally.) Hamilton, much hurt by a strike that started among journalists whom he considered should be personally loyal to him, remarked to me, with unconscious innocence, 'I can't understand our chapels. All my life I believed in giving them what they want and they still seem to ask for more and don't appreciate what I am trying to do.' I felt sorry for him. His faith in the chapels – which he had used to undermine me during the shutdown – had finally been shown to be based on an illusion.

As soon as Rupert was installed as proprietor in Gray's Inn Road he dismissed the entire senior management team and many of the leading executives. The butler went in double quick time. One of the first of the new guard to arrive was Richard Searby, the tall, elegant and highly intelligent chairman of News Corporation. We hit it off at once and he became a great friend. He once gave me a fascinating insight into what motivates Rupert.

'When he was a little boy, he liked train sets, but what he liked best was to find another little boy whose train set was broken and then make it work. That, broadly speaking, has been what he's done ever since.'

One morning soon after the takeover Rupert's secretary rang up to say he was coming to see me. I assumed that this was my turn for the departure lounge. He came in, very cheerfully, and immediately told me that he planned to make Harry Evans editor of *The Times* and Frank Giles editor of the *Sunday Times*. What did I think of that? Having nothing to lose and expecting the sack, I told him. 'The quickest way to wreck two marvellous newspapers I can think of! Harry is an inspired editor of a Sunday paper but he lacks the organizational skills to do it six times a week. Frank is an able number two with very considerable knowledge of foreign affairs but I doubt whether he is right to edit the *Sunday Times*.'

'What would you do then?'

'I would leave Harry where he is and make Charlie Douglas Home editor of *The Times*.'

'I'm not going to do that.'

'Well, that would be a big mistake. Charlie may not be such a dynamic, inspirational figure as Harry but Harry will get in the most fearful muddle. After six months of Charlie, *The Times* will be in much better nick than it would be otherwise.'

Rupert took no notice. Why should he? He called me a year later and said, 'I've ballsed it up. Harry's going so I'm putting in Charlie.' I knew that already because Charlie had come to see me the night before and was doubtful whether to accept the job. 'For heaven's sake,' I told him. 'I've spent five years trying to secure you the editorship – if you want out now I'll never speak to you again.'

Back to that initial meeting. Having told me about his plans for the editors, Rupert now turned to me. 'I hope you will stay on as a consultant on a salary of £10,000 per annum and you can keep your secretary and have a car.' I was amazed but assumed that I would be the normal ex-chief executive called a consultant who turns up occasionally and is never consulted. It didn't work out like that at all. Rupert quite often asked for my advice, didn't always take it, but sometimes did. He liked me to keep him in touch with anything I had heard or any views I had which I thought might be of interest. With all my connections with the newspaper proprietors and the unions, friendly now, I think I was quite helpful.

In June 1983, we were getting on so well that Rupert made the third proposal that I should become chairman of the NPA, but I was blocked by the *Mirror* who thought, probably wrongly, that the unions wouldn't like it. I was also asked to take over everything to do with the bicentenary of *The Times* in 1985. A raft of souvenirs and a magazine celebrating the 200 years did well and turned in a profit. We also issued a commemorative facsimile edition of the first edition of *The Times* in January 1785. Fascinating reading – not least for a notice among the personal ads on the front page about a divorce in which the husband cited seven co-respondents. Several of them were named. Pretty contemporary really.

We had a huge gala at Hampton Court, attended by the Prince and Princess of Wales. With orchestras playing and bands marching, it was a great success and, to Rupert's surprised delight, came in within the budget of £100,000.

I was also asked to organize an auction for Prince Philip's birthday in aid of the twenty-fifth anniversary of the Duke of Edinburgh's award scheme. We gave a hefty boost of £65,000 to this imaginative project which provides a vital impetus to children and young people of all ages and all classes. It encourages enterprise, self-confidence and a wholly admirable spirit of independence.

In 1984 John Patten, then a Minister of State at the Department of Health, called me at home to ask if I would like to be Chairman of the Royal Marsden Hospital. 'Good God, no,' I said, 'too gloomy.' John persisted. It was a good hospital, doing marvellous work in cancer care, but it needed someone tough to tackle its problems. 'Unlike most hospital chairmen,' John pointed out, 'you know a lot about hospital life from the position of the patient and that will be a help. And, if you can handle NATSOPA, you can certainly deal with the consultants.' I was tempted. I owed a lot to the hospitals I had been in, so it did not seem right to shirk this job. I agreed to go and meet Phyllis Cunningham, the chief executive, and was impressed. She was an efficient, tough manager, a little autocratic perhaps, but someone who ran a tight ship. I was persuaded to take it on.

The Marsden, based on two sites, one on the Fulham Road near my London home and the other down at Sutton in Surrey, had a very distinguished history. It had been the world's first cancer hospital and was in the forefront of international research into and treatment of cancer. However, lack of investment and the prejudice in the health service against single specialty hospitals had left it with many problems. It desperately needed substantial rebuilding, but on top of that we had to remove a question mark over its future.

When I started, I was given excellent advice by two people. Professor Gerald Westbury, the leading consultant at the Marsden, told me that my absolute priority must be to bring the Marsden and the Institute of Cancer Research closer. We were supposed to be allied to each other and indeed the Marsden was responsible for the clinical research, but for various reasons – mainly jealousy, personal or professional – they were hardly on speaking terms. I was lucky again here because shortly after I joined Kenneth Stowe was made chairman of the Institute. By a simple procedure we resolved the whole issue. I joined his board and he joined mine. Things started to get better at once.

The other person was the distinguished surgeon, Professor Ian McColl, who told me that I must sit on appointments' boards. This was an excellent way of understanding what was happening in the hospital, he said, and of exerting some control over the quality of the top medical staff. I made a note of this and the first appointment that came up was, of all things, for a gynaecological oncology consultant. We had a strong board of top-line consultants, so I was not too worried, until a fierce row broke out – and the board split two versus two. I had the casting vote. I suddenly had visions of all these women patients of whatever age whose lives might, in some respect, depend upon my decision. I asked whether there was anything to choose between the two applicants on either research or clinical experience. 'Nothing. We leave it to you.'

I really hadn't expected this after only six weeks at the Marsden. However, I tried to look wise, while weighing up the qualities of White and Black. I paused for at least three minutes while I thought through all the evidence we'd had. I came down in favour of Black. It turned out to be a brilliant appointment and in later years I was frequently congratulated on the wisdom and perspicacity of my choice. 'How had I done it after only six weeks?' 'Well, I suppose experience,' I replied rather pompously. Actually what I did was have a quick glance at the relative ages and chose the youngest. It took half a second. I always go for the youngest if there's a problem in an appointment. It usually works.

Virginia Bottomley, the Secretary of State for Health, came to visit us one day and I was taking her through a ward when we suddenly saw three men in a small side room, sitting at a table laid for five in very festive circumstances – wine and crackers. 'What on earth is going on here?' she asked.

'I haven't a clue, Virginia. You'd better go and ask them,' I replied.

So she did. 'Well, Secretary of State,' one man replied, 'we've all three been cured and the two other places are for the nurses who helped achieve this miracle. We're going home tomorrow.'

I could hardly believe my luck. It could have been a disaster. But then, being a politician, she said, 'Now what I want to know, is have you any complaints?'

'Yes, we have a serious complaint.' My heart sank. It was too good to last. 'And what is that?'

'This is a wonderful hospital with marvellous doctors and superb nurses. Why is it restricted to people with cancer?'

I nearly cried. It was so typical of what the Marsden is all about. Virginia was obviously moved.

Soon after taking over as Chairman, I asked to lunch one of the Marsden's chief supporters, Johnnie Wynne-Williams. He had been involved in fund-raising for various pieces of equipment but wanted to do something much bigger. We started with Phyllis and asked what she thought she needed. Hesitantly she suggested £9 million. So Johnnie and I set off cheerfully to the

Berkeley to make our plans. To lubricate the thought processes, I ordered a bottle of champagne. After the second glass we had lifted the target to £15 million. Feeling increasingly bonhomous we finished the bottle and had one more glass each, for luck. By the time we were done we had upped the goal to £25 million – in the middle of an economic slump.

Phyllis was astounded – almost appalled. 'What do I spend it on?' she asked. 'We re-equip the hospital,' I replied. And that is what we did and it was Johnnie's initiative that may well have saved it. The £25 million which we raised provided an entirely new block for the central London site, with theatre suites, two wards, a kitchen and a staff restaurant. Down in Surrey it refurbished the breast diagnostic unit.

My own role was a modest one. I chaired the fund-raising committee, co-opted some talented people onto it and then encouraged them to do their best. And they did. As with any job I take on, I saw it as my responsibility to get involved, not to be some remote figurehead. So I would attend the fun runs and charity concerts, I would go to the hospital as often as I could to meet the staff and patients, and I did my best to make sure that the name of the Marsden once more became synonymous with excellence. Again I can take only a small part of the credit. Diana, Princess of Wales, who was a devoted patron of the hospital, did much to raise awareness of the important work going on there and was wonderful with the patients, and so incidentally was another patron, Terry Wogan.

We built a children's ward down in Sutton with most generous help from the Wolfson family. I visited it often. You would think that one could hardly bear to walk through a ward occupied only by children with cancer, but they were so brave and the nurses so cheerful and inspirational that it became a joy not a pain to go there. There were tragic moments. The Duchess of Kent came once and was going through talking to all the children. About halfway round, the sister in charge whispered to me that the child in the next room but one had only two or three days to live. The parents wondered whether the Duchess would agree to be photographed with them. I thought this was imposing a heavy strain upon her, but nevertheless I told her.

'Of course,' she said. The photograph was duly taken and stands proudly on the mantelpiece of the parents in memory of their little boy.

Phyllis was magnificent. She led the Marsden from the front, giving countless interviews, talks and addresses to members of the House of Commons and the House of Lords. The battle to save the Marsden became a national campaign. By the time the moment of decision arrived, I had joined the BBC as Chairman. I had grown to love the Marsden and made it a condition of taking the BBC job that I could carry on at the hospital. Obviously there was potential for conflict of interest. If I took too prominent a part in the battle to save the Marsden, and if that battle then received air time on the BBC, as inevitably it would, people would start pointing the finger. Therefore I took a step back and left the crusade to Phyllis Cunningham who coped splendidly.

A further complication arose because by then I was also Chairman of the King's Fund inquiry into the future of London hospitals. There was a strong bias against single specialty hospitals on two grounds: one, better all-round care would be available if cancer was always treated in large general hospitals (not true); and two, arising from jealousy, that the single specialty hospitals got exceptionally generous treatment from the NHS budget (true). Incidentally at that time there were twelve special health authorities of which the Marsden was one. The twelve chairmen were the only members of the health service, at that time the largest employer of labour after the Russian army, not to be paid. It took some nifty steering to stop my report coming out against the single specialty hospitals. Some were, of course, unnecessary, but those like the Marsden, Great Ormond Street, the Hammersmith and the Brompton Hospital, were and remain unique.

One of our patients, with throat cancer, was John Bute. A great public servant and the inheritor of a distinguished family tradition, he was often in the hospital in an ordinary ward. He demonstrated daily the most tremendous courage. One day, his wife, Jennifer, rang Sue to say, 'John has bought a new dinner jacket and he is determined to wear it, if only once. So we're having a dinner party and he's very anxious for you and Dukie to come.' We accepted, of course, and had dinner at their London home surrounded by superb pictures. Sue sat on John's right and halfway through he said to her, 'Dukie must save the Marsden.'

'Well, he's determined to,' she reassured him.

John then said, 'Being a patient there is rather like being a member of White's Club.'

'I don't think he's ever seen it quite like that,' Sue replied.

'You see, there is a great variety of people and we have a great bond in the condition in which we find ourselves. We get to know each other very well and become friends. Sometimes people go and come back later, new members arrive, who also become friends. Sometimes people go and don't come back, but you have this common interest. You all have plenty to talk about. And, you are waited on by marvellous staff. Just like White's really!'

Outlandish though it sounds to compare the Royal Marsden Hospital to White's Club, as he expressed it, it made sense. A brave man.

If an opportunity arose when I could exert pressure behind the scenes, I would. I set up a meeting with Tony Newton, by then Leader of the Commons under John Major but once the Secretary of State for Health who had appointed me as Chairman of the Marsden. My crafty secretary, Carole, had indicated I would want to talk about the BBC but that the Marsden might come into it. The joy of being Chairman of the BBC was that, if you wanted to see someone, you did. I think this was the only occasion, other than on BBC business, when I used that privilege.

As luck would have it, just as I was leaving Carole slipped into my hand the latest copy of the *Evening Standard* which had a totally inaccurate story about the BBC on its front page. It made my visit, as Tony volunteered, particularly apposite. Just before I left, I added (and this is abridging the conversation), 'About the Royal Marsden. If I may say so, your government is in terrible difficulty. A decision to close the Marsden would be a public relations disaster of spectacular proportions. You have enough problems already. Don't make another for yourself. Give the Marsden five years to prove it can run successfully on its own. If we succeed, you have shown wisdom. If we fail, you have shown sympathy but would be justified in closing us. You don't have to decide now.' In the event, the Prime Minister personally took the opportunity to tell me that he had decided himself to keep the Marsden open. By the time Phyllis and I had retired in 1998, the future of the Marsden was secure.

In the summer of 1986, I had been asked by Hugh Astor to join the board of the King's Fund. It had been founded by the Prince of Wales in 1897 for Queen Victoria's Diamond Jubilee. Its purpose was to support the voluntary hospitals of London. As King Edward VII, its founder, successfully expanded the fund – with great help from many of his very rich friends – into one of the country's major charities. Indeed, until the formation of the NHS in 1948 it was the major financial organization supporting London hospitals.

What it had failed to do, though, was to make any impact on the shape of hospital provision for the capital's rapidly changing population. As long ago as the 1880s, a House of Lords' inquiry had concluded that the distribution of London's hospitals was unsuitable to meet the demands placed on them. A map published in the *Daily Mail* in 1902, and still in the possession of the King's Fund, showed clearly how the major hospitals remained in a tight circle in central London, close to the major railway stations, while the majority of its population was moving out to the new suburbs to the west and south. By the 1980s when I joined, I felt that the management committee had lost sight of this primary purpose and were concentrating on developing the neglected parts of the NHS such as community services, primary care and management by investing in small but worthy ventures. Yet this was a time when the NHS seemed to be in constant crisis, particularly in London where a combination of costly services, medical intransigence and union disputes had brought the hospital services close to the brink of chaos.

I thought that in this situation the King's Fund should assert itself. I had in mind the Rhodes Trust at Oxford of which I had for some time been a trustee. They thought nothing of giving a quarter of a million pounds to a college in need and sometimes to more than one college. This was the example we should follow. So I went to see the chief executive of the NHS, Duncan Nichol, a long-time associate of the King's Fund, whom I knew well, and said, 'Look Duncan, you and I know that the King's Fund is hugely rich [about £175 million at that time]. Can't you think up a proposal which would contribute to health in London? Even if it costs a million pounds, the King's Fund has got the money. We would be re-establishing the King's Fund, fulfilling its original objective and helping London's hospitals and their patients at the same time. I think I can persuade it to disgorge the cash if you can produce the right idea.'

He was all for this. He said he would ring me back in a fortnight's time when he had made enquiries. 'Be bold and imaginative,' I urged. When he came back, he revealed, unbelievable though it may sound, that the NHS had not a single set of contemporary statistics on London's health needs. They were operating on figures that were fifteen to twenty years out of date. It is not surprising they got into such a mess. Duncan suggested that what he wanted most of all was a comprehensive investigation into the hospital services in London.

Since 1886 there had been sixteen reports on London hospitals, all saying the same thing, and virtually nothing had changed except that St George's had moved from Hyde Park Corner to Tooting. And now Kenneth Clark, the Health Secretary, was planning to introduce an internal market into the NHS forcing hospitals to compete to provide services. London's hospitals looked vulnerable. Expensive, unresponsive and unwieldy, with no up-to-date statistics, they presented a tremendous problem.

The King's Fund responded nobly and promised the £1 million. In 1990 we established the King's Fund London Commission which I chaired for the next two years. Robert Maxwell, the highly experienced and intelligent chief executive of the Fund, picked a high-quality team. I wanted a prominent member of the government and of the Labour Party. We had Julia Cumberledge and Patricia Hollis – both outstandingly able and now members of the House of Lords. At the first meeting I laid it down that we wanted no politics in our discussions. We were meeting together to help the NHS in London and I would rule any political comment as out of order. We had none.

We published twelve working papers and our final report, 'London Healthcare 2010', recommended a complete overhaul of hospitals, their training, research, specialist services and especially primary care services, supported by detailed facts and statistics. To our relief (I must admit) as well as attracting a huge degree of attention, our final report stimulated action by successive secretaries of state. Rather than dodge the difficult decisions, they picked up the challenge and instigated radical restructuring. The result was a complete overhaul of medical education in London, and most controversially, the merger of Barts with the London and Guy's with St Thomas's.

Three years after that first report, I made another suggestion to the Fund. I felt what we had done had been massively helpful to London hospitals (and to the Fund) but we hadn't got everything right. And, above all, because there were so many targets, we couldn't hit them all in one burst. We had deliberately excluded two of the most pressing – services for the elderly and for the mentally ill. The Fund generously agreed a further subsidy and we got to work. With a team from the Institute of Psychiatry we subjected the mental health services to the most comprehensive review ever attempted and found them close to meltdown. Professor David Goldburg of the Institute was invaluable and superb. The picture that emerged was shocking.

Because of political sensitivities, publication of the second commission's findings was delayed until after the 1997 election, but the report, 'Transforming Health in London', made manifold recommendations about mental health, old people and public health and provided valuable material for the incoming government as they put more resources at the disposal of the NHS. In this report, we were tremendously helped by Margaret Jay (who had asked if she could be on it) and Diana Eccles. Again, no politics. I think it is not immodest to say that these two reports set alight the whole debate about health care in London.

At about this time, Robert Maxwell felt that it might be the moment to hand over as chief executive of the Fund. I discussed this with Donald Irvine, a fellow trustee and President of the

General Medical Council. I also invited along Rabbi Julia Neuberger who had tremendous experience in the health field (and indeed in many others). We all agreed on the general principle when suddenly Julia asked tentatively and modestly, 'Do you think I have a chance?' It had been half in my mind when I asked her to join us and I was delighted when she took the bait. Donald too was enthusiastic and between us we promoted her candidacy so effectively that she got the job. When it was all over, Donald congratulated me and said: 'I don't think I've met a genuine revolutionary before.' I was surprised, but frightfully chuffed.

After ten years, I thought it was time I left and they gave me a wonderful farewell dinner, along with a beautiful silver bowl thanking me for my efforts, all accompanied by some gratifying – although I'm sure overblown – compliments. Best of all, from Sir Graham Hart, who had been the Permanent Under Secretary at the Ministry of Health and was now chairman of the Fund. He generously described my activities, adding '. . . but lastly and best of all he can spot a load of bullshit at 200 paces'.

Meanwhile, I was still wondering about my own future. My father, who had left me no money because he never had any, gave me one piece of advice. 'You must save something, every month.' And I did. Starting at £5 per month in 1949 and working upwards as my career progressed. I only stopped the monthly saving in 1996 and had therefore accumulated a certain amount of capital.

In 1984, my accountant, a wily old bird, suggested there might be profitable opportunities for investment in local radio which he believed would ultimately prove commercially very successful. As chance would have it – there's that word again – the local station in Bristol approached me almost at the same time and asked me to be their chairman. It didn't look too good on paper. Basically, the station was bankrupt. We had to raise some money, so to show a lead I invested a substantial proportion of my not very large Thomson's settlement of £20,000. We started to improve Radio West on the back of the successful rights' issue which my money had launched, but it was clear that it was not a strong station – unlike its neighbour, Radio

Wiltshire, run by a dynamic and imaginative chief executive, Ralph Bernard, supported by an able and, in broadcasting matters, experienced board. We had neither, so I negotiated a merger of the two as GWR on the basis that they had the managerial and broadcasting skills and we in Bristol had the rich potential market. Just before the merger was completed, I became Chairman of the BBC and so had to resign. But this was another lucky stroke. When my candidature for the BBC came up at the cabinet, I am told the Prime Minister asked, 'Does he know anything about broadcasting?', to which the reply came, 'He is chairman of a local broadcasting company.' 'That settles it,' she is reported as concluding.

When I joined the BBC, I believed those shares presented a conflict of interest and although my accountant urged me to put them in a blind trust, or spread them around the family, I refused and sold them. I knew the BBC would be difficult and I was determined to start with no baggage. Ten years later, the fact that I had done so was featured by Ray Snoddy in a story in *The Times*. Because, as he said, you told everyone that you'd sold them. Ralph Bernard couldn't resist the opportunity to ring me up and tell me what they were now worth. £3.2 million! To be honest, if I had to choose between the £3.2 million and ten years at the BBC, there would be no competition. That was one of the cards I've been dealt in my life, just as another card was the loss of a leg. In neither case did I hark back and wish it had worked out differently. No regrets. None at all. What you haven't got, you don't miss.

Meanwhile, back at *The Times*, Charlie Douglas Home had, as I expected, proved the right man not just to edit the paper but to stand up to Rupert. Early on in his editorship, Rupert asked one of the leading executives to see him while Charlie was away. 'Don't do that again,' Charlie said on his return. 'Of course you have the right to see the executives but not to summon them without my knowledge. I should be there too.' Rupert agreed, and never did it again.

There was a cloud of increasing density on the horizon. Charlie kept falling and breaking bones and I gradually realized and was eventually privately advised that he had cancer – and in an incurable form. It was an appalling tragedy – especially for Charlie, Jessica, their children and their huge circle of relations and friends. And also for *The Times*.

Charlie told me in strict confidence and soon became an itinerant patient of the Marsden. He made me swear not to tell Rupert. 'I know what he'll do. He'll fly doctors over from the States to see me or me to see them. I don't want it to work like that. I will go on as editor for as long as I can.'

That night I thought it over. Rupert was pouring millions into *The Times* and his editor was dying. I went to see him the next day and told him that Charlie had cancer and that I thought it was almost certainly mortal. I added that in telling him I was breaking my word to Charlie. I don't think I had ever broken my word solemnly given before or since. Rupert was very upset and asked how long he had got. I didn't know. It turned out to be four years.

'All right, Duke,' he said, 'I'll tell you what I'll do. So long as he's able to edit the newspaper, Charlie must continue to do so until he wishes to give up. I'm not having any assistant editors moving in to take over while he's alive. Whatever Charlie needs, you give him. Sign all the bills yourself and I will give an instruction that those bills are to be paid immediately, whatever they are.'

'All right,' I said, 'leave that to me. But Rupert, I've broken my word telling you this, and I'll never forgive you if you let me down.'

We continued on that basis for longer than I had expected. There was a tricky moment when Charlie had to have an electric chair costing about £2,000. All Homes have a very Scottish attitude to money. He said, 'What on earth am I going to do. They are terribly expensive. But I am told I have to have one.' 'Don't worry, Charlie,' I said, 'I can handle this and bury the cost under some other heading. No one will know. I've been doing that sort of thing for years for one reason or another. You learn a few tricks about presentation when you are Chief Executive.' That was enough to persuade him. We got the electric chair within a week, Rupert paid, and it was a huge success.

Charlie's health gradually and steadily deteriorated but not his spirit. He continued to edit the paper with courage and skill. His illness became increasingly apparent. Eventually he asked me to come down one day to see him. He said, 'Oh Dukie, I just wanted to tell you that I've told Rupert now. He was very surprised. He didn't know. I thought he must have guessed.'

Rupert Murdoch has a deserved reputation for being hard, rough and tough with his executives but I don't know any other newspaper proprietor who would have behaved with the generosity and sensitivity he showed Charlie. However unlikely, it proved a very close relationship. It was just so sad that it ended as and when it did.

At Gray's Inn Road, Rupert's patience with the unions was running out. 'All I want,' he said, 'is the new technology and uninterrupted production.' (Now where have I heard that before?) He had begun to prepare a plant at Wapping in east London. Officially it was to print a new London evening paper. This was all I was ever told. However, I was not surprised when in January 1986 this plan was revealed as a smokescreen. Having manoeuvred the print unions into calling a strike, Rupert overnight transferred the whole production of all his papers to Wapping where they would be printed by the electricians' union with whom he had done an exclusive and highly secret deal based on the application of the new technology.

I wasn't in the loop on the plans for Wapping – that was wisely restricted to very, very few people – but as Rupert kept on mentioning it to me, either directly or indirectly, I had a rough idea of what was happening. The move to Wapping outraged the unions. There were mass and violent pickets at the new plant. Rupert, showing a steadfastness the Thomson board had never managed, didn't budge an inch. He broke through the pickets and got a few papers out on his first night. After that, as I had foretold, he couldn't be beaten.

The pickets at Wapping took a long time to realize that. Picketing also started outside our premises at Gray's Inn Road. All the editorial and production staff were at Wapping but the advertising and clerical staff stayed put. The pickets were offensive and unpleasant. The secretaries were often followed down the streets, verbally abused and physically frightened. They were terrified of leaving the office alone and tried to depart in groups to get through the pickets. I was one of the few executives left and did my best to deflect some of the hatred by personally escorting people out of the building and through the picket lines. One night I left with Carole. She got into the car first and I followed. And as I did so, one of the pickets leapt forward and slammed the door on my leg. It was the false one and the door bounced back with an almighty clang. You should have seen his face.

That was a further slice of good fortune. My other leg is paralysed below the knee with little circulation. If it had been that one, the damage from the car door would almost certainly have meant a second amputation. Two days later, quite by chance, I met Ken Graham, Len Murray's deputy with whom I had worked closely during the shutdown. I told him the story. 'Oh Duke, that they should do that to you,' he said. 'That's terrible. If only they had listened to you, they wouldn't be in this mess now.' It had crossed my mind that he would repeat this to Len Murray and I think he did. The pickets were much quieter thereafter.

In early September 1986, the Chairman of the BBC's Board of Governors, Stuart Young, died after a long fight with cancer. There was great speculation in all the newspapers about his potential successor. I was staying with Dick Troughton up at Ullapool, salmon fishing. Not much success, but a glorious holiday. I was leaving on Sunday to catch a plane from Aberdeen and as we lunched, Dick asked me, 'Who do you think will get the BBC job, Dukie?' 'I have no idea,' I replied, 'but the BBC is in a terrible state, obviously out of control, with some pretty unreliable characters there too. They'll be hard pushed to persuade some idiot to take it on.'

That was Sunday. On the following Thursday the telephone rang about 9.30 in the evening. 'Oh Dukie, it's Douglas Hurd here, with a very odd question to ask you. Would you like to be Chairman of the BBC?'

'Good Lord, no!' I said. 'That's a ridiculous idea. I'm far too old and it's an appalling job anyway.'

'No,' he said, 'this is a serious proposal which I am making to you, formally, on behalf of the cabinet. The only problem is that I must have the answer by lunchtime on Saturday.' He told me where he was staying on that day and asked me to call him.

It all came as a tremendous shock. Brian Griffiths, who was a key adviser at No. 10 to Margaret Thatcher, had even asked me for suggestions. He and I had worked together on what was known as the [Ian] McColl ALAC Committee on a report that we had prepared on the provision of artificial limbs and wheel-chairs. My involvement was due to my position at BLESMA – the British Limbless Ex-Servicemen's Association. I had gone to see him in Downing Street and provided him with my list – not a very intelligent one actually – of retired Field Marshals and titans of industry. He wasn't very impressed. He threw out as I left that Rachel, his wife, had suggested I should do it. 'That's absurd,' I said, and never gave it another thought. It never occurred to me in a million years that I would hear any more, though I learnt subsequently that my name had come up several times in various discussions.

I put down the receiver after Douglas's call and went to bed in a state of shock, leaving all the lights on. Sue had been at the opera. When she came back she found me lying motionless in bed, as white as a sheet. She thought I might have had a heart attack. I told her what had happened. She took the same view. It was an appallingly difficult job, I was far too old, the BBC was having a terrible time, at loggerheads with the government and virtually everybody else. We could only assume that about eighty-seven people had already been offered the job and refused it. It was, of course, a great honour but really . . . We had a sleepless night. It kept going round in my head. It seemed wet just to turn a job down because it was a challenge, but this really was some challenge. It would be massively in the public eye – far more than we had suffered already, and that had been pretty bad.

The next day I had to travel down to Bath for a board meeting of a small engineering company of which I was a director. I left at 6.30 a.m. I still couldn't get Douglas's call out of my mind. I was at once appalled and excited. One of the great jobs in Britain. But could I do it? I was called out halfway through the board meeting with a message that Sue had telephoned. I was to ring her back immediately. Her brother William, then a junior minister, had called her with a message from Douglas Hurd. Douglas had informed William about the offer, she said, and had told him that I had been so taken aback by the proposal – not to mention distracted by our dogs barking in the background – that he had completely forgotten to tell me the two most important things. First, no one else had been offered the job and second, the whole cabinet wished me to accept it. Put like that, we had no alternative.

On the Saturday I got on to Douglas and said that I was much flattered, honoured and apprehensive but in view of what he had said, I would accept. At that moment Sue took the telephone and said, 'You know Dukie, Douglas, he's very old and lame. You've got to look after him.' 'Of course,' Douglas replied. 'The money is appalling but he will have all the comforts – cars, good hotels when he is abroad, all the help he needs.' I took the telephone back at that point, and said, 'All right then, I will try my best. What about a briefing?'

'Oh, don't worry about that,' he said, 'you'll find out what's necessary when you get there.' So contrary to all expectation, all gossip and all the stories in the newspapers, that was the only briefing I got. No one in the government or in politics gave me any advice (plenty later on, of course). I was on my own.

The announcement from Downing Street was to be at midday the following Wednesday. We were sworn to secrecy, even going ahead with hosting a long-planned drinks' party the night before the announcement was made, doing our best to act as if nothing unusual was happening. We were not even allowed to tell the children until the night before. I made one exception. Sue had said, 'You must take Carole [Haynes, my secretary from *The Times*] with you. You will never manage without her.' She was going on holiday on the Tuesday so we told her. There is no one more discreet than Carole.

When the news was announced, it would be fair to say that my appointment did not receive universal approval. Gerald Kaufman, the Shadow Home Secretary, described it as 'outrageous and provocative' (Sue and I made a point of asking him to dinner and a Prom) and said I would be sacked after they had won the next General Election (they lost the next two). One newspaper suggested I would be a 'prime contender for Monty Python's Upper-Class Twit of the Year Award'. Journalists questioned my knowledge of broadcasting – arguing that a medium sized commercial station like GWR was hardly a preparation for the BBC – and, of course, they raked up the whole business about the *Times* shutdown. Most assumed I was a Tory toff. Wrong on both counts. Some suggested I was too close to Rupert Murdoch for comfort, others that I was Margaret Thatcher's place man. In fact I hardly knew her at all. We had met only once or twice at large parties. I was in close consultation with the Prime Minister's Private Secretary about the mechanics of the announcement. The particular problem was the Vice-Chairman, Joel Barnett. He had been filling in since Stuart Young's death and must have hoped to take over permanently. Due to a series of accidents which were nobody's fault, he was not going to be told until 10.30 a.m. on the Wednesday. I asked the PM's Private Secretary to tell Lord Barnett that I had always admired him and that I had reserved a table for two at the Berkeley Grill so that we could at least have a good lunch before we started out on this adventure.

I also rang Rupert Murdoch to tell him. Although I trusted him, I took the precaution of not doing so until Wednesday morning in case the temptation to slip it into his paper was too much. He was congratulatory and encouraging. I said, 'I thought you must have known, Rupert.' 'No no,' he replied, 'I only told Margaret that the new man must understand the media otherwise he was sunk from the start. That's all.' I didn't believe him for a moment.

By five past noon all hell had broken loose. Every telephone was jangling incessantly. I got to the Berkeley at 1.15 p.m. I took an immediate liking to Joel. We have been close friends ever since. As we left I was about to hail a cab to head off for Broadcasting House, but Joel insisted that I take his car – the Chairman's official car. It was a generous gesture. I saw this as a team job, the two of us, and so I ensured that Joel should have his own office at BBC headquarters, plus a secretary and a car – to great opposition from the top BBC executives who, incidentally, were noticeably carefree about the number of cars and secretaries they each had. Joel was the first Vice-Chairman to play such an active role, but he was an invaluable adviser, friend and colleague for seven years. We only had one disagreement, which comes in the next chapter. And, of course, as a former Labour treasury minister, he was well to the right of me.

I arrived at Broadcasting House to a characteristic media frenzy. I decided neither to be too overawed nor to be too serious. The first question I was asked was, 'Are you intending to make many changes, Mr Hussey?' 'That begs the question as to whether changes are necessary,' I replied. More lightheartedly I said I was so astonished by the appointment, I had had to look up the BBC in the telephone directory to find out where the Chairman's office was. That went down badly with the BBC, but well with everyone else, particularly as it was carried on the radio. I didn't intend to be intimidated either by the journalists surrounding me or in the background by the grand top BBC executives. It was a measure of how little they moved around London that I had only previously met one (Alisdair Milne, once, at a dinner party).

After about fifteen minutes of this, a smart young lady came up to me and said, 'Chairman, I am the Secretary. Perhaps I can take you up to your new office.' I thought, 'Well, she looks as if she can type, that's the good news.' I didn't know that the Secretary is one of the most senior and important positions at the BBC and that Patricia Hodgson had the invidious job of being the link between the governors and the management and confidante to both.

Up we went to my grand apartments and I was immediately subjected to a barrage from the woman who was the Chairman's real secretary. 'Chairman, we don't know what to call you. Is it Mr M. Hussey, Mr M. J. Hussey, Mr Duke Hussey or what? What's your name?' In a fury, I shouted 'Marmaduke Hussey'. I had never been called Marmaduke in my life but this proved to be one of the public relations coups of all time. No one is called Marmaduke (except the odd cat in a children's story). Certainly no one forgets anyone who is called Marmaduke. A brilliant stroke, entirely by mistake.

Chapter Ten

My first priority was to meet the BBC's Board of Governors, the ultimate source of power in the BBC, and immediately afterwards the Board of Management who, it rapidly became clear, resented the governors and any exercise by them of their authority. I was later told several times that the Board of Management meetings were largely occupied by discussions on how little they could tell the governors.

On my first day at work at 9 a.m. I sat down with my new colleagues at Television Centre. I told them how proud I was to be appointed and didn't hesitate to make clear that I knew very little about television and radio. But I did emphasize one thing because of the reverberations in the media about *Real Lives*, an allegedly uncritical documentary about terrorists in Northern Ireland. I would never preview any programme either on television or radio. My philosophy, based on having been managing director of two newspaper groups, was that editorial content was the business of the editor. It was not my function to tell him or her what to write unless it imperilled the paper's finances. I applied this principle broadly to the BBC in regard to the Director-General and Board of Management, except that the Chairman and Board of Governors had an added constitutional responsibility for everything that the BBC did. Nevertheless, I said, I will never preview a programme; I will judge it after transmission. And I stuck to this absolutely.

It was perfectly clear from the start that there was much wrong with the BBC – or at least a lot that very many people thought was wrong. In my early days, crisis after crisis or mistake after mistake seemed to hit us, on top of the fundamental problems I inherited. Two days before my appointment, a First World War drama series, *The Monocled Mutineer*, which was billed as history, turned out to be fiction. There is a greater truth, the BBC retorted. Not a very convincing alibi.

The problem facing the BBC was the renewal of the Royal Charter in 1996. Crucial to the charter was the continuation and size of the licence fee by which the BBC was financed, and for the first time the hitherto periodic reaffirmation of the mandate to the BBC by the government appeared anything but a foregone conclusion. Originally the BBC had been a monopoly broadcaster. The birth in 1956 of ITV, funded by advertising, turned a monopoly into a duopoly. The arrival of Channel 4 and the start and expansion of commercial radio, into which I had been venturing, created much greater competition, fuelled by a rapidly escalating income. The BBC was facing new challenges. Moreover, there were other changes in the wind with satellite, cable and digital technology. In my first fortnight, the Managing Director of Radio, Brian Wenham, told me I need not worry about satellite television. It would never take off.

The Prime Minister knew better. Margaret Thatcher was certainly aware of the implications of potential changes. She had a favourite phrase to damn the licence fee – a compulsory levy enforced by criminal sanctions. I didn't like the sanctions – the thought that people certainly would be fined and might even go to prison for not paying their licence fee. I believe that sanctions have quietly been softened.

My term of office was for five years. Towards the end of that there would be a Broadcasting Bill. Many predicted that the BBC would be stripped of its traditional means of funding, shorn of a television channel and a couple of radio networks. And even if the BBC survived that Bill, it would then have to face the charter renewal. While my time as Chairman would not, I assumed, reach up that far, I knew we had to prepare the ground by taking the BBC out of the arena of political debate into which it had naively strayed. The management seemed totally oblivious of the rocks towards which they were blindly sailing.

Relations between the BBC and the government were always likely to be difficult unless the government – and the leaders of the opposition parties – believed that the corporation was in trustworthy and impartial hands. It is a problem the media always have. People who go into the media tend to believe that the world is not as good and as well ordered as it should be. They want to change the established order, some dramatically, others more smoothly. They tend to be on the left. People who go into the armed services, the civil service, the City, the law and the land are inclined to believe that everything is pretty good as it is. They tend to be on the right. People who go into politics straddle these two positions and are sensitive to anyone else adopting them.

I needed top-class advice so I consulted Lords Rothschild and Annan. Victor Rothschild I knew because he was head of the Downing Street Think Tank. If he wanted to enquire about the media, he summoned me. I would then be grilled by him for two hours, with my replies taken down by my young brother-in-law, William Waldegrave. Pretty intimidating. Victor invited me to an excellent lunch at the family bank. The house wine was delicious, but no mention of the BBC. So with the cheese, I said, 'Now what about the BBC, Victor?'

'How much power have you got?' he asked

'I'm not sure.'

'Can you fire the Director-General?'

A long pause. 'I think so.'

'Well, that's all that needs to be said, isn't it?'

Typical of Victor – the basic problem as always is power. If you have it, use it. How you use it is the problem. Having considered the constitution it was clear to me that the governors, if they chose to exercise it, had tremendous power.

Noel Annan had chaired a report on the future of broadcasting in 1977 which had condemned 'administrative fog' in the upper reaches of the BBC. We met at Brooks's Club, of which we were both members. Looking down St James's Street from Brooks, he said reflectively, 'The problem with the BBC is not that it wants to do what everybody else is doing, which is bad enough. It is that it wants to do more of what everybody else is doing.' As I write now, in the year 2001, that lesson needs to be relearnt.

I quickly decided to work through the governors and establish them as the ultimate power, but equally I had to work through the Board of Management by whom I was not impressed. They were all clever technocrats, but were marooned in Broadcasting House and Television Centre like a couple of Boer contingents holed out in a laager. They seemed totally unaware of the world outside, and what was worse, unaware that they ought to be in the world outside. The BBC was a self-indulgent organization. It took its lead from the top. And the top seemed to me not to be in the outside world at all. I planned to move the BBC back into the centre of British life and told Patricia Hodgson (the Secretary) I was going to do just that. I meant to restore the supremacy of the governors and reinvigorate the Board of Management. I intended also to visit as many places in the BBC as often as I could so that I could be seen and make myself available to all ranks.

This in the end went on for ten years. Whenever I went to a centre, I used to ask the Controller to call the staff together and tell them that I would like to meet them and talk to them. They could ask me any question they liked. There was never any preparation, let alone any analysis of questions. I took the view that if I couldn't answer, then I wasn't up to the job. So they had a free run. It is rather moving how this still pays off. At the Aldeburgh Festival last year, a couple of broadcasting technicians came up to see me. They said they had been to one of these meetings and just wanted to say hello. That has happened often. I thoroughly enjoyed those unscripted, uncontrolled meetings and I think the staff did too.

The first visit I made was to *Breakfast News* on television. It was a new departure for the BBC – rather good I thought, and getting a raw deal from the critics. So off I went, hopefully, to encourage them. After the programme had gone out, we all had breakfast. Hardly had I lifted the coffee cup to my mouth before the presenter, Sally Magnusson, said, 'Now, Chairman, what's your objective as Chairman of the BBC?'

'That's a bit rough, Sally. I've only been here a fortnight and it's very early in the morning.'

'That's not good enough,' she replied. 'You are the Chairman. You must have set yourself an objective. What is it?'

'Well,' I said, thinking quickly (because I hadn't thought it out beforehand), 'I suppose I would like to think that when I leave the BBC, I would leave it with its range of programmes and services across television and radio, and its system of payment, the licence fee, intact.'

Though I say it myself, that was an excellent summary of what, in my subconscious, I had already worked out and realized I had to do. Frankly, at that time, it was a most unlikely proposition. I knew what the media thought of the BBC and I knew what public opinion was.

The immediate task was to repair the non-existent relations between the Board of Governors and the Board of Management. My first Board of Governors' meeting loomed up. As I was going into the Council Chamber at Broadcasting House, I found Bill Cotton, the Managing Director of Television, and Brian Wenham sitting outside. 'What on earth are you doing?' I asked. 'Waiting to be called in,' came the reply. I was appalled. In the chamber there was a huge table – very like that at the NPA headquarters. The governors sat on one side – all twelve of them, with the Secretary on the Chairman's left and the Director-General, Alisdair Milne, and his deputy, Mike Checkland, on his right. Then each executive was summoned in turn to answer for his or her conduct of affairs. I wasn't surprised that relations were so strained.

In due course I completely changed this. First, I said I wanted all the Board of Management at all governors' meetings so they could all hear the discussions that were going on and hopefully take part in them. Second, without telling anyone, I arranged that they would mix round the table, with first a governor, then a member of the Board of Management, then another governor and so on. It was a trick I had pulled once with the unions during a dispute which immediately resolved it. At least, I thought, they could pass notes to each other saying what an ass I was. Of course it didn't stop me from having a private governors' get-together before the main meeting to discuss anything confidential – but every board does this.

The entire BBC was infused with an essentially civil service background. That stemmed, I imagine, from its birth under

Reith, so its conduct of affairs was far more like the civil service than a commercial organization. Not unnaturally. But it was being pitchforked into an increasingly commercial climate. That's why I tried to make the changes, like answering the telephone myself if everyone else was busy. No one else did. But Roy Thomson always had. I thought if it was good enough for him, it was good enough for me.

I decided that my first outside London visit would be to Bristol, one of the major centres of the BBC where all the natural history programmes were made. Very palatial, beautiful buildings. Also, I wanted to visit my old radio station to say goodbye after my sudden and unexpected departure. When that was completed I went up to the Television Centre. They had arranged for all the top executives to be there, as I had asked, under the chairmanship of the regional controller who welcomed me warmly. I said I was very pleased to be there on my first visit, with my West Country background. I had only come to listen. Basically it was one long dirge – complaints about the BBC being misunderstood, shortages of money (there was masses of it, of course) and general unhappiness.

This went on for about an hour and a half and then the controller said, 'Now, Chairman, have you anything to say to us?' I had, of course, given this some thought while I listened to the catalogue of complaints.

'No, no,' I said, 'I've just come to meet you and to listen. That's all.' I paused. 'Oh yes. There's just one thing. I'm a little surprised there is not a woman in the room.'

'Funny you should say that,' said the controller, 'we were just discussing this last week.'

'What a coincidence,' I said.

I went back to London, determined to do something about that. At Times Newspapers we had had a woman editor of the main feature pages. Our resident lawyer had been a woman. Our advertising director had been a woman. They had been all over the place, and very good at their jobs. So when I got back, I told Patricia I wanted with the governors to see the six most senior women in the BBC. The meeting was set up in the Council Chamber, with armchairs, like a drawing room – not the normal cold formality. After Patricia herself, the most senior woman was Jane Drabble, then the editor of *Everyman*, the religious documentary strand. I recounted my Bristol experience and asked was it our fault, or theirs? We had a stimulating discussion and Jane summed up on behalf of her colleagues by saying it was 60 per cent our fault and 40 per cent theirs. Young women did have a challenge, she pointed out, combining work and children, but it was manageable. And they didn't want to get involved with all the managerial jealousies, discords and the competition ladder. I couldn't blame them for that.

With the support of the governors, I gave instructions that from that day onwards the promotion of women must be one of the major personnel policies of the BBC. It takes time, of course, to develop but over the next ten years we made very substantial progress. Now it is automatic. We have women controllers of television and radio networks and several women on the Board of Management – all able and most enterprising. I was pleased to have started that.

One of the things that struck me most when I joined the BBC was the amazingly cavalier attitude to money. Staff flew to America by Concorde and back. Our resources department, I discovered, was so well equipped with outside broadcasting units that if the entire royal family died, a third world war broke out and England won the Ashes, all on the same day, we could handle it quite easily.

I was surprised also by the size and grandeur of many of our buildings. Partly, I think this was the responsibility of one of my predecessors, George Howard, who lived in Castle Howard, a wonderful castle and estate. He felt that BBC buildings should be somewhat on the same scale as his home. They were all architect designed, regardless of cost. I discovered also, incidentally, that at every local radio station – and there were nearly forty of them – the consoles were individually designed by the BBC engineers who were brilliant but not cheap. A quick call to GWR established that these consoles could be bought off the peg for a fifth of the price, but the BBC culture was that everything had to be bespoke.

Drink flowed. Janet Morgan, a brilliant writer and a clever

consultant (not consulted enough) told me that when she was Special Adviser to the Director-General, Brian Wenham came to see her one morning. She offered him a drink.

'I'd love one,' he said.

'Tea, coffee or orange juice?'

'No, I want a drink drink.'

'I don't keep any.'

Later that morning a case of wine was delivered to her office from Wenham. Great example to the staff.

The Board of Management met every fortnight for lunch – drinks before lunch, two wines over lunch, liqueurs after lunch. A close associate of mine told me that when he was quite junior, his job was to bring in to the Board of Management luncheon an unopened box of cigars. Only one member smoked cigars and he took two. At the end of the lunch, the junior had to give the rest of the box to the cigar smoker and then produce a fresh box of cigars for the next Board of Management luncheon.

Another thing which became immediately apparent to me was the disdain with which letters of complaint were treated. The BBC management felt that they were not accountable to anyone. I demanded to see all such letters and laid down that every reply addressed to a member of either House of Parliament would be topped and tailed by me. (It was surprising how often, subsequently, people commented on this and also on the refreshing speed of replies.) This was common courtesy.

I was appalled by the content of many of the letters. Later that year I was invited to speak at the Institute of Directors' AGM and in among my explanation of the BBC's purpose I made a joke about the extraordinarily arrogant replies to correspondents from the Board of Management. The policy appeared to be: first, deny any possible bias or incompetence in the programme; then imply the correspondent had no right to write; then deny any responsibility; and finally, if there was clearly a fault in the programme, say it had been shown on ITV. My comments were reported and welcomed in the press – not, however, in the BBC. I was making a serious point. The first six letters I was shown by Patricia, I put a straight line through. The attitude of arrogance was stupefying.

As the weeks and months flowed by, I became more and more worried. We had a charter renewal ahead and before that a Broadcasting Bill expected in 1990. We appeared to have no strategy with which to face them. I consulted Alan Hart, who had been cruelly ousted from the position of controller of BBC1 in 1984 because he had fallen foul of the ruling elite, who ran the BBC. 'The producers,' he told me, 'make the programmes they like or want to make regardless of what the audiences, the governors or even the Director-General might think.'

In my first week I was given a startling illustration of this. Patricia told me there was a court libel case starting imminently, about a *Panorama* programme called 'Maggie's Militant Tendency' which alleged far right infiltration of the Conservative Party. Two Tory MPs, Gerald Howarth and Neil Hamilton, were suing us. I immediately asked Joel. He knew nothing about it and was apoplectic. I don't know much about the law, but if you've run two newspaper groups, you do know about libel. As soon as I saw the reports in the press of the first two days in court, I could sense we were in deep trouble. The Director-General, however, seemed very unconcerned. The case, he told me, had been mentioned in the monthly briefing of current legal cases which was sent to the governors. No further information was necessary. But it was to me.

As an instance of our problems, the programme alleged that the MPs concerned had been present at an outdoor fascist revivalist meeting. The facts were that it was an informal lecture given by an academic professor ten years earlier. Moreover, Milne had given an undertaking that there would be no executive action against those responsible if the libel case went wrong. It was when discussing this with Alisdair I made a point about the pictures on television not quite fitting the words.

'You don't understand television, Dukie,' he said. 'That's wallpaper.'

I replied that I didn't understand television. I was used to the newspapers where there was only one media concerned. 'It seems to me, Alisdair,' I said, 'that in television we are using two media. One illustration on the screen, the other the spoken word. If one makes a lie of the other, the whole is a lie. In future if we show an historic picture it must be labelled as such, like an illustration of the type of aeroplane that has just had a disastrous crash.'

This was clearly going to be a very, very expensive case, which we might easily lose. And what was more, there were several other cases waiting in the wings. We had already spent £150,000 of licence fee payers' money. I rang up our QC, Charles Grey. I had a bit of luck here. His junior, Andrew Caldecote, was my godson – a connection which I declared immediately to the head of legal affairs at the BBC. I asked Mr Grey what our chances were of winning it.

'Very unlikely.'

'Why are we fighting it?'

'Those are my instructions.'

'Well,' I said, 'you've got fresh instructions now. I have been named the Chairman of the BBC and am speaking in the company of the Vice-Chairman, Lord Barnett. We instruct you to settle this case this afternoon for whatever you can manage.'

It was another case of a total disregard for expenditure of public funds. Norman Tebbit – an enthusiastic scourge of the BBC – wrote later: 'The BBC had a well-known record in committing libel and then trying to brazen it out knowing that few victims would dare risk bankruptcy in legal battles where costs might run to many hundreds of thousands of pounds.' It was outrageous – which is what the BBC thought of my behaviour.

Another insight came in my first month when Joel and I had a meeting with the Director-General and his deputy to discuss the Peacock Report which had been published just before my arrival as Chairman and had recommended that the licence fee be tied to the retail price index (RPI). Patricia, as Secretary, was present. Joel and I thought the Peacock recommendation was a fair solution and would be accepted by the general public, who had to pay it, as fair. The management thought it should be increased by, I think, £2–£3. We overrode them. Joel and I thought it extraordinary, with the BBC under such pressure, that the senior managers should fail to understand that to tie the licence fee to the cost of living was a just way of handling it – and would be seen as such.

After the meeting, I said to Patricia, 'That talk about the licence fee reminds me of something. I have two homes in London and Somerset and have been told that I don't have to pay a licence fee for both.' Patricia went white. 'Not paying your licence fee,' she told me, 'is the only crime for which you can be dismissed at the BBC' (just about right, actually). I rang up Gladys, the postmistress at Chewton Mendip, wife of the baker.

'Oh, Mr Duke. We're so proud of you in the village. It's been all over the papers about you and the BBC.'

'Actually, Gladys, that's what I'm ringing about. The licence fee.'

'Oh well, as you're Chairman I'm sure you don't need one now.'

'Well, it hasn't worked out like that, Gladys. I think I ought to have two. One at each end.'

'Oh no, I've looked it up.'

'Gladys, I think I'd rather have two.'

'Oh well, I'll give you another one.'

'Be a darling – just backdate it to the beginning of the month, will you?'

'I'll do it at once.'

She was a lovely lady. Her post office was the heart of the village. She died suddenly in January. There were over 300 people at her funeral in the village church.

So I steered past that rock. I never quite discovered what the legal situation was. I believe that if you had two homes, you had to demonstrate that the television wouldn't be used simultaneously in both. Anyway, it's no longer a problem – being over seventy, I get a free one now.

Another worrying governors' meeting. There was going to be an announcement from the government about the BBC World Service – funded by the Foreign Office. John Tusa, head of the World Service, brushed it aside. 'We have our rebuttal already prepared,' he assured us. 'But surely that depends on whether a rebuttal is required,' I replied.

With all this going on, and Joel and I feeling so isolated, it was imperative to get Carole, my former secretary, in as soon as possible. Later Joel often used to say, 'It's the three of us against the BBC, Dukie.' I asked to see the personnel director, Christopher Martin, on some spurious reason and as he was leaving said, 'Oh, by the way, I want to have my old secretary from *The Times* here. She knows how I work and she knows my wife and the children. It'll be much easier.'

He came back into the room and sat down. 'If I may say so, Chairman, that will be a very great mistake.'

'If I may say so, Christopher,' I replied, 'you can chalk it up as the first of a great many mistakes. She's coming on Monday.'

Carole was not welcomed. They tried to freeze her out with minimum information, but she's a tough girl and sorted it out within three days. She followed the golden rule for a chairman's secretary – always be polite and welcoming on the telephone and to everyone who walked into our office, except me who frequently got stick.

The next crisis was an attack from Norman Tebbit, then Conservative Party Chairman, about BBC bias over the American raids on Libya in the autumn of 1986. He didn't like Kate Adie's reporting of the destruction. Joel and I watched the tapes and believed we were vulnerable – not actually in Kate's reporting but in the headlines introducing it. Ron Neil, the head of news, issued a strong statement. (He was, I soon realized, one of the best members of the Board of Management.) I wrote to Norman telling him to back off. Alisdair Milne, to whom I showed the letter, told me not to send it. Extraordinary! My job was to defend the BBC and tell the government to back off if it was in the wrong.

Alisdair's reaction was, I think, typical of a certain view which the top BBC management had of me initially. They thought I was a stupid ex-Guards officer with no intellectual capacity. Ian Trethowan, Alisdair's predecessor as Director-General and an old friend of mine, told me he had tried to warn them. 'Do your homework,' he told his ex-colleagues, 'and you will find that Dukie is no fool. He got an open scholarship to Oxford and a First' – not quite accurate, but near enough.

Anyway I have always enjoyed being thought a fool – at least not to be clever. It gives you an immediate advantage over those around you.

So I took no notice of Milne over the letter. I'm told there was a great cheer in the newsroom when the text was distributed. I was already distancing myself from any hint of political partiality. Not that I had any, incidentally, as I have already said. I have voted Conservative, Labour and Liberal in my lifetime. When the first Tebbit letter came in, I likened it to the attacks on me by Gerald Kaufman when I was appointed – 'not a bad left and right'. And those who knew me well were aware of my political neutrality. 'I sometimes suspect,' Paul Channon once remarked, 'that you are a closet socialist, instead of the die-hard Tory everyone takes you for.'

I have a theory about the whole Libya episode. Kate Adie, whom I like and admire enormously, is a superb reporter. She was in Libya on a different story and woke up to hear the bombs falling and saw corpses of women and children in the street. She was genuinely horrified. There is a generational problem here which was increasingly apparent when we approached the Falklands War and the Gulf War. Forty years after the Second World War a generation has grown up which subconsciously, though not of course literally, believes that when you drop a bomb or fire a shell it only hits the uniformed enemy. The truth is that it very frequently hits unarmed civilians and only too frequently more of our own troops than the enemy. Friendly fire they call it now.

Norman didn't let go. He continued to attack an anyway unpopular BBC as a political weapon, winning cheers at the Tory Party Conference. I knew what he was at and didn't want the BBC to be a party political football. On the other hand, I have never blamed politicians for trying to bully the BBC. It is, after all, the most powerful political influence in the country. I only blame people in senior positions within the BBC if they submit to such pressures. I'm happy to say that no political complaint made to me in ten years ever resulted in a programme change.

Several years later I was at a media dinner where Jim

Callaghan made a great speech. He talked of the power of the
media (everyone sat up with a smile on their faces) and went on
to extol the power of the BBC. 'We prime ministers,' he said
with a wonderful gesture implying that everyone in the room
was a prime minister or might one day become one, 'we all
knew about the appalling famines in Ethiopia but it was not
until Michael Buerk on BBC television exposed the dreadful
privation and suffering of the women and children on the *Nine
o'Clock News* that public opinion was mobilized so that we
could do something to help. That is the great power you can all
exercise.' Loud cheers. 'But with that power,' he went on to say,
'comes a great responsibility for impartiality, honesty and accu-
racy which must always be exercised.' Silence.

One Friday, soon after my arrival, when I was planning to
leave early to get down to Somerset, Carole took a call from
Conservative Central Office telling her that an important letter
was being sent round. I delayed my departure and waited for the
letter which was embargoed for 6 p.m. on Saturday – just in
time for the Sunday first editions. I suspected they thought I
would have left for the weekend. It was another complaint from
Norman about alleged bias. I called in Patricia Hodgson, who
advised me that if the management and the governors presented
a united front, Norman's only option would be to involve the
Home Secretary and spark a major row. I judged that he would
not go that far and so dictated a strong, terse reply to Norman
which I released to the press and embargoed for five minutes
after six. My newspaper experience taught me the response
letter always gets the headlines – particularly if it's punchy. And
this was. The BBC was chuffed.

They were strangely innocent, the heads of the BBC. They
didn't seem to understand that all these shenanigans weren't
personal. They were just politics. On another occasion, Mike
Checkland told me I couldn't send so rude a letter to Norman
Tebbit as the draft I had shown him.

'Why on earth not?'

'It will cause trouble and, if I may, I will compose a letter for
you to send instead.'

I had anticipated that one and had already posted my version.

Next time I saw Tebbit he banged me on the shoulder and said, 'I did enjoy your last letter. You were on very good form.'

After a fortnight or three weeks, when it was difficult not to be disturbed by the way the BBC was conducting its affairs, Joel and I had a talk together. He made it quite clear that he thought Alisdair Milne, for whatever reason, was not giving the BBC the leadership it required. In fact, he thought he was not up to the job. Neither did I. In my opinion it was the whole attitude – contempt for the governors and contempt for any normal principles of conducting a business, like the ludicrous and arrogant way we were embarking upon a series of libel actions which our advisers told us we had no chance of winning. Cautiously, under a pretext of talking individually to all the governors, I discussed the Director-General's position with each of them. One by one they told me that they thought he ought to go. He simply wasn't in control either of the BBC or, for that matter, of himself. He epitomized a failing management culture that was leading the BBC to disaster.

We had got off to a bad start. After greeting me on my first day, he took a ten-day holiday – well, everyone is entitled to a holiday but there has to be some sensitivity in the timing. This rang a bell with Joel who, not unreasonably, had wanted to have lunch with Alisdair after Stuart Young's death and been told he wasn't free until mid-December. These are details but they reveal the atmosphere. Alisdair is a man of great personal charm and intellectual ability, but his judgement was wildly erratic. On one occasion, he shot into my office, unannounced and unexpected, telling me, 'Dukie, you must ring up the Prime Minister immediately and tell her to stop her cabinet ministers attacking the BBC.' This from a man who only days before had told me not to write to Norman Tebbit in such strong terms. This time I told him I would do no such thing, but privately reflected that the pressure had now got to him as it did to wartime soldiers. He seemed to me to be unbalanced and irresponsible.

As my enquiries extended, I discovered that Stuart Young had decided once or even twice that Alisdair Milne should go. The last time, shortly before Stuart's death, had been when the governors examined Alisdair's conduct in the ousting of Dick

Francis as Managing Director of Radio to make way for Brian
Wenham. Dick Francis had appealed to the governors, who
found they had a great deal of sympathy for his charges, but
Stuart was mortally ill and the governors believed that the row
that would follow sacking Alisdair would be too much for him.
So the Director-General remained but stupidly, in my opinion,
refused to see the writing on the wall.

Once Joel and I had decided on the policy, we had to work
out how to execute it. Timing was difficult. There's always
something. Christmas was coming and that was clearly an inappropriate time. Joel then had a holiday arranged, so it seemed to
us that the right time was as soon as he returned – 28 January.

The dismissal of the Director-General of the BBC would
cause a major sensation. It had never happened before. I was
therefore determined to do it quickly and brutally. My rule for
these difficult situations had always been the same. Be clear,
decisive and fast (actually that applies to all decision making –
particularly in the media). Obviously it is important to be
sympathetic and above all generous in the settlement.

Meanwhile, awaiting Joel's return, I took the opportunity to
ring Michael Swan, by now in the House of Lords and my only
living predecessor. I knew him slightly and got to know him
much better up to his death in September 1990. We would
often meet for a drink. I would tell him of the latest problem at
the BBC. 'Wait a moment, Dukie,' he'd say and puff on his
pipe. 'I must ponder on that.' I rang to tell him what I intended
to do. It was likely he would be involved in the controversy
given his position in Parliament. His reaction surprised and
comforted me. 'I admire your courage,' he said. 'I knew that
Alisdair was not up to the position of Director-General, and one
of the reasons I retired when I did in 1980 was to avoid being
involved in the decision whether to appoint him.' Surprising,
but very reassuring.

I started to make detailed preparations. The first thing I
discovered was that his file and employment conditions were not
in my office. To initiate a search for it would be to give the
game away. I rang up Arnold Goodman. 'I have a problem,' I
began.

'My dear Duke, in that place, I should imagine you have hundreds.'

'I want to dismiss the Director-General.'

'That is not a problem, it will be a merciful release to us all.'

'That's not the problem. I have to do it without knowing what his contract is.'

'That is more interesting. You'd better come down and see me. Bring your secretary.'

The deed had to be done on the day of the governors' meeting because Alisdair had the right to appeal to the full Board of Governors. They had to be on hand to avoid any delays. Unfortunately the first meeting after Christmas was at Television Centre, so I had to create a wheeze to get Carole down to the office I used at the Centre to type the correct one of the two alternative notices Arnold had given us, dependent on which way the interview with Alisdair went. Meanwhile I continued to consult the governors. Joel returned and said immediately, 'I will be there, Dukie, with you.' I said it was kind of him but he didn't have to be, that was my job. 'No, no,' he insisted, 'it is important I am there because when you ring up the government and tell them [Douglas Hurd], I will ring up Neil Kinnock and David Steel and tell them there is nothing political in this. It is only a matter of fitness for the job.' That was loyal, considerate and wise. But Joel is all those things.

I then told the Secretary, Patricia Hodgson, on the Monday, stressing to her that I was now speaking to her formally as Chairman of the Board of Governors. I passed her a piece of paper and said, 'This lists the three occasions on which each governor has been consulted about this policy and agreed it. They will confirm their agreement on the morning of the board meeting.'

The evening before we had a governors' dinner for a retiring governor and poor Sue had to sit next to Alisdair knowing what was to happen the next day. Patricia said that was the traditional form and, if I departed from it, Alisdair might smell a rat and disappear, as he had a habit of doing. After the dinner, Patricia approached me white as a sheet. Alisdair had made a very bad speech (mine was not much better). When he sat down, a lady sitting opposite John Boyd, a governor and a splendid trades unionist in the old-fashioned mould, had said, 'That was appalling.' 'Don't worry about that, lass,' John replied within Patricia's hearing, 'we're firing the bugger in the morning.'

The governors' meeting started at 10.30 a.m. After it had ended Joel and I went to my office and I asked Patricia to send in the Director-General. It was swift. I told Alisdair that the governors were determined on widespread changes in the BBC and that those changes had to start at the top. He had two alternatives. He would probably agree with Joel and myself that a dignified resignation, for personal reasons, would be the course most in the interests of the BBC. Much less satisfactory would be instant dismissal by the governors.

He was shaken but behaved with great dignity. He paused and then said, 'I will take the way that is in the best interests of the BBC, which I have loved all my life.' He left within twenty-five minutes. We then called in Michael Checkland and told him what had happened. Until a successor was appointed, he would be Acting Director-General. We also told Bill Cotton and said that as a senior executive and a man of great experience, we expected him to steady the ship. We then went and had lunch, starting with a bald statement that the Director-General had just resigned for personal reasons. Conversation was a little strained.

The governors then broke up and the management, as anticipated, collected together and said I hadn't the authority or the support of the Board of Governors and that they should act together and stop it. At this point, Patricia intervened and told them about the piece of paper with the triple agreement of every governor. That ended the incipient revolt, but it didn't end a certain malevolence towards Patricia, who had acted honourably as a Secretary of the BBC should act. Many never forgave her for behaving with integrity and counted it against her in her future career, which, nevertheless, has been most deservedly successful. To complete the tale, over the next few years every member of that Board of Management subsequently told me privately that I had done the right thing in getting rid of Alisdair.

If events at the BBC itself passed off reasonably peacefully on the day of Alisdair's dismissal, the media reacted with frenzy. After all, no Director-General had ever been sacked before. It caused a sensation. Reporters besieged our London flat, persuaded our faithful housekeeper Maria to open the door, and forced Sue to take refuge in a neighbour's flat until they could be persuaded that I was not at home. In the face of such intense interest, I could see no sense in a long-drawn-out appointments' procedure. I told the personnel director that day that we would select a new Director-General on 27 February – the day before a joint Board of Governors and Board of Management conference started. He said that was impossible.

'Why?'

'It can't be done in the time.'

'Why not?'

'Well, we have to advertise.'

'I know all the papers. I will have the advertisement in this Sunday and the following Sunday. We will stick to a rigid timetable.' Which we did.

There were three potential internal candidates – Mike Checkland, Michael Grade, Director of Programmes at Television, and Brian Wenham, Managing Director of BBC Radio. And three external candidates – Jeremy Isaacs, Chief Executive of Channel 4, David Dimbleby, a very able and experienced broadcaster in the best traditions of his father, Richard, and Tony Smith, a programme maker, supported by Richard Attenborough. Joel and I also interviewed Paul Fox, a distinguished former controller of BBC1. He didn't want to enter the race, because of the attendant publicity which might affect his current post at Yorkshire Television, but agreed to be available on the night in the event of a deadlock.

My private preference was for an outsider who would see the need for reform and would know what to do. We mentally dismissed Wenham from the start. He was able but, I thought, idle and had no support from among the governors who did not trust him. Michael Grade, coached by Bill Cotton, gave a wonderful interview, but we felt he was not yet ready for so big a job, although he was a brilliant and charismatic figure, popular with the staff. He was, we felt, a little young for such a difficult political and administrative position.

Joel backed Isaacs, I backed Dimbleby. It was a long debate. Both gave good interviews. They had contrasting disabilities. Isaacs was, in a caustic phrase of mine (immediately leaked to the press), 'Alisdair writ large', the producers' pet. Dimbleby had the prestige, the political nous but was unpopular. An internal campaign was mounted against him and leaked to the governors. I thought he was the best man for the job and it has always been on my conscience that I never explained to him why he didn't get it. I apologize to him now. But at the back of my mind I had the similar advice given me by two great friends I much admired – Arnold Goodman and Dwyn Bramall, Chief of the Defence Staff and a man of many talents. They both said, independently, if you want to make radical changes, Dukie, you must appoint a man who has the support and confidence of a good proportion of the staff. If he hasn't got a decent constituency within the corporation, he will never succeed.

This brings me to Michael Checkland, the number two whom no one had seriously considered. His interview was absolutely superb. He just walked in, seized the job with both hands and walked away with the prize.

We appointed Mike on the condition that he brought in a deputy who could successfully undertake the much needed overhaul of news and current affairs. That was the department that was doing the BBC the most damage – both in the eyes of the public and of the politicians, which, in my book, was the right order of priority. Mike would not accept Dimbleby. John Birt, then at London Weekend Television as Director of Programmes, was strongly recommended to me both by Paul Fox and Peter Jay, whom I had known well in my *Times* days. This was, in bloodstock terms, a good line. Mike's appointment was announced immediately before our joint Board of Governors and Board of Management meeting which he conducted ably.

That was the start of the great adventure. The BBC was under new management and would have to adopt new policies. It would have to show courage, determination and above all, an understanding of the responsibilities it owed to the people who paid for it.

I went home to sleep, remembering this timely quotation from Edmund Burke: 'Those who would carry on the great public schemes must be proof against the most fatiguing delays, the most mortifying disappointments, the most shocking insults and worst of all, the presumptuous judgement of the ignorant on their designs.' I had been in the country at some stage during my first three months at the BBC and had seen this hanging on our host's wall. It seemed totally appropriate for the job I had so rashly taken on.

Chapter Eleven

At the end of my first year, I felt more confident. There were, of course, huge problems still to be overcome if we were to survive the test of the Broadcasting Bill and the renewal of the royal charter. On the other hand, we had made a start. The governors were more confident. We had appointed a new Director-General who was able, popular with the staff and working more closely with us.

An accountant, Mike Checkland knew where many of the bodies lay, though he was weak on programming. But for that we had appointed a new Deputy Director-General, who came highly recommended and understood the art of programme making. He was an old colleague of Michael Grade's, so that created a consensus at the top. David Hatch, the successor to Brian Wenham, who resigned as Managing Director of Radio shortly after he was not appointed Director-General, was a lively, companionable, enthusiastic man of great personal charm. He was also funny – an original member of the *I'm Sorry, I'll Read That Again* team. And, my goodness, didn't we need someone with a sense of humour. In my ten years at the BBC I was determined to get some fun out of it. And it was fun. The BBC needed teasing, which it didn't appreciate, being too serious and fraught.

We needed one further appointment, and that was to create a new position on the Board of Management for a Director of Corporate Affairs. If there was ever an organization which needed to improve its presentation to the outside world it was the BBC. It had no idea how to handle journalists, corporate relations, or for that matter, internal relations. Corporate Affairs was in the hands of a charming Welshman who came to see me and openly said he knew nothing about it and didn't know what to do – a refreshing and rare honesty.

I rang Arthur Brittenden, now a senior executive in Tim Bell's public relations company. We went out to lunch at L'Etoile and I explained what I wanted – a highly experienced, young, energetic PR executive, the best young man in the business. I promised Arthur a second lunch when he had a name to give me. Three weeks later he claimed his lunch and over the first glass of wine produced Howell James, a thirty-three-year-old marketing and PR man who had already worked with great success at Capital Radio and TVam and was now adviser to David Young, Secretary of State at the Department of Trade and Industry (brother of my predecessor). We advertised the post. There was a shortlist. Howell walked it.

There was one issue which I particularly wanted tackled and that was the total departmental fixation and jealousy within the BBC. First, BBC1 versus BBC2. They saw themselves as bitter rivals for BBC resources, so bitter, I discovered, that on one occasion they were both covering a London event with live cameras (there was a massive duplication in all news departments). In the event, BBC1 could not get their coverage onto the *Six o'Clock News* but absolutely refused to make it available to BBC2. They disputed this, but I proved it.

The thought that BBC Television was in any way connected to BBC Radio was outrageous. They saw themselves as all competing against each other. But they were in the same company. The enemy was not internal but external. I told Howell we had to establish, fast, the concept that BBC1 promoted BBC2, Radio 4 promoted Radio 3 or 2 and that radio and television would each promote each other. It was almost inconceivable to think that that was necessary. Now they do it with will – too much will actually. I put it down to the zeal of the converted.

Just as you think things are beginning to go well, an unexpected and unnecessary crisis blows up in your face. John Birt and Michael Grade had been colleagues and friends but in his new position as Deputy Director-General, John immediately exerted authority over Michael and specifically demanded to be on the board that selected new controllers for BBC1 and BBC2. This was not tactful – never John's long suit. Of course he had a point, he was the Deputy Director-General and these were very important appointments. I supported him and told Mike Checkland so. But Grade was furious.

We selected the two controllers – Jonathan Powell and Alan Yentob – in the face of Michael's opposition. He was trying to propose Ron Neil, Birt's very able deputy. However, he personally announced the appointments saying that they were his. It was awkward. With a little more grace and tact on both sides, the row could have been avoided.

A few days later, Mike Checkland came to see me, white and shaken. Grade was allegedly in Hollywood purchasing a variety of programmes for the BBC which he had discussed with Mike on the day of his departure. But he hadn't departed. He was reported to be in London negotiating his appointment as Chief Executive of Channel 4 to succeed Jeremy Isaacs. This was a great loss to the BBC, and should have been avoided – or perhaps with Birt and Grade in open rivalry, it couldn't have been.

I like Michael. I admire his chutzpah and inspirational style and his inherited Grade nose for theatrical success. He also understood the business. He told me, shortly after my arrival, that one of the real problems at the BBC was that when a producer embarked upon a programme, he or she only controlled 30 per cent of the costs. The other 70 per cent was wished upon him or her by the vast resources department which needed employment for their equally vast staff. It was an integral part of the complex financial mismanagement that was the BBC. It went on the agenda.

So we lost Michael. He could have been a real strength. Where to go for his successor? We looked but there appeared to be no one we could see of the necessary stature and talent. Already there were murmurings from our staff and the press that we didn't know what to do (true). Suddenly Mike popped into my office and said he had had an extraordinary call from Paul Fox who offered himself for the job. 'Grab him,' I said. 'It's more difficult than that,' Mike replied. 'We mustn't make a move, particularly in public, until after he's cashed in his share options in two months' time.' I didn't blame him for that, although I've never had an option in my life. If you're lucky enough to have them, you don't want needlessly to throw them away. Criticism mounted of our weak and indecisive approach to the vital vacancy. The weeks ticked by with no announcement. Finally, the appointment was made; loud cheers all round. Paul would add stature to the Board of Management, it was said, and he did. We were praised for our initiative. As so often happens, we had done nothing but answer a telephone call.

At the end of January 1987, straight after Alisdair Milne's departure, the police in Scotland raided our Glasgow offices and seized material to do with a planned series called *Secret Society*. BBC Scotland had commissioned it from a radical journalist, Duncan Campbell. I nearly fell off my chair when I heard that he'd been engaged to make the six parts. He had total control of the content. There was no check on what he might say or do, and no system for submitting his programmes to his seniors for approval. 'What happened to the referral system?' asked Daphne Park, an exceptionally well-informed governor. Any proposed programme with dicey material of whatever sort – language, content, pictures – was supposed to be referred upwards, and if necessary as far up as the Director-General. 'It didn't work,' she was told. 'It never does, does it,' she replied.

Whatever the rights and wrongs (definitely wrongs in this case) of the commissioning process, the police action appeared extraordinarily heavy-handed and I wrote in the strongest terms protesting to both Malcolm Rifkind, Secretary of State for Scotland, and Douglas Hurd, the Home Secretary. Fortunately for us, the warrants were wrongly drafted so we evaded any breach of the Official Secrets Act. It was an unhappy episode which only served to re-emphasize the need to control programmers.

The whole incident was not helpful to our relations with the government or Parliament. Hardly had we survived one crisis than there was another, over a radio programme called *My Country, Right or Wrong*. It was along the same lines as *Secret*

Society so I immediately enquired whether we had submitted the programmes to the D-Notice Committee, charged with protecting official secrets. We had. Twice. Phew!

The row mounted in the press. It so happened that I was lunching that day with Brian Griffiths, the Downing Street adviser to the Prime Minister on Media Affairs.

'You're in real trouble this time, Dukie,' were his opening words.

'No, I'm not. It's been through the D-Notice Committee.'

'No, it hasn't. Downing Street has checked.'

'Well, you'd better go and have another check after lunch.'

The government sought an injunction to stop the series being broadcast. We fought all the way through the courts until they were forced to submit because we had the approval of the D-Notice Committee. A great relief to find someone else dropping such a clanger. The series, incidentally, was excellent.

After their third election win in spring 1987, the Conservative Party was intent on dismantling the BBC. Margaret Thatcher was not a fan and made little secret of it. Certainly, the hotheads within the BBC who wanted a higher licence fee, and said so loudly, had no chance. I believed most strongly that as long as the BBC could show that it was a lean, efficient and creative organization, at the heart of national broadcasting, offering something for everyone, it could survive and thrive, with its licence fee, as the bastion of standards and quality in the increasingly deregulated and downmarket world of satellite, cable and digital. Our mission had to be that set out by the BBC's founder, Lord Reith. 'As we conceive it our responsibility is to carry into the greatest number of homes everything that is best in every department of human knowledge, endeavour and achievement.' The first step, however, was to get that proposition accepted at the top.

On Joel's advice, I wrote to the Prime Minister as soon as I took over suggesting we might together discuss the problems of the BBC. There was not an immediate response but early in 1988 Joel and I were invited to Downing Street. It was the first proper conversation I had ever had with the Prime Minister. She was primarily concerned about Northern Ireland and the tragedies our troops and the police were suffering. I believe she wrote in her own hand to every family that suffered a loss. We sought to reassure her that we were well aware of the problems and were rapidly reorganizing the BBC's News and Current Affairs Department to handle them more responsibly.

Joel and I decided before the meeting that if it went well, we would invite her back to the BBC to meet some of the executives. It did, so we issued a verbal invitation. She finished the meeting, which was fairly short and with only four people present, by saying how grateful she was for what we were trying to do. I heard later that some ministers thought the meeting had gone wrong. 'The problem,' my brother-in-law, a junior minister, said, 'is that you gave the impression of having everything so well under control that you'll soon be running rings around the independent sector.' That was nice to hear but not what the Tory party wanted.

Mrs Thatcher did not take up our invitation, but in February 1989 invited me, Joel, Michael Checkland and John Birt to dinner at Downing Street. She had also included Bernard Ingram, her press secretary, and Brian Griffiths. I had assumed that I would be sitting on her right. Not a bit of it. We were in the small dining room, just off the main one, seven of us. She put me opposite her, bang in the line of fire, and started with a few preliminary salvos with the soup. I replied, 'That's a bit hard before we've finished the first course.' (I think I must have been strengthened by a couple of glasses of whisky.)

Then we were at it hammer and tongs for an hour and a half. All the regular issues: Ireland, the Forces, political bias, incompetence and the licence fee. It was friendly but tough. I argued back ferociously but you can't get into an argument with her without getting into difficulty and I did – on the World Service which she, grossly unfairly, thought to be an instrument of left-wing propaganda. Always the loyal colleague, Joel, who knew her very well because they had been opposite each other in the House of Commons, leapt in to try and rescue me. She rounded on him. His hand happened to be on the table and she slapped it, like nanny, saying as she did so, 'Now, now Joel, we had all that nonsense in the House of Commons. We don't want it here.' She had to leave a little early for the salmonella in eggs debate, and as she paused at the door, she said, 'Well, I hope you don't think I've been critical. Well, I am critical, but I am also very grateful for what you are doing in tackling such a difficult and important issue.'

She waltzed off looking, the chauffeur said, like a girl going off to a good dance and we thought we'd go in search of a drink. My upbringing was totally unpolitical. My parents would have thought I had done very well if I had once had tea with a Member of Parliament. To have a two-hour battle with the Prime Minister was way beyond the Hussey family comprehension. But she was very fair. Joel and I felt we had given as good as we got and scored a few direct hits.

One of the things that most impressed me about her was the number of letters she answered or wrote in her own hand. I have already mentioned her habit with grieving families in the forces, but there were many others too. She opened a BBC Radio exhibition for young industrialists for us two years later in Birmingham. I had her letter of thanks in her own handwriting the next morning, before I'd even had time to dictate my own to Carole (I never send important letters in my own handwriting – I can't even read it myself).

Two years later she wrote and offered me a knighthood. I discussed this with Sue. I thought my work wasn't finished and the acceptance of an honour would imply the opposite, so I wrote back politely and much conscious of the honour to say no. But there was another reason – the more important. I happen to believe, and it was a view widely held some years back, that people of stature and influence in the media should not taint their political impartiality by the acceptance of a political honour while still in office. I think that to be a still relevant principle, though one not often observed now. It may be an old-fashioned view but it remains mine. Anyway, I received a charming letter back with a PS in her own handwriting. 'All right. We have all taken note. *Not* until after you have retired.' And indeed this was the case because at least once a senior civil servant referred to it in those terms.

As always, and rightly, Northern Ireland and standards were

the two most sensitive areas between the government and the BBC. It was alleged, I suspect, correctly, that the establishment of the Broadcasting Standards Council in 1988 as a watchdog, was partly as a result of Mary Whitehouse's conversations with the Prime Minister. William Rees-Mogg, who was Joel's predecessor as Vice-Chairman of the Board of Governors, was appointed as its first chairman, which some elements within the BBC felt was deliberately provocative. To a certain extent, they had a point because the creation of this council could be thought to overlap the functions of both the BBC governors and the Independent Broadcasting Authority. Certainly, William had strong and clear views on the BBC – and on virtually everything else as well – but he was an old and close friend. I didn't think that we were likely to fall out. He was well aware of what needed doing at the BBC and a great support.

Northern Ireland was a constant concern. The BBC had an excellent custom according to which each year we held a governors' meeting either in Belfast, Cardiff or Edinburgh. In my first year, it was to be Belfast. So I asked Patricia Hodgson to brief me a little as it was one of my first such gatherings. 'There's nothing controversial on the agenda,' she said, 'but I ought to warn you that governors' meetings in Belfast are not always very well attended.'

'How extraordinary, it's a lovely country,' I innocently replied. 'You might mention that I would regard non-appearance at Belfast as very close to a resignation issue.' They arrived.

My own attitude to the IRA is well illustrated by an episode at the height of one of their periodic attacks on London. I had to go to a major charity reception in black tie, and then to a royal dinner in a suit. Halfway between the two, I got stuck in a traffic jam on Park Lane caused by terrorist disruption. 'You're not going to make this,' Alan, my chauffeur, told me, 'you can't get back to Broadcasting House. There's nothing you can do.'

'Oh yes there is, Alan,' I said, 'I'm not going to be frustrated by the IRA, I'll change here.'

'You can't!'

'I can!'

I got out of my dinner jacket, down to my vest and pants

and had to change my leg. This was observed with some interest by the cars crawling along side us.

'It's all very well for you, sir,' Alan said, 'but what do I tell the wife if the *Sun* has taken a picture of me with my naked chairman on Park Lane?'

We had a huge office in Northern Ireland – both television and radio – and its operation was vital to the economy and morale of the whole country. It also shared the distinction of being, with the Irish International Rugby Football Union, a rare place where Protestants and Catholics worked or played along-side each other as a matter of course. I went there every year, often accompanied by Sue (I don't think they'd had the wife of a chairman before. Sometimes one is ashamed of one's contemporaries). I always went round the office but also I always met the Secretary of State and the heads of the police and the armed forces. It was absolutely vital that with all the crises that arose there we should know each other and understand each other's points of view. I think, to be honest, it helped that I had been badly injured in the Grenadiers.

There was a terrible incident in March 1988 when two British soldiers who had accidentally stumbled into an IRA funeral were murdered. It was appalling. Douglas was on to me at once. Some of the BBC cameras had covered the funeral and therefore might have shots which could help the security forces. He asked for the coverage. I refused to hand over the tapes. Our cameramen, with all their heavy equipment, our sound recordists and reporters were all well known to the IRA, as were their homes, their wives, their children and the schools to which they went. To submit to this request could permanently put their lives at risk and might even result in a reduction of our vitally important coverage. Douglas and I had three increasingly angry exchanges. He was under great pressure from the Prime Minister, which I understood. But I felt I had to safeguard the life and livelihoods of our staff.

I also knew that more subterranean sources on both sides were trying, discreetly, to resolve the problem. The pictures, Mike Checkland told me, would turn up in London. But, of course, I couldn't say this. However, nothing stops the Prime

Minister. Just as Douglas and I were trying to sort everything out, she made a furious speech in the House of Commons (getting herself out of another difficulty, Howell James told me) accusing us of hindering the course of justice. That's politics. You have to laugh.

The next problem was the imposition in March 1989 of a gagging order preventing the voices of members of Sinn Fein being broadcast. I could sympathize with the Prime Minister's concern about such individuals being given, as she put it, 'the oxygen of publicity', but equally I could see that such a move, meaning that on screen they had to have their words spoken by actors, was damaging to pure broadcasting independence. I was perfectly prepared to admit that the BBC had not been rigorous enough in the past in interviewing members of Sinn Fein – indeed there was a long history of what I regarded as passive treatment. Yet my doubts about the legislation were strong. The governors wrote to the Prime Minister with the 'unanimous expression of their deep concern about the BBC's abilities [in the light of the new ruling] to represent the full range of opinions and activities in Northern Ireland'. I did not, though, think that this was an issue on which the BBC should be seen publicly to clash with the government. I think ordinary people saw this deviation from the pure ideas of freedom of speech as not unreasonable in the circumstances.

I was much more robust in shooting down an appalling idea that emerged under David Young, from his Department of Trade and Industry in 1988. They proposed moving BBC2 onto a satellite. Heaven knows what satellite – or when it would appear in the sky and how many people would be capable of getting it. It was an absurd idea which would tear the heart out of the BBC's national role. David, who always looked very far ahead in his anxiety to stamp his mark on all aspects of government, simply couldn't see that the BBC was different from other industries. Fortunately Douglas supported me strongly in the rapid demolition of this proposal.

Douglas and I had established a good working relationship. We seemed automatically to understand the parameters of our powers and positions. He was very helpful when I was doubtful about a nomination for a vacant slot on the Board of Governors (frequently I was not consulted) for someone with an arts background. The man in question was a businessman with no conspicuous service to the arts. Douglas accepted my veto and happily appointed instead Phyllis James (better known as the crime writer, P.D. James), a senior official for many years at the Home Office. She served with great distinction.

When the BBC covered the 50th anniversary of Dunkirk in 1991, they did it superbly. It transpired afterwards, however, somewhat to my surprise, that our commentators were so exhausted by the strain of broadcasting for twelve hours in emotional circumstances that they required counselling. There was a governors' meeting shortly afterwards where it came up. I decided to make no comment. Phyllis, with her customary directness, said, 'May I ask you, Chairman, whether you had counselling on the beaches of Anzio?' I said nothing. Her remark fell like a stone in a stagnant pool.

My relations with the Home Office, and later the Department of National Heritage once it took over responsibility for the BBC, were always good. After about a year at the BBC, Douglas Hurd rang me up and said he would very much like a private lunch with me – i.e. no advisers or civil servants – to have a general chat about the corporation. I, of course, agreed. He took me to an extremely discreet but excellent restaurant of which I had never heard. We ordered and sat down.

'Douglas,' I said, 'I want to just clear with you the conditions of this lunch and that is that we will ask each other questions and reply in absolute truth regardless of anything we might have said in the past or will in the future. Secondly, that no one but our personal private secretaries will know about it.'

'That's right,' he said.

'You fire first.'

'The thing that worries me,' he said, 'is how really strapped for cash is the BBC?'

'Not in the least,' I said. 'There are rivers of gold running through the corridors of Broadcasting House. Don't give it a thought.'

I asked him whether he thought I could persuade the government that I really was trying to tackle a very complex and difficult situation at the BBC. He was encouraging about that. 'The Prime Minister, of course, is not an enthusiast and it will be difficult' – and sometimes it was – 'but in the end, she is fair when she thinks that the right steps are being taken.'

That was the beginning of a series of lunches I gave, starting with Douglas and finishing with Virginia Bottomley, always thereafter at an excellent little French restaurant near to my home called Hilaire. They proved invaluable. It was the only time I lunched alone with ministers but we always had a totally free exchange. I outlined my plans, they outlined their reactions or feelings. No one ever knew they were even taking place, since we were always alone. I saw Clive Whitmore, the Permanent Secretary at the Home Office, over a year after he retired. He couldn't believe it when I told him about the lunches.

They took much of the steam out of any political tension there was between the government and the BBC. It was the only contact of that sort I would countenance. I liked to see ministers in their office or mine – usually theirs. I much dislike and disapprove of constant meetings over lunch or dinner – demeaning and questionable. If you want to discuss the BBC, you do it in your office.

My dealings with some ministers are worthy of recall. I had an amusing encounter soon after I was appointed Chairman with David Mellor, whom I like. He is engaging, talented and up to all the tricks. He was then Minister of State at the Home Office under Douglas. Joel and I were summoned to see him on an issue where we had a very weak case and were in some doubt as to what to do about it. As I left, Carole thrust a copy of *Broadcast* magazine into my hand. On the front page was an account of the rocket he was about to deliver us. As we went in, I threw the copy of *Broadcast* onto his desk and said, 'I am not standing for this; someone on your side of this table has leaked this to *Broadcast*. That's it, as far as I'm concerned; come on, Joel, we're leaving.'

David looked very discomfited, his civil servants delighted. He pursued us down the passage and besought us to return, which, grudgingly, we did and won a totally unjustifiable case.

When I next saw Douglas, he asked if everything was all right. 'Any problems?'

'No, not at all,' I replied.

'Well, I'm glad to hear that. I had been told that the wrath of the Chairman echoed down the corridors of the Home Office.'

When I saw Kenneth Baker, as Home Secretary in 1992, about sports rights, I was arguing that some significant events ought to be reserved for showing only on the main terrestrial channels – the BBC, preferably, or ITV. He wanted them thrown open to Sky, or anyone else willing to bid. 'Oh,' he said, 'you don't understand about sport, Dukie. The people controlling those events will never sacrifice their audiences and let them go anywhere else but BBC or ITV.'

'I'm sorry, Kenneth,' I replied, 'I may not understand about sport, but you do not understand about money. They will be offered money they cannot refuse.' I think I have been proven right, though it gives me no pleasure.

My first rule when dealing with ministers was that the independence of the BBC, rooted in its licence fee, could not be compromised. In the early 1990s, I was invited by the Russian government to speak about how you could have a broadcasting corporation which was independent of the government – not an easy concept to convey in a country which had been under an all-powerful dictatorship, monarchist or communist, for a thousand years. My host was the head of Russian state broadcasting, Mr Popsov.

'You are the Chairman?'

'Yes.'

'You are responsible for everything that happens in your great institution?'

'Ultimately, yes.'

'If the government complains, you do not have to take notice? You make your own decision?'

'That's right.'

'So you can still transmit the programme and do so?'

'Yes.'

'And you cannot be sacked?'

'Yes.'

'My friend, you are most fortunate.'

A very difficult situation arose when Geoffrey Howe was Foreign Secretary. He rang me about a programme we were going to run based on a visiting Sikh of extremely violent and revolutionary views. He was very worried about it. I told him, truthfully of course, that I knew nothing but would enquire. He rang again two days later stressing his great anxiety. The government was most concerned. I said, 'This is an issue for the BBC, Geoffrey.' He accepted that without much enthusiasm.

I made enquiries to check out that the basic points of the story were true. I gave the handling of it very considerable thought. In the end, I decided to tell Mike Checkland and John Birt what had happened. They came up to my office together, sat down in front of my desk with some papers on their knees which I took, though I never asked, to be a script or programme plan. I told them of the three conversations I had had with Geoffrey – plus a hurried exchange at a dinner party at the Wolfsons. I had taken careful notes and repeated them to Mike and John. I paused and said, 'Of course, the race issue in Birmingham is a very serious and explosive issue but one which it is quite proper for the BBC to explore. On the other hand, it should not be done in such a way as possibly to incite violence and maybe injury to person or property. You are both experienced and responsible executives. I leave it to you.'

That's all I said, but I watched the programme with care and hardly had it finished than Patrick Wright, Permanent Under Secretary at the Foreign Office, rang and thanked me. I don't know and have never asked whether any changes were made. It was a matter for the broadcasters. I promised from the start I would never preview a programme and I never did. I believe that editorial control is much more effectively secured in the long run by pointing out after the programme has been shown where we had made a mistake. And thereby setting up a signpost for the future.

I quickly learnt that the BBC management did not like me to move around and see people. About six months after the new Director-General's appointment, I was rung by Charles Powell,

the Prime Minister's Private Secretary, who told me that Mrs
Thatcher had that morning had a meeting with the Kenyan
President Daniel Arap Moi who had launched a vicious attack
on the World Service, concerning its inaccuracy and bias. The
PM had made no comment except to say that it was a matter for
the Chairman of the BBC. Charles said, 'It is a matter entirely
for you, Dukie, as to how you handle it. But if you feel it is
appropriate to see him – and I stress that is a matter entirely for
you – you ought to know he is leaving London tomorrow night
and is staying at the Dorchester.' Like my predecessor, Michael
Swan, I pondered a bit. It seemed wrong to let this attitude
fester without trying to counter it. I knew also that the Director-
General was away at a conference. So I decided the best thing
was to go myself, unaccompanied. The meeting was arranged for
later that day.

I went to the Dorchester where the President was occupying,
as far as I could see, two floors at the top with a very large staff.
After a short wait I was shown in to see this enormous man with
two equally big ones standing immediately behind him – well
armed, it appeared. After the initial courtesies I said I was sorry
to hear he was unhappy about the World Service, which was of
course within my domain, and that I would be very grateful if
he could outline to me what were his complaints. This he did,
at some length and with some heat. Listening carefully, it
seemed to me the complaint was that we had interviewed, more
than once but not excessively, an opponent of his regime. This
did not strike me as an especially heinous crime.

So I said I was very sorry to hear that he was unhappy and
that I would certainly look into the matter. I emphasized how
particularly important it was in the World Service that we
should report the news accurately and without bias. I would
certainly stress this most strongly when I returned back to my
office. After this exchange of fairly fatuous platitudes, I made
my respectful way out. I reported the conversation to Mike
Checkland when he got back to the office and suggested he had
a word with John Tusa, but to stress that in my opinion, where
there was discord and opposition in a country, it was right for
the BBC to report the fact without, of course, either over- or

underemphasizing the issues. That was rather successful and a Foreign Office official rang me the next day to thank me. He said that for various reasons Kenya was, at that point, important to Britain and that my visit had been most helpful.

I saw the World Service as one of the real beacons of not just the BBC, but of world broadcasting. I supported it with enthusiasm and pride. I always kept in mind Terry Waite, on his release from captivity in Lebanon, saying that the World Service helped keep him alive both spiritually and mentally. But I never regarded the World Service as an extension of government activity despite it being funded by the Foreign Office. Later on in my period as Chairman, I travelled quite widely on behalf of the World Service – particularly in the Middle East. I always informed the government of where I was going, not least because it gave me an entrée to the ambassadors and it would have been very bad mannered not to have done. They briefed me about the situation in whatever country I visited but we never discussed government policy. It is an oversimple generalization, but not all that far from the truth, to say that the World Service supplies the only true, fair and free source of information from the east coast of the Mediterranean to the west coast of the Pacific. That is its strength.

The reach of the World Service is such that there were always those who wanted to try and influence its contents. Soon after my appointment, I was given a forcible reminder of this when in the course of one day I had first the Israeli ambassador and then the Crown Prince of Jordan suggesting that the World Service was rather too sympathetic to the other's case. I took the fact that they both, from opposite standpoints, regarded it as biased as a mark of how successful it was in treading a middle and impartial line.

If it was sometimes tricky handling the politicians, my job was made ten time harder when my own colleagues at the BBC needlessly offered our opponents ammunition. In fairness John Birt worked very hard as head of the new directorate of news and current affairs to ensure that the bias and straight howlers of the past were avoided. His merging of radio and television news in 1987 brought a new strength in depth to our programmes, seen in particular at key moments like the Lockerbie crash at Christmas 1987 or during the uprising in Tiananmen Square the following year. On that occasion, the students surrounding our reporter, Kate Adie, held up banners saying, 'Thank you BBC – tell the world.' The one standing beside Kate was shot through the chest and died next to her. Kate and her cameraman went on reporting. She hid the video in her shirt, climbed over a wall, fought off soldiers and handed it to a courier. That's how those pictures reached the world. The radio correspondents had it easier, they just dialled the BBC from their hotel rooms and dictated.

In the light of such heroism the foolishness and sloppiness of others within the BBC was doubly hard to stomach. Most unfortunately we produced a *Spotlight* documentary, made by the BBC in Northern Ireland, which alleged that three suspected members of the IRA were murdered by the SAS. This was, of course, seized upon by our detractors. In my opinion, it was an ill-argued, second-rate programme which did not justify the allegations it made. At the last minute, John Birt tried to save the situation by re-editing it himself. Geoffrey Howe, the Foreign Secretary, was on the phone urging me to pull it. The press was baying for our blood. Neither John nor I wanted to stop the programme at the behest of the government. This could have caused, in the long run, more problems than it resolved. In the end, we just managed to escape greater condemnation because ITV's *Death on the Rock* – about the shooting of IRA suspects in Gibraltar by the SAS – drew the politicians' fire.

Mike Checkland and John Birt, though very different characters and from very different backgrounds, were working well together. John, though much maligned personally, made a series of good appointments and began the mammoth but essential task of clearing out the dead wood and slimming down the numbers in the news and current affairs directorate. I knew, and he realized, that we could never hope to keep our privileged position unless confidence was restored in that area.

Mike and I soon established a partnership. On a personal level, I liked him enormously. Professionally I respected his eye for detail, the esteem in which he was held by the BBC staff and his commitment to the corporation. He had spent virtually the whole of his career there. The easy chemistry we demonstrated when we appeared on *See For Yourself* in January 1988, a programme where for the first time the public could challenge the people in charge of the BBC on air, was merely an extension of how we operated on a daily basis. The BBC was horrified at the initiative. I was, they thought, an inept broadcaster and Mike wasn't much better. Funnily enough that wasn't how it appeared to the listeners and viewers who admired the fact that we were prepared to go public and answer questions off the cuff. We drew a bigger audience than a Frankenstein film on the other side – quite a compliment.

I had hardly ever appeared on television – just a few times lambasting the unions during the *Times* strike – so it was suggested that a little coaching might be appropriate. Luckily, it was done by Anna Ford, whom I knew quite well. She conducted a mock interview with me to polish up my methodology. Was there, she asked, any difference between chairing the BBC and managing a newspaper group?

'Not really. Both are about communication. Both seek to entertain people. The same problems arise in both, with politicians and their audience. The only difference I can think of is that at newspapers we were fighting hard for every pound of revenue, while at the BBC £70 million of licence fee payers' money flies in through the window each year without anyone lifting a finger to get it.'

That went down very badly with senior managers, but Anna persisted.

'There must be something, Chairman,' she said, 'that's better at the BBC?'

'Well, there is one advantage,' I replied. 'Now I'm at the BBC, Claridge's is much closer than the Savoy!' (It's a good thing to tease the BBC. Sometimes it can be a little short on humour.)

As we steadily increased the pace and scale of change at the BBC, I kept a watchful eye on the press. The really important sphere of influence was Parliament where I knew that I had MPs' and ministers' confidence. Nevertheless, I remained vigilant. To the newspapers, the BBC was an infinite source of gossip and speculation. They were well served by a constant range of tip-offs, speculative stories from a myriad different sources within the BBC – many of them paddling their own canoes. The internal speculation that followed Alisdair Milne's resignation had alerted me to this. One aspirant for the vacancy used to visit Carole every day, trying to look at her diary to discover who I was seeing. Broadly speaking, *The Times*, the *Financial Times*, *Telegraph*, *Daily Mail* and the *Mirror* – and the *Sun* sometimes – were supportive of the changes I was advocating. The *Observer* and *Independent*, both avidly fed by discontented producers, were hostile.

I didn't take active steps to promote my objectives with journalists any more than I did with politicians. I thought quiet action was more effective than lunch in expensive restaurants. However, one day in 1989, Robert Maxwell, owner of the Mirror Group, got on to me. I'd known him, of course, for some time and didn't trust him an inch – or even a millimetre. However, he rang me on my private line (he always knew everyone's private numbers). 'I'm not one of your enemies like Murdoch, Duke, I'm one of your supporters,' he told me. 'Bring a few people with you and we will have a general discussion.'

Clearly this was not an invitation to be neglected because Mirror Group was a powerful company. So along we trooped to Robert's lavish new headquarters in the old WH Smith building, now furnished like the entrance to an eastern brothel (not that I'd ever been to one). I had taken with me Mike Checkland, John Birt and Joel. We were greeted by Peter Jay, Maxwell's chief of staff, who was an old friend dating back to my early days at *The Times* where he was economics editor until 1977. These had possibly been Peter's greatest days. He used to claim that his far-seeing articles on economics had only been understood by about three people. I'd always liked and admired him and was delighted we could have a glass of champagne together. Robert then arrived. 'Come on, Duke,' he said. 'We're going in to lunch now.'

'Should we go in together, Peter?' I asked.

'No, no,' he said, rather embarrassed. 'I'm only here to serve the drinks. I don't get invited to lunch.' The last time I'd seen him was at the British Embassy in Washington where he was ambassador for two years until 1979.

The lunch was hilarious and bizarre. I sat on Robert's right and was immediately faced with an enormous plate of smoked salmon and invited to add some caviar from a pot. Having helped myself rather sparsely I was mildly miffed to observe that everyone had their own pot of caviar. At this juncture the butler insinuated himself between Robert and myself – a gap of only a few inches – and said, 'Your host would like you to choose the wine, Mr Hussey.' He proffered two bottles of German and French white wine. A little taken aback I opted for safety – French. Conversation was general – Robert had three of his executives there – until we reached the coffee stage: business. At this juncture it became clear that totally conflicting instructions had been given by the two team captains. I had said, 'When we get to the business I do not intend to play any part at all. You must all do that. I know this bastard. If I say anything, we will wake up one morning to read with horror on the front page of the *Mirror* "The Deal I Have Just Made With The Chairman Of The BBC". I'm not taking that risk.' It became increasingly clear that Robert's instructions to his employees were the reverse. 'When we get to general conversation, you buggers don't open your mouths. This is my business.'

So we emerged from that trial well-watered and unscathed. Two years later in 1991 *Panorama* decided to do a stitch-up on Robert – a large and tempting target. He was on the telephone at once. Several times. Carole handled it with customary aplomb, saying, 'I'm terribly sorry, Mr Maxwell, it's very unlike him, but I don't know where Mr Hussey is.' This was followed by a massive letter threatening every known legal process against us and the *Panorama* team. I thought about this carefully and decided it was a matter for the Chairman – partly because Robert wouldn't deal with anyone else, and partly because I felt I had the experience to handle it without copious enquiries, inquests, meetings and all the other panoply of discussion that normally accompanied major BBC issues.

I contented myself therefore by ringing our solicitors and indeed our counsel to check that they were fully aware of what we were saying (I didn't ask) and we were confident that legally the programme was watertight. As the deadline for *Panorama* grew closer, the pressure from Maxwell increased. I took no action until 5 p.m. on the day it was due to be broadcast. I then sent him a short note saying how sorry I was that I had been unable to take his telephone calls or answer his letters but this was to assure him that the *Panorama* programme would be going out as forecast, as scheduled and unaltered.

This turned out to be a critical decision. I watched the programme and in fact, to an old media hand, there wasn't all that much in it – some slippery work about competitions and how the winners turned out to be conveniently placed, but I knew all about that. The strength of the programme lay in the number of incidents when Maxwell had clearly lied or in other ways dissembled. The weight of these incidents cast legitimate doubts on his whole exercise of power – though, of course, we knew nothing about the pension scandal at that moment. The day after *Panorama* his shares slumped on Wall Street and panic selling took over. I have no doubt in my mind that it was the BBC *Panorama* programme that unhinged the fading confidence in Maxwell's empire. A few days later, he disappeared off the end of his boat. At the time, I could not believe that he had committed suicide. I thought he was so vain he would never accept potential defeat but a wiser head than mine put me right. 'No,' he said, 'he was so vain that he couldn't bear the shame of being found guilty in a court and led away by warders facing sentence.' The programme was a seminal incident and proved yet again the power of the BBC when properly and responsibly exercised.

If I had any lingering concerns, it was that Mike was not showing the same relentless determination to get on with major changes as John Birt had in the news and current affairs director-ate. Mike wanted to take it slowly. Sometimes his reassurances that all was well did not quite ring true. I am not as bad at figures as I make out and at one meeting I happened to notice that those quoted for staff numbers did not add up with the figures we had been shown previously. I queried it with the personnel director. Sensing he was fobbing me off, I got a bit testy.

'To put it more simply, how many people are we currently employing?'

'That, Chairman,' he answered, 'is not the right question to ask.'

'Well, it's the question that I'm bloody well asking. What is the answer?'

It became clear he had no idea. I was shaken.

On some matters, inevitably, Mike and I clashed. Mike was enthusiastic about plans to move radio out of Broadcasting House along with the central BBC directorate, 'governors and all'. Even our offices at a new building in White City had been allocated. I was totally opposed to the concept of exiling radio – and the governors – from the heart of the capital, the centre of political, economic, cultural and social life. Moreover, the new building was to be filled mainly with bureaucrats, with very few programme-makers to liven it up.

The governors shared my views. Mike wouldn't budge. In the end I had to force his hand by sitting him down and saying that, as Chairman, I was entitled to decide from where I operated and that would continue to be as it always had been, in the centre of London, at Broadcasting House. Therefore the governors and the Director-General and senior managers would have to stay there in order to work with us. As far as the rest of the staff were concerned, it was a matter for him. I left him with no choice. Mike was very angry indeed about it, but he accepted my decision. And in the end, it worked out very well. The new building is now a centre of programme-making and it enabled the BBC to concentrate its staff in several large buildings rather than have them scattered across London at small and expensive locations.

There were some issues where Mike was right and I was wrong. When I arrived at the BBC, I was doubtful about the value for money represented by our huge investment in the local radio network. In particular I regarded our stations in London,

Birmingham and Manchester as superfluous when the commercial alternatives did so much better. Mike argued otherwise and turned out to be absolutely right. As local commercial radio became increasingly wall-to-wall pop, our commitment to speech-based programmes and local news meant that we were distinctive. By 1990 we were achieving 11–12 per cent of radio audience with our local stations. We know now that when there are storms, floods, railway disasters or traffic congestion, BBC local radio is the prime media. For that Ron Neil, who became the director in charge of all regional broadcasting, deserves great credit – as he did for everything he touched. I am now a stalwart supporter of local radio. When the snow falls in Somerset, we reach immediately for BBC Bristol.

In the end the Broadcasting Act of 1990 was something of a triumph for the BBC. We were clearly on the right track. The dire prediction of losing a television channel and some radio stations proved misplaced. We emerged scot-free. Indeed, we were hailed as the cornerstone of British broadcasting in an age of new channels. There were new obligations – to make 25 per cent of our output with independent companies (a jolly good idea, I thought), a situation to be monitored by the Office of Fair Trading (not so good). Most of the Broadcasting Act was about the future of ITV and the distribution of the franchises. The pressure was on them to make more money by going downmarket, leaving the quality end free for us, a highly desirable result. This, to my mind, was due entirely to the more clear-sighted and resolute determination of the governors, in many areas, but above all in changing the management. We had cleared Becher's Brook and were now heading for the Canal Turn, and the winning post of a new charter on 1 January 1997.

Chapter Twelve

The passage of the Broadcasting Act in 1990 did not, as I had somewhat optimistically hoped, silence the licence fee debate. A new Home Secretary, David Waddington, had previously been the Chief Whip and did not carry the weight of Douglas Hurd, a long-established cabinet minister and now Foreign Secretary. The Prime Minister, understandably, needed reassurance that all was continuing to go well at the BBC and so David was persuaded to commission Price Waterhouse to examine, once again, the link between the licence fee and the retail price index. When I met him for my annual off-the-record lunch, I offered to make a concession, namely that that year, when inflation was running very high, we would accept a rise of less than the current rate, and then revert to the RPI link the following year. It could have saved a lot of time on all sides, but Downing Street was not enthusiastic. So we all went through the motions and Price Waterhouse completed their report proposing exactly the settlement I had suggested in the first place.

The report did, however, make some sound recommendations. It identified potential savings of £203 million, and criticized our overstaffing. These were, of course, objectives that Michael Checkland had been asked by the governors to tackle, but I was beginning to suspect he wasn't making much progress because he didn't really want to. The 1 per cent savings per annum that he had been achieving were just not enough, but try as I might I couldn't push him further. He flinched from the difficult decisions which would extend this efficiency drive and make it bite. Moreover, I wanted the impetus to come from him in order to avoid any suggestion that the governors were calling the shots.

So, at the governors' instigation, Ian Phillips, the director of finance, was commissioned in 1989 to look at staffing and outlined a potential for a further £75 million in savings over three years. At this moment, we had a strike over wages. Much to the concern of the governors, who wanted Mike to stick to his guns, he raised his offer. Finally, when he'd been told by us to go no further, without any consultation he offered an additional 1 per cent. I was horrified when I heard it on the BBC radio news. So was Bill Jordan, a governor who was president of the engineering workers' union. Mike had not consulted either of us. Bill and I always kept in close touch on labour affairs and almost always agreed. Bearing in mind our backgrounds, this was hardly surprising. That whole episode undermined our confidence in Mike.

About three years into my time at the BBC, the electricians called a strike. In any industrial process a strike by the electricians is devastating. The governors and management were extremely worried when suddenly I received a call from John Grant, one of the group of Labour MPs who had joined the SDP in 1981. He said he could act as a mediator in the dispute and that Eric Hammond, the general secretary of ETU, would like to meet me. This was familiar territory, so I said I'd ring back shortly. I called Mike Checkland and told him. He made it clear he didn't think such a meeting was the job of the Chairman. It was his responsibility and I certainly shouldn't go alone. 'Look, Mike,' I said, 'I know this business. I know these people. I've had countless encounters of this nature. I really think you should let me do this. Just give me the parameters of the issues.'

He put a brave face on it and told me that there was no leeway, save for a small adjustment on pensions. I rang Grant and said I would be delighted to meet Hammond and suggested tea at the Stafford – a luxurious hotel in central London. I arrived first, sat down in the lounge and ordered sandwiches, cakes and tea. Eric Hammond ambled in.

'How nice to see you, Eric. Come and sit down and have a cup of tea.'

He helped himself to a sandwich. 'Now Duke, what are we

going to do about these stupid buggers?' Encouraging as an opening shot.

'I don't really know,' I replied. 'With the best will in the world, there's very little I can do.'

'I told them not to be such bloody fools and now they've dug themselves into a hole,' said Eric.

We got down to business and I, rather apologetically, put forward our minor adjustment in their pension entitlement.

'That'll do,' he said. 'It's their fault. I'll instruct them to go back to work tomorrow.'

This took five minutes. We then had twenty minutes reminiscing happily about all the events at Wapping and in no time I was back at the BBC to tell Mike what had happened. I think he was surprised at the ease and speed of the solution, but he shouldn't have been. Eric and I had been at this game for years and knew how to handle it. It stems from confidence in each other's integrity.

After the coup which deposed Margaret Thatcher in November 1990 I hoped that relationships with 10 Downing Street might get better. So at Christmas that year, Sue and I went to tea with our local MP, Chris Patten, whom John Major had installed as Tory Party Chairman. I explained why I believed all this ill-feeling between the BBC and the Conservatives was bad for them, bad for us and bad for the country. It had politicized public service broadcasting and continued to do so. Chris listened carefully, largely agreed with what I said, and indicated that John Major felt the same way. Five weeks later the Prime Minister, in a speech in the House of Commons, went out of his way to praise the BBC. Whether it was connected in any way with my meeting with Chris, I never asked.

Although Margaret Thatcher had been a fierce critic of the BBC (so was I in many ways), she had been fair to me. She asked us to her Boxing Day lunch at Chequers (very inconvenient actually – miles from Somerset). Sue and I went, with me sinking down in the car seat as we arrived, hoping not to be spotted by photographers, but realizing that it was her way of saying, 'I am a critic, but thank you for doing a good job.' During a gap in the conversation the first time we attended, Nico Henderson, a former diplomat well known for his impish humour, said, 'Tell us, Dukie, what are the governors of the BBC like?' I hesitated to frame a diplomatic reply. It wasn't necessary. The Prime Minister intervened. 'I'll tell you what they're like. They've got no guts, no bloody guts at all.'

A little harsh, but it made the point – the governors are ultimately responsible for what happens at the BBC. If or when they abdicate that responsibility the BBC will be in difficulties. The experience and knowledge of the outside world the governors can bring should enable them to prevent the management making unnecessary mistakes and amply demonstrate their power if they were prepared to use it.

For all the talk of a new atmosphere of goodwill with the government, the 1991 Conservative Party Conference reverted to business as usual with the new Home Secretary, Kenneth Baker, attacking us with all the venom of Norman Tebbit in his heyday. The only comfort was that the seventy-nine people who called our duty desk that day all supported the BBC against the Home Secretary. Later, when I had been invited to a reception to mark Britain's hosting of the Group of Seven major economic powers summit in London, I shook hands with the Prime Minister and congratulated him on his success at the event. John Major took me by surprise by seizing my lapels and saying, 'That isn't what the BBC is saying.' I argued the point with him, defending our reporters, and put his outburst down to his extreme sensitivity over the constant attacks from within his own party about his performance as premier. Yet it was a disturbing encounter.

There were undoubtedly still both individuals and incidents that invited controversy. Polly Toynbee, for instance, hired from the *Guardian* in 1988 as social affairs editor, reporting on health, was, I thought, over-gloomy about the NHS. In retrospect, she was right. In the health game, as I knew well because of my chairmanship of the Marsden, there was always bad news – and still is – but there is also much that is good. On the other hand, Polly was enormously helpful to me when I had to address the Friendly Society from the pulpit of Worcester Cathedral on

the occasion of their annual general meeting. It went well –
entirely due to Polly.

Then there was a most unfortunate incident. A play called
Man in the News, which included a character based, as far as I
could see, very closely on the journalist Duncan Campbell (who
had already caused us so much trouble), landed the BBC in the
libel courts once again. The jury agreed with me. That libel suit
cost us £250,000, with a substantial amount going to Campbell
in damages. I was livid. So were the governors – particularly
Curtis Keeble, a distinguished ex-ambassador to Russia and
a wise voice on the Board. The governors thought that the
producers concerned should be dismissed, but neither Checkland nor Paul Fox (who took the line 'I must support my
producers') agreed. That was a seminal issue in the minds of the
governors who were shocked at the attitude of the Director-
General.

I liked Mike very much, but his position was not easy. I
suspect he didn't get support from the Board of Management as
he was delicately poised between them and the governors. He'd
grown up in the BBC, he knew them all and they all knew and
trusted him. He was once described to me, unkindly, as the 'staff
representative', with the implication that he saw his job as being
to protect the status quo for BBC employees. That was only
partly fair, but we, the governors, had our eyes on the next big
jump – the charter negotiations. We could not afford to weaken.

There were some encouraging signs of change. Mike was
undoubtedly making the BBC more commercial, upping the
number of co-productions with foreign broadcasters and building
up the enterprise division (although the initial profits from this
would scarcely have covered one series on BBC1). I supported
this. I was convinced that we could make much more money
from reselling our programmes and developing world markets –
a job I used to do for the *Daily Mail*, so I knew something of the
potential.

BBC Enterprises was making progress, but it was somewhat
haphazard. The success of the *Radio Times* was spectacular and
still is, even when there are millions of free supplements with
listings supplied by the newspapers. Some tough decisions had

been taken in this division – like the closure of the *Listener* in 1991. It was a sad end for a worthwhile publication, but it had been swamped by the ever-growing Saturday and Sunday news-papers. Weekly magazines, unless they have a rich patron like Conrad Black at the *Spectator*, are living on borrowed time – with the exception, of course, of the 'sexploitation' market. Only *The Economist* can stand on its own feet and most of its circulation is overseas.

Elsewhere we had made a start on the task of rationalization. We had closed the Lime Grove Television Theatre, a white elephant, and relocated the finance department to Cardiff (a Phillips' committee recommendation). John Birt was trying to build up centres of excellence in the provinces. Moving produc-tion out of London to where it could be done more cheaply, but no less efficiently, made good sense. I had always believed, and frequently said publicly, that the media were far too concen-trated in London and the south-east. Little things, small begin-nings, but we needed to go further. John Birt pointed out that, whereas the BBC sent teams up once a week for two nights to do one programme in Manchester, ITV sent one team to Man-chester to make four programmes in two nights.

We undoubtedly had our triumphs: the launch in March 1991 of World Service Television (only a small beginning but a start); our comprehensive victory over ITN in news ratings; the launch of Radio 5; the televising of Parliament. Controversial but I strongly supported it. The reporting of Parliament had started in the eighteenth century when, with great reluctance, the Lords and Commons agreed that the names of the speakers could be published. From there, the development was a straight line through summaries of speeches to total speeches, reports on the radio and now television. There was no logical argument to my mind for not making it possible for the electors to see and hear on their screens what their representatives and the peers were saying and doing while governing the country in their name. Televising Parliament led to some ill-discipline but nothing like its opponents had anticipated. What it did do, I was amused to see, was to rearrange carefully the most photogenic members of the Cabinet or Opposition to sit next to their leaders.

John Simpson's reporting from Iraq during the Gulf War in 1991 was excellent – as John's reporting always is. We were attacked for allowing our reporter to remain in Baghdad during the conflict but I was confident that John's stories would be the most accurate and responsible. Jenny Abramski's inspired decision to run a rolling news service on Radio 4 FM during this conflict was a forerunner of major developments in radio. David Hatch, the Managing Director of Radio, was initially opposed, but that experiment increased audiences by 50 per cent in the first few days and by 25 per cent throughout the war. It was an example of the inspired and innovative thinking that the BBC so badly needed. No one's promotion has been more deserved or more welcome to me than Jenny's.

Coincidentally at this time I was asked to address the Senior Services Division. It was a difficult agenda, surrounded by Field Marshals, Admirals of the Fleet and many senior officers – not least for a lieutenant. I was brutally frank. I told them why we were broadcasting from Baghdad and why we were giving full-time coverage on radio. The audience's response was gratifying. Field Marshal Lord Vincent told me that our coverage had been superb. I stressed that I had deliberately told the BBC to prepare the public for the possibility of heavy casualties. We might have lost several hundred on the first day if it had gone wrong according to the Field Marshal. The BBC had been criticized for being too pessimistic in this assessment by Sir John Keegan, the military historian and *Daily Telegraph* defence editor, a man for whom I have the greatest respect. But I believed that nothing could have been more irresponsible of the BBC than not to make the British public aware of the potential dangers. It was far better to err the wrong way like that than the other way round.

Overriding all these positive pointers was my sense that the pace of change was too slow. I was evidently not the only one thinking it. John Birt, in powering ahead in his pivotal role of reforming news and current affairs, had brought in Ian Hargreaves, a resolutely clear thinker and analyst. Suddenly in 1990 he decided to leave to become deputy editor of the *Financial Times*. He went on to edit the *Independent* and *New Statesman* and is now an established commentator, frequently on the BBC's airwaves. He came to have a farewell drink with me and told me that one of the major factors in his decision to leave was what he perceived as the failure to push through reform. It was a tragedy to lose one of the brightest hopes of the new Birt generation.

That sense of foreboding was reinforced when John Harvey-Jones, the ebullient ex-chairman of ICI, took a look at the BBC and recommended we got rid of a third of the management, drastically cut back the lower levels of the bureaucracy and speeded up our decision-making processes. I was one of the few within the BBC to applaud his conclusions.

John Harvey-Jones had estimated that there was a 20 per cent excess in resources in television. Paul Fox had been appointed as Managing Director of Television for three years only. And much though I liked him, the governors felt it had not been a total success. He certainly restored our confidence in the conduct of television and, on several occasions, showed courage and powers of decision. But the governors had been upset by the way Paul had presented us with his plans for a new soap as if it were a fait accompli. There was in 1991 simply a sudden announcement at a Board of Governors' meeting that the BBC had decided to start another soap called *Eldorado* the following year and was building a large village in Spain in which to film it. No one had been told, not even Birt, the Deputy Director-General, a programmer of distinction. He was livid. A pistol was held to our heads. We were told all contracts were due to be signed that week, or even that day. It was a classic BBC coup that amply validated all my suspicions of the management. The project hadn't been thought through, was going to be extremely expensive, was rushed onto the screen before either the actors or the sets were ready and was predictably a flop. It was axed within a year.

The question of Paul's contract was due and the governors felt that we ought to stick to our initial agreement of three years and appoint a younger man. Paul had given much to television and the government's decision to give him a knighthood was nothing but a just reward for a lifetime's service to the broadcasting industry. There was, in the BBC, an able executive, Will Wyatt, who had somehow never been made a controller of BBC1 or BBC2 but was, in fact, cleverer than the people he worked for. He had great charm and a crab-like approach to decisions which he almost invariably got right. We appointed him although Mike was unhappy about the treatment of Paul. We wanted younger men running the BBC, more sensitive to the political imperative and the huge changes about to break over the broadcasting industry.

Towards the end of 1990, Mike began to press me about his future. He was on a five-year contract which expired in February 1992. I told him, honestly, that I had made no decision about renewal, let alone discussed it with the governors. But the governors met regularly for dinner and there was inevitably gossip. One told Mike that his position had been fully discussed at a dinner (untimely and untrue) and a decision had been taken to promote John Birt in Mike's place. There may have been a general discussion about the two, and about the pace of change, but nothing more. However, Mike was upset and angry, as he had every right to be. I told him that in no way could I take part in any decision about his future until I knew what mine was. My five-year contract finished in November 1991. Any renewal of his contract would, like as not, be a matter for a new Chairman.

About six months later, in April 1991, I was sitting dictating to Carole and said, 'By the way, what's the name of that word processing course you're on? When I am thrown out – as the newspapers say I will be' – (I have the cutting from the *Guardian* hanging in my loo) – 'I'll have to learn to do my own typing.' 'You certainly will,' she replied and before we could draw breath the phone rang and someone called from the outside office, 'it's the Home Secretary for you.'

'Hello, Dukie, it's Kenneth here,' he said. 'I've been talking to John about the BBC chairmanship. You're doing a bloody good job in difficult circumstances and we'd like you to do another five years. I hope that's fine with you. I must dash. I'm seeing the Prince of Wales in three minutes.' 'Christ – that's an awfully long stretch,' I replied.

'Oh God, don't say no,' said Kenneth, 'it's all settled as far as we are concerned.' He was in a hurry so I agreed, thinking I could easily get out of it in two to three years.

It was a great honour and one that I had not been expecting. I had privately wondered if I might be given another year, to see the BBC over the coming General Election in 1992. I would, if asked, have liked two years to take us a stage nearer to the charter renewal, but it never crossed my mind for a single second that I would be given five years. When Kenneth had more time, I negotiated a renewal for Joel for two years. I held him in the highest regard and would have liked him there for the full five years, but could see the wisdom of separating the two retirements.

Clive Whitmore subsequently told me after he retired as Permanent Secretary at the Home Office that, when the subject of the chairmanship came up in 1991, he told Kenneth Baker that I was the only man who could deliver the BBC for the charter. And I believe, although he may not have said it, that the other reason was, in spite of or maybe because I kept so far apart from the politicians, I was the only man whom all three parties believed could ensure fair play.

With all that sorted out, I knew the time had come to confront the question of Mike. It was one of the most difficult things I have had to resolve. I spent months worrying. I rarely lie awake in bed at night, but I did over this. I had come to the conclusion that Mike was a man of great talent, but who hadn't got it in him to take necessary steps to bring the BBC into a position where it could retain its charter without being butchered. Even when Mike tried to appear a modernizer, it could backfire to reveal deeply ingrained attitudes, whereas every decision I took was aimed at charter renewal.

Mike, anxious to have his contract renewed, wanted to make a splash. He suddenly announced that he was splitting up the Radio 4 long wave and FM frequencies to create a rolling news service on long wave (like in the Gulf War). Radio 4 listeners marched, with as much militancy as the passive middle classes could summon up, on Broadcasting House. A protest march by Radio 4 listeners! Who'd have thought it. The governors overturned the decision. I had already caused trouble because I couldn't tune in to Radio 4 on FM. Carole told me once there was something in the BBC known as the Chairman's Test. It referred to the use of technology. 'If the Chairman can do it, any fool can.' About right I should think.

I was modest about my criticism of the FM wavelength and tentatively raised it at a governors' meeting. To my surprise and delight, they all agreed. However, the management rejected our concerns. FM, we were assured, was available to 90 per cent of the country and 90 per cent of the listeners liked it. I remarked rather testily, 'If you are correct, all I can say is it is your misfortune that I seem to know all the ten per cent who don't and I can tell you they are intelligent, articulate and angry.' Later I discovered that we were not alone. To get good FM reception, you needed upgraded equipment, or had to hang out of a window with a coat hanger. No one had told us that. It was the radio producers who were pushing FM, because it was a more sensitive wavelength, if you could get it. It suited them, but not the market. Now the technology has improved, and reception on FM is excellent, but at the time it was another sign of the blinkered BBC management.

I had grown to suspect that Mike's hope was that Labour would win in 1992 and then everything, in his terms, would be all right. If this was true, he was showing a massive naivety. He failed to realize that the BBC will always have an antagonistic relationship with the government of the day – that is in the nature of its independence – and likewise will always be courted by the opposition. In my experience, Neil Kinnock and later John Smith were less worried about politics in regard to the BBC than with making it accountable, via the governors, to the public, who effectively owned it.

What reforms Mike brought it then were, I suspected, a way of buying off demands for greater and more radical alterations ahead of what he anticipated would be a Labour victory. When the 1992 election took place, Sue and I watched the results at Television Centre with Bob Runcie, in every way a wonderful man and widely underestimated. (In my opinion, like Alec Douglas Home, the further we get from his period in office the more he will be admired.) We witnessed a senior political correspondent of the BBC storming out as Major's victory became obvious, shouting, 'This is disgusting! I can't stand it!'

We had successfully kept the politicians at bay during the election campaign. I had refused three requests from Jack Cunningham, Neil Kinnock's campaign chief, to see me. I would see the campaign managers of all parties or none. None was preferable. 1992 was the campaign when Kinnock had that great revivalist meeting at Sheffield, just before the poll, and assuming victory announced his future cabinet ministers and their jobs, one by one. I watched the broadcast with deepening gloom. For the first half I thought at any minute I will get a call from the Chairman of the Conservative Party saying this is a party political broadcast for the Labour Party. For the second, I wondered if we might receive another call from the Labour Party saying, 'Stop it, it's becoming a party political broadcast for the Conservatives.'

As a matter of interest I had only one complaint during that election campaign (from Norman Tebbit in the middle of the night), which I totally ignored. On the morning of the results, we had a Board of Governors meeting and I got the tip that the Labour Party had conceded defeat. I felt sorry for Neil Kinnock. I had always liked him since the time he came to have lunch just after we had fired Alisdair Milne. He didn't raise it. He merely said, 'You have a new Director-General to appoint, that is not a matter for us. I am sure you'll make a very good choice.' I am one of the few who believe that Neil and Glenys might have been very successful in Downing Street. If he could tame the left wing of the Labour Party, I thought, he could run the country. And he had a wonderfully natural way with people, as I saw for myself when he was our guest at a Prom. I felt so sorry for him and Glenys that I waited for a fortnight after the election and then sent Alan, my driver, to deliver a huge bunch of flowers for them. Didn't tell anybody though.

Assessing Mike's achievements as Director-General, while mulling over his future in 1992, I saw that overstaffing remained endemic. We still had too many outside broadcast units lying around unused. Our studios were only used for 65 per cent of the time. Until the introduction of producer choice, the cost of making individual programmes remained shrouded in mystery. No one could put a figure to it. That didn't surprise me. No one in the Marsden could tell me what an operation cost either. Producer choice taught the BBC what the cost of individual operations was and threw up some bizarre comparisons. It was thought up by John Birt but actually introduced by Mike Checkland. Stories abounded. The one I remember was the black tie which was needed for a television broadcast and cost at least £50 because someone had to go, by taxi, from Television Centre and back, to buy it.

Taxis were one of the legendary BBC scams. There was no check on them and no one in the management wished to tackle it. It was not unusual for two or three people to book a taxi, drive to a smart restaurant (often the Gay Hussar), have a two-hour lunch while the taxi driver waited to drive them home. Funnily enough, while writing this chapter, I took a £20 taxi ride from a company of which I am a director. The driver said, 'How are you getting on without the BBC, Mr Hussey?' It's rather heartwarming how often that happens. He went on: 'I've got no time for this Greg Dyke. He's cut down on the taxis. No more loverly luncheon dates. I used to reckon the money I made out of those paid for my licence fee several times over.' Good old Greg, I thought, at last someone has had the courage to deal with it. That had to be a management decision.

The BBC's carefree disregard for costs was the absolute antithesis to the success of our charter renewal. We needed to score on three vital points. We had to make quality programmes that appealed across the spectrum. We had to be more efficient than our competitors since it was public money we were spending. And we had to show commercial enterprise. My verdict was: on point one – not enough; on point two – nowhere near enough; on point three – getting better, but a long way to go. The governors had been pushing points one and two for months to no avail. The failure was a failure of management and Mike Checkland led the management.

One of the things that most incensed the governors was Mike's handling of a £38 million overspend by television in 1991. TV finances were his strong suit and he had been in charge of television, yet he didn't appear to have known about the overspend. Why hadn't he seen it coming? Now it had come, he appeared anxious to cover it up.

As a final example of the mindset the BBC presented, I was told by the Rugby Union officials that the reason why we were beaten by ITV for the 1991 Rugby World Cup was that our bid had been a shambles, drawn up as if the event was the BBC's by divine right. The fundamental problem was, many of those who worked for the BBC couldn't see that the licence fee was a privilege, not a right. It would go if we didn't put our house in order. The complacency I had seen when I first arrived had been driven underground, but still flourished.

When I finally confided in Joel that I had decided that Mike would have to go, he told me that his mind had been made up six months earlier and with the same reluctance. At the end of July 1991 I organized a governors' dinner. It was a long, gruelling session. Joel and I carried four other governors with us. The six others were, to various degrees, opposed. It was stalemate. Our deliberations were not made any easier by the fact that friends of Mike had leaked to the press that he would not accept anything less than a two-year renewal. To some governors this sounded like blackmail, but I believed that Mike, a puritan at heart, was being ill served by his friends.

In the end we compromised. We agreed unanimously to offer Mike one more year when his present contract expired. That would take him to February 1993. We couldn't just let him go after he had worked so hard. It would have been a public relations disaster and would have gone down badly with the BBC staff by whom he was held in high regard and would not have been fair. The extension would also allow him to complete the next stage of the charter renewal process. After that he could go with the honour accorded to so many of his predecessors. We agreed we would appoint a Director-General designate to shadow Mike and to take over when he left.

Joel and I were adamant that there was only one man with

the breadth of mind, the experience, the intellect and the dedicated determination to face the problems ahead and that was John Birt. We carried the day. It was agreed not to advertise the post but to offer it at once to John. There were question marks about him, of course. There are always question marks. But we were playing for high stakes – back to my original objective, thought on my arrival to be impossible, of leaving the BBC with its range of programmes, channels and its licence fee intact in the new charter. There was still much to do. George Russell, head of the Independent Television Commission – the ITV and Channel 4 regulator and a wise man – said, 'Birt has the best brains in the BBC and the best idea of what has to be done for it. But has he got the management skills and the qualities of leadership?' That is what we were going to find out.

I saw Mike the next day and told him. He was hurt but dignified about it. The decision was very unpopular within the BBC. John Birt was not universally liked and I understood him to be difficult and dogmatic, but he was head and shoulders above any other candidate. Joel and I were convinced that, whatever his awkward management style, he was the one man who had the intellect and the drive to do the necessary. Jane Glover, a governor, argued strongly for John Tusa, the head of the World Service, who soon afterwards came and complained to me that he hadn't had the chance to apply for the post. He put his case with characteristic eloquence. I tried but failed to explain to him that he would not have got the job and I didn't want him to suffer the indignity of applying and being turned down. He was a brilliant presenter, an able and attractive man – and particularly good on the arts. Those qualities would have been beguiling in a Director-General but there were two other points. He was a convinced defender of the BBC as it was and had not the appetite that either Checkland or Birt had for change. Moreover, to take Tusa would have meant losing both Checkland and Birt. Neither would have served under him. That was the kernel of the argument. John did not see it that way, but that was the unpalatable truth.

There was another factor. At a major presentation on the World Service, John had countenanced a blistering attack on

the Foreign Office. Sir Michael Palliser, a retired Permanent
Under Secretary, refused to be drawn on the substance of the
attack, but pointed out that the Foreign Office was the only
friend the World Service had in Whitehall. Such an approach, I
believed, was not what we were looking for in a new Director-
General. You don't need to demonstrate your independence of
mind by kicking your only friends where it hurts.

So there it was – nasty, unpopular but settled. There was
much criticism but less of a row than I expected. Very few
observers whose views I respected challenged our decision. Only
Douglas Hurd queried if we'd got the right man.

Initially at least, Mike and John worked well together,
although it required something of an effort on both sides. There
was much discontent and plotting within the BBC, some of it
directed at getting rid of me. What the rebels didn't seem to
understand was that the appointment of the Chairman of the
BBC has to be agreed at the Privy Council. Equally, if the
Chairman is to be dismissed, that is also a Privy Council matter.
Funnily enough, shortly after I joined the BBC, I met at Brooks
a previous Clerk to the Privy Council who said, 'You are in a
very strong position. You can't be fired. That has to be a Privy
Council decision. It only came up once and you will be amazed.
Anthony Wedgwood Benn who was Postmaster General in the
1964 to 1966 Wilson government, asked me whether the Privy
Council would agree to his request to dismiss the current
Chairman on the basis that he wouldn't take advertising. That
didn't get off the ground.'

It was the partnership of John and Mike that delivered
'Extending Choice', our document on the future of the BBC
published in December 1992 at the same time, coincidentally,
as a government green paper on broadcasting. Psychologically
we stole a march. We sold our offering for £2.50. The government's pamphlet was £7. The response to 'Extending Choice'
convinced me that we were on track in the charter negotiations.
The launch was expertly handled by John and the whole package, I believe, changed the perception of the BBC in the eyes
of the mandarins. John Hunt, the former cabinet secretary,

remarked to me at the time, 'I don't know how you've managed to capture the agenda. I thought you were going to get filleted.'

The title, 'Extending Choice', was brilliant. It expressed in two words the justification and purpose of the BBC. The document, which developed out of the charter renewal process organized by John Birt within the BBC and fourteen internal focus groups, was a compromise between John's reforming zeal and Mike's determination to hold the line. Its key theme – that the BBC should add something extra across the spectrum of broadcasting and not simply reproduce what was there already – was one that I had been stressing since I joined. There were radical new ideas – like the suggestion of a Public Service Broadcast Council which would share out the licence fee revenue between all channels that carried out public service work (an idea which was rejected by the ITV companies) – and more straightforward detail on the role of governors and the question of standards. It also sought to make the BBC more accountable by setting clear objectives in terms of programming, finances, staffing – and then measuring our performance. It spoke too of quality as well as ratings. This was something about which I cared. Much as I admired Murdoch for his handling of the unions, in the newspaper industry I had seen his arrival drive down standards. Now in broadcasting, through his satellite channels, he was doing the same. I was determined the BBC would not succumb.

The publication of our document and the government's own green paper were followed, for once, by a calm, civilized and constructive debate. There was one small glitch. John Birt's remark at the press launch that our share of television audiences might drop to 30 per cent was soundly based in a changing marketplace, but attracted some criticism. What needed emphasizing though was that across the range of our broadcast services we reached 90 per cent of the population. What he should have emphasized was not ratings but reach and range. (And indeed BBC's share of the peak-time TV audience still regularly tops 40 per cent.)

Mike Checkland had indicated that he would serve out his

extra year to the full – setting a leaving date of February 1993. I had hoped, once 'Extending Choice' had been prepared, he would take the opportunity to bow out with dignity, rather than cling on to the bitter end. However, his mind seemed made up, when suddenly the most unlikely event dramatically changed the scene. In October 1992, there was an international television festival held in London and at it Mike launched a highly personal attack on me, questioned my capacity to lead the BBC at the age of seventy-three – actually I was sixty-nine (seventy-three if I had served out my full quota). I don't know whether he had planned it, whether he suddenly lost his temper or whether it all just arose out of a sense of smouldering resentment. Anyway my possible departure was now on the agenda and was carried, needless to say, on all programmes, including the World Service.

Howell and John McCormick, who had succeeded Patricia Hodgson in 1987 as Secretary of the BBC, were my two trusted advisers and came to see me with long faces and deep apprehension. Haltingly they reported Mike's bizarre attack. To their astonishment I roared with laughter. 'That's a full pitch outside the leg stump. We will hit it for six. He can't stay after this.' And indeed, that proved to be the case.

Compared with some of the things that have been said about me, a glancing blow about my age was a compliment. Mike came to see me afterwards and explained but didn't apologize for his remarks (bewilderingly, he said they were not meant to be personal). I told him it would be inappropriate for him now to present 'Extending Choice' to the public alongside John Birt, which he accepted just as Birt grabbed with delight the chance of doing it himself. Meanwhile, the governors were unanimously furious and a party of three – I don't know whom – told Mike that, after this, he could not remain as Director-General. A few days later, he came to see me to say that he had decided to leave at Christmas.

I was genuinely fond of him, but was irritated by his mastery of management by fix and fudge. He was a long-term BBC prisoner, trapped and bound by historic attitudes. Nevertheless, his contribution to the BBC has been underrated, not least by his successor. He did what no one else within the BBC and certainly no one without has ever done – taught the BBC it had to change. Maybe his view of the scope of the change ranked lower than others, but nevertheless change was now firmly on the agenda. He preached that with great courage and determination. Only he could have done that. The staff might have taken it from the governors. They certainly would not have taken it from Birt. Mike was loved and admired throughout the BBC, especially at the shop floor level.

After Mike had left John Birt came with Margaret Salmon to discuss his future plans. It was all drawn up on a chart, I suspected by McKinsey. It included moving radio into the heart of television so that the same executives would control both television and radio output. This would also involve moving radio from Broadcasting House in central London to White City under television. I said that I would not agree to that. It was a step too far. As anyone who has read this far will know, I have a strong belief in radio. I believe it is different from television (another art form). One is based on sight and the other on sound. One is a huge consumer of cash, the other modest. They would never mix. Any merger would be disadvantageous to radio which, in its own funny way, has a singularly unique hold on its audience. Their channels, like Radio 4, extend choice, have little competition and supply outstanding quality to BBC output.

The division between broadcast and production which John suggested was, I thought, bold and might work. So I gave it halting agreement. I looked at the plans for appointments and noted there was no place for David Hatch, Managing Director of Radio, who had done more than anyone else in the BBC to smooth over John's abrupt and difficult management style. 'What's happened to Hatch?' I asked. Birt replied, 'There wasn't a place for him on the chart.' Ridiculous! 'Draw another chart, with a place for him,' I suggested. 'And make him your assistant. He has wisdom. I know he's old BBC but he knows how people react. He knows how people in the BBC feel. He knows how to calm the malcontents. If you use him properly, he will be an enormous help to you.' Unfortunately John didn't, and David therefore wasn't.

There was one piece of good news. When John became Director-General, I told him he had a sound Board of Management, but it needed strengthening. I suggested two names. The first, as a deputy, was Bob Phillis who had wide experience in Fleet Street and in managing media companies with all the various problems that that involves. Bob was wise, intelligent and straight. My second suggestion was Liz Forgan – brilliant, funny, energetic and in every way a delight. She would light up the Board of Management like a Christmas tree. He followed my advice and they both contributed the talents I knew they had to the Board with great effect. What they also contributed was forthright honesty. They said what they thought, and what they thought was based on a wider management experience than John's. Sadly, that undid them.

With John Birt at the helm, assisted by the new recruits, who joined in January 1993, I was increasingly optimistic. My own view was that the Conservative government had been badly bruised by the fallout from the 1990 Broadcasting Act and now desperately craved a period of stability. That Act, which left the BBC almost unchanged, had altered the way ITV franchises were awarded to place much greater emphasis on money than quality. I was amused that, though the great drive from the Conservatives had been to carve up the BBC, it was ITV which was turned upside down. When the Act came into effect in 1993, even Mrs Thatcher's favourite TV channel, TVam, lost out. She wrote a letter of commiseration. ITV standards fell as advertising revenue became the sole arbiter of what appeared on the screen. This suited me admirably. In my conversations with ministers, I always urged that they would be wise to accept the status quo with the BBC for ten years to see how these major changes panned out in the commercial sector.

Due to the reorganization of news and current affairs, we were having less trouble about political bias. Much of this was due to Joel's parliamentary contacts. Inside the BBC, of course, I remained in many people's eyes the leader of an interfering bunch of right wingers. I own up to being right wing in one sense only – if it was right wing to argue that the BBC had to be just as accountable to the public as all other nationalized industries had been forced to be, then I was right wing. We weren't, of course, a nationalized industry, but, like them, we existed on public funds.

During this period, I continued to travel on behalf of the World Service. In 1992 Sue and I went to India where we stayed with Mark Tully, a man of great charm, understanding and knowledge. A fierce row broke out just before arrival because an interview with Rajiv Gandhi by *Panorama* had been, Mr Gandhi alleged, altered by the inclusion of new questions which were not actually the questions to which his responses had been made. A distressingly typical incident. Mark warned me that we would get a very hostile welcome and recommended us not to come. 'You might even get pelted with camel dung,' he added cheerfully. 'I've never had camel dung Mark,' I said, 'that will be a new experience. We're on our way.'

At first his prediction was borne out but luckily on the evening of the first day we met an important behind-the-scenes figure in the Indian cabinet and got on well with him. I don't know how, but we did. Perhaps by being honest. Mark was in a state because he was giving a party for us and the refusals were flowing in. Overnight, it changed. Guest after guest accepted. We had a marvellous evening, including a treasured meeting with Bede Griffiths, a Benedictine monk who had made his home in India. Sue was hugely moved and impressed by him and said, 'You are a saint', to which he replied, 'No, there is only one saint in this room' and pointed to Mark (an old pupil of Bob Runcie). I still listen every Sunday morning to his radio programme *Something Understood*.

One of my most interesting visits stemmed from an invitation to Russia to explain to President Yeltsin's media advisers the principles under which the BBC worked – primarily its total independence. This, of course, was an improbable cause in a country that had, for over a thousand years, been under the direct rule either of autocratic tsars or cruel tyrants. However, I embarked upon this unenviable mission in the interests of creating further good relations with Russia.

What made it particularly difficult was the mutual contempt between President Yeltsin and Mr Khazbulatov, the general secretary of the Communist Party. Each had his own army. Shortly after I left they engaged in an historic pitched battle in the White House, the seat of the Russian Duma, for hegemony. Khazbulatov was one of the nastiest men I have ever met – eyes like a snake. I was accompanied by a World Service colleague and an interpreter – a charming lady who shared my opinion. My host, the head of Russian state television, Mr Popsov, was also there, along with banks of cameras and reporters.

Khazbulatov launched a vicious attack on the impossibility of giving broadcasters independence: 'How can you trust a lump of shit like this?' he asked pointing to Mr Popsov, an ally of Yeltsin.

'General secretary,' I replied, 'every country approaches the ideal of democracy in their own way and in their own time. We do not all proceed at the same pace. For instance, in my country, we executed our king in the seventeenth century. In France, they executed theirs in the eighteenth century. You in Russia did not execute yours until the twentieth century. So we march towards democracy, but at a different pace.'

The next day I saw Mr Popsov. 'Oh, you are a diplomat,' he said. 'If you had tried to defend me it would have been . . .' he drew his finger across his throat.

In 1991, I was invited to visit Prague, two years after the Velvet Revolution ended communist rule. I met and talked with President Václav Havel. At the end of a fascinating conversation, he asked me if I would like to visit their Chamber of Deputies – parliament as it were. As this was the first democratic government in Eastern Europe, I assented with alacrity. Half an hour later I was shown in. It was, like most political chambers, in a half circle, not the confrontational seating in our Parliament.

A debate was in progress when suddenly someone appeared by the small box in which I was sitting with my World Service Czech escort. To my surprise and apprehension he told me that the Speaker (I use the English term) wished me to come forward as he had something important to say. I joined him as he rose from his chair to greet me. He then said (it was translated to me and I will repeat only the final sentence): 'On behalf of all the deputies here present, and on behalf of all my fellow countrymen, I want to welcome the Chairman of that great institution which kept the flame of truth alive in our country throughout the forty-five long, dark years.' I was moved and proud and in reply emphasized how much my country had always admired the courage of the Czech and Slovak peoples.

His tribute crystallized for me the ultimate motive and purpose of the BBC and our World Service.

Chapter Thirteen

Early in 1991, I set off with Sue for a visit to Australia and Hong Kong – both areas of great importance to the BBC. They bought vast quantities of our programmes, were profitable places for us and generally were very pro BBC, depending on us for news, features and archive material. There was another reason for the trip – to attend a board meeting of Colonial and Mutual, the Australian company of which I was director. That directorship – as well as my role at the Marsden and the King's Fund – ran in parallel with my time as Chairman of the BBC.

Colonial Mutual Insurance was an old-fashioned Australian insurance company which I and David Adams (now the chairman) were trying to revive. Among our objectives was the appointment of a dynamic new chief executive (typical). The English directors were all invited out once a year. They particularly liked me to visit because they thought (more flattering than accurate) I knew what was going on in England where they had substantial interests. Also, I had earned a spurious reputation for forecasting election results.

In 1991 we had arrived in the middle of an Australian general election. At the board meeting every director was asked his or her views. They all went for the conservatives. When he turned to me, the chairman said, 'Well you won't have much of a view on this.' 'I have actually,' I replied. 'I think Keating will win it.' There was general consternation round the table. But he did. Greater consternation.

They thought I was a clever fellow, but I followed the old taxi routine. Every taxi driver I met opted for Keating. On my next trip in 1992, I forecast a majority in the twenties for John

Major in the British General Election. They thought I was a genius. Two lucky guesses. I have always believed it is better to be lucky than clever.

From Australia, we went to Hong Kong where the BBC had started up a Far East service in co-operation with Li Kai Shing. It was an extremely important development which extended into China and the Indian subcontinent the BBC World Wide television news service, of which Chris Patten, the governor of Hong Kong, was a great admirer. Unfortunately the deal came unstuck. Lunch was arranged for me with Li Kai Shing, the richest and most powerful Chinese businessman in Hong Kong. He spoke in a low guttural voice, difficult to understand, but the meaning was clear. He complained that our news service was embarrassing 'my friends in Peking'.

'Why?' I asked.

'You keep referring to Tiananmen Square.'

'Well, it happened.'

'But it upsets my friends in Peking.'

'Mr Kai Shing,' I replied, 'when you were proud to sign this contract with the BBC, you made a contract with the most famous and admired broadcasting service in the world, but there is one snag.'

'What is that?'

'We tell the truth and do not intend to hide it.'

Our notice to cease came shortly afterwards, followed by a contract between Kai Shing and Rupert Murdoch. I did not regret sacrificing our commercial advantage by maintaining our impartial reputation, but it was a setback.

When I arrived in Hong Kong in 1993 a storm was blowing up over John Birt's contract. At the time that he was appointed Deputy Director-General, he had wished to continue with the not unusual contract he had had previously with London Weekend Television. It was a similar arrangement to that enjoyed at the time by Michael Grade and John Tusa at the BBC. He had a private company which was paid by the BBC as if he were a separate unit. When he had raised this with Checkland, it was cleared by our personnel director and also by the tax authorities.

At the time of his appointment as Deputy Director-General, I told the governors that he was expensive, which we had expected, and there were some unusual but not unprecedented add-ons. Joel and I didn't go further. The arrangement included a payment for his wife, as a director of the company, and an extremely inadequate pension subscription. Because he was in effect a company, John was able to charge the cost of his cherished Armani suits against the company.

These I had long considered particularly bizarre. A month before the row blew up, I had said to Michael Stevenson, BBC Secretary since 1992, 'Now John is Director-General, I really ought to tell him to go to a better tailor. His suits are appallingly cut. They make him look like a square gorilla.' 'You can't,' Michael warned me. 'Those are Armani suits and John is inordinately proud of them, and they cost about £900 each.' I was staggered. I had never heard of Armani and still thought they were dreadful, but I let it go. I have never paid more than £285 for a suit in my life.

The row which broke while I was in Hong Kong arose because the *Independent on Sunday* had got the story of John's contract. It was, they suggested, a very odd arrangement for the man running the BBC not to be in its employ. What they didn't make clear was that he was not Director-General when this deal was made. And from there, it rolled and rolled. What fuelled it was that John was unpopular with many old BBC hands because of his commitment to reform. He was also obstinate and had refused to accept advice from some senior and influential friends inside and outside the BBC to the effect that it was fine to have such a deal when he was Deputy Director-General, but that once he held the top job he should rapidly conform with normal BBC arrangements.

This was indeed what I had been saying. The day before I had left for Australia, I had instructed the personnel director, Margaret Salmon, to tell John that he had to change the contract. 'No contract change, no job.' On my return, I checked up with Margaret and, as I expected, she had delivered the message. These facts were not, of course, covered in the newspaper reports. The implication was that the new contract had been specially agreed by me on his appointment as Director-General. The exact reverse of the truth.

The anti-Birt faction was whooping it up and what was called the great Armani suit scandal became headlines in all the newspapers with pious outcries from editors and journalists who, as I very well knew, had been enjoying that type of contract for years. What started as a put-up job to get at John and halt the march of reform through the BBC, not without some help from at least one governor, switched into an attack on me. The critics had latched onto the one vital fact – getting rid of Birt wouldn't alter the strategy that the governors had embarked upon. The way to do that was to get rid of me. So I became the objective of the mob. Presented with a garbled version of events by reporters, two governors told the *Evening Standard* that I should resign. Mike Checkland weighed in to call for my head.

Throughout my stay at the Pattens (I managed to do some business), I was permanently on the telephone from Government House in Hong Kong to Joel and Michael Stevenson. They kept me fully informed. Faxed headlines reading 'Hussey to go' enlivened my breakfasts. We returned on our due date to London and the chief steward on our plane warned Sue that I would get a hostile reception from a barrage of journalists who were awaiting our arrival. I had a good dinner and slept like a top, helped by a good slug of Johnnie Walker Red Label (my favourite).

The steward's report proved accurate. As we disembarked, we were besieged by the press. 'Is this your last day at the BBC?' 'Are you ashamed of your husband, Lady Susan?' Alan Mabbs, our loyal chauffeur, pushed through the crowd with our luggage, flooring several journalists on the way.

The day after our return there was a memorial service at the BBC church, All Saints in Portland Place, for our legendary and much loved tennis commentator, Dan Maskell. Naturally we went. We sat, as the Chairman and his wife always did, in the front pew. The crowds were substantially larger than those at Heathrow and no less vocal or offensive. We followed Dan Maskell's family out of the church. As I went down the aisle, I caught Brian Johnston's eye. He gave me an encouraging wink and a smile. In the history of the Grenadiers, Brian, who won a Military Cross, was specifically mentioned for appearing without fail in the most unpleasant circumstances always with a smile and a joke. That cheered the troops, just as it cheered me.

As soon as I was clear of the church, I went up to my office to test the water. It had looked a bit rough. I called Carole in and sifted carefully through the correspondence, the newspaper cuttings and the messages. There was no political comment and no political messages. It was then I suspected that this was a spurious crisis got up by the malcontents. They had won the journalists round – even *The Times* reported that I was on the way out if not immediately, then certainly by the summer – but had failed to enlist anybody who mattered. There were no ministers, no MPs, nothing from anyone of substance or import- ance, just journalists and BBC staff.

Clearly the first thing was to call a board meeting that night. Meanwhile, some of the loyal Board of Management were energetically lobbying the journalists on John's behalf, with some success. John appeared before the Board. Hitherto he had consis- tently and obstinately refused to change his contract although his job had changed. The governors went through the whole position with John and made it clear that whatever the ques- tions, whatever the position, this contract was inappropriate for a Director-General of the BBC. As it turned out, it wasn't even financially beneficial (apart from the suits). And his pension would be worse than if he were a member of the BBC scheme. Finally, with reluctance, he agreed to change. Round one satis- factorily completed, but not before one of the governors had asked to be excused from the discussion because he enjoyed a similar contract – but not with us.

The next day, there was a meeting of the General Advisory Council to the BBC – a watchdog body with no power, used for general consultation and discussion about our affairs. This, they thought, was their moment. At the start of proceedings, they asked the governors to withdraw, which we were happy to do – the meetings were always pretty dreary. Immediately they passed a vote of no confidence in the governors and me, without even asking us what our position was, what decisions had been taken, when and what was the truth of the whole matter. Several of them then went out onto the streets and gave television interviews. One of their leaders, Mark Fisher, Labour's arts spokesman, who knew nothing about the issue, said I ought to resign and that my behaviour was a disgrace. Several governors, including Phyllis James, were so outraged that they never went to another meeting of the General Advisory Council. Neither did I. In fact, I think that was the end of the General Advisory Council – probably the most productive result of the whole affair. It staggered on, ill-attended, and was finally put down in 1996.

That day ended with Mike Checkland's farewell dinner – eccentric timing as it turned out. Mike had rung to ask me if I would like to cancel it, but I said certainly not. 'I am not a believer,' I told him, 'in cancelling important events because they are inconvenient.' Afterwards Mike described the dinner to waiting journalists – and there were plenty of them – as 'a typically English occasion'. I had used the event, not to reflect on our current difficulties, but to praise Mike for his substantial (and still underrated) contribution to getting the BBC back on course. When Sue and I came to leave, we found another governor, Keith Oates and his wife, trying to find an exit to avoid the press. 'Rubbish,' said Sue, 'come on, Keith, take my arm and we'll give them something else to write about.' And write they certainly did – but not about that pairing.

The following day, there was a normal governors' meeting, held at the World Service headquarters, Bush House, again preceded by great press excitement. It was short. I outlined the position. Bill Jordan, who knew his way around a crisis, immediately put the one question I wanted asked. 'Chairman, you are a man of great experience. Tell us, do you think you ought to resign?' I replied that to my mind there were four moments at which I might resign. 'Today; at the end of the month; in six months' time when the hullabaloo has died down; or when my contract expires in 1997.' Immediately Phyllis and Joel said that if I resigned, they would too. All but two of the governors followed suit. That was the business of the day closed. I called in the Board of Management, told them that the governors had reviewed the matter, that John's contract was now satisfactory and that there would be no resignations from the Board of Governors, nor from the Board of Management.

It was over – a huge, unnecessary, malicious fuss about nothing. I spoke to no journalists, gave no interviews and the whole crisis went away in three days. We had arrived back on Sunday; it was a dead duck on Thursday. The critical point was finally persuading John that if he didn't alter his contract his job was at stake. Of course if John had agreed to alter his contract when he'd been advised to, the mess would never have arisen in the first place. The whole row was a classic display of the power of the press who blew up the issue with no factual support from anyone except malicious sources within the BBC (and, I suspect, one of the governors).

In the early stages Sue met Bernard Donoghue who had been senior policy adviser to both Harold Wilson and Jim Callaghan when they were at 10 Downing Street. 'Tell Dukie to stand firm on all accounts,' he said. 'The press is now taking up the position the unions used to occupy when we were in power, seeking the right to appoint or dismiss cabinet ministers. Someone must stand up to them, show them they won't be bullied and driven out of public life. He must stay there.'

On my return, Birt had told me he had the support of John Smith. I don't know what he had to do with it. I never spoke to any politician at any stage, but after it was over several wrote to me. Douglas Hurd: 'You have been through a troubled time and have carried yourself manfully. I hope the waves have now subsided.' John Wakeham: 'What a rough time you've been having. The hypocrisy of some people knows no shame.' Willie Whitelaw: 'Do not consider resigning. You are badly needed at the BBC and I'm sure the governors will stand totally behind you.' They did. And this from a member of the public: 'I have been following the news very closely regarding events at the BBC recently and can sense the enormous pressure you must be under. Well done with your stance against the national press. It is good to see they cannot destroy the lives of all the prominent people of this country and call it the freedom of the press.'

Three days later I was due to speak at the National Liberal Club with David Steel in the chair. He asked, 'What will you say about the Armani suits and the crisis?'

'Well, if they ask about it, I'll tell them the facts, but I don't think they'll bring it up.'

'Neither do I,' said David. And they didn't. Nor did anyone in the fifty public meetings the BBC held in the next three months.

Best of all was a postcard from Peter Brooke showing a picture of Harold Larwood. 'You must have felt like Bradman and Woodford facing bodyline bowling.' I much appreciated that and wrote back: 'I thoroughly enjoyed your card because I followed, I think, the classic recipe for playing bodyline: offer no strokes, duck as often as you can and hope not to get hit.' (I was, incidentally, an appallingly bad batsman.)

The BBC, of course, thought that I had been damaged by the row. Even Michael Stevenson and Patricia Hodgson told me so. 'Rubbish,' I said. 'It's a one-week wonder.' And it was.

I've spent some time on this issue partly because I believe, in spite of my long time in the newspaper industry, that the power of the press to debase public standards of accurate reporting and critical comment has smartly increased. The secret in these situations is to avoid talking to journalists and politicians. If you say nothing, they can't get back at you. Every time you open your mouth, you invite a counterpunch. If you don't open it, they're left punching empty air.

Journalists and dissatisfied members of staff continued to make mischief. In the autumn of 1993 the *Observer*, not one of my most fervent admirers, reported on its front page that John Major planned to replace me at the BBC with David Owen, the former Foreign Secretary and co-founder of the SDP. I was, it reported, a discredited public figure. It was another characteristic leak by the ancien régime of the BBC reflecting what they would like to happen and bearing no relation to the facts. The Prime Minister's office at once put out a statement dismissing the *Observer*'s report as rubbish. It was a ridiculous story. I knew and liked David Owen and I knew also that he would never have accepted the job. He had other objectives.

Far from being discredited, later in 1993 I successfully oiled my way through a National Heritage Select Committee inquiry into the BBC. Gerald Kaufman, who had been so horrified when I was first appointed, was in the chair. The first question was a nice gentle half-volley outside the leg stump. 'Aren't you a toff?' one MP asked. 'Well, I may look like one, but I'm not,' I replied. It continued much in that vein – a thoroughly enjoyable occasion with a good-spirited debate on both sides and few aggressive questions. Unbeknownst to me, the World Service had invited my old friend, Mr Popsov, the head of Russian state television, who was in Britain on a reciprocal trip, to attend this public meeting. This only emerged at a dinner I held for him that evening. I asked him what he thought. There was a long pause. 'Well, Mr Chairman, I think your deputies are just about as stupid as our deputies.'

The committee's report, when published, was a triumph for the BBC and another step on the road to charter renewal. It underwrote the position and authority of the governors, it backed the BBC in its current form, and it recommended that the licence fee continue for the last three years of the current charter with its link to the RPI.

We were approaching the crucial moment for the renegotiation of the charter, but first we had to agree a level for the licence fee for the next three years. We wanted the RPI link maintained, but the government had insisted on employing Touche Ross to look into our finances once again. I had spoken to Peter Brooke, the minister responsible, about the level of the licence fee but Phyllis James, drawing on her many years' experience as a senior civil servant, strongly advised me to put it in writing. 'A letter has to be on public record.' I therefore wrote to Peter just before Christmas 1993. My letter made, I hoped, an unanswerable case. So, I think it is appropriate to quote from it in some detail.

The Touche Ross report concluded: 'In our view the BBC has pursued appropriate opportunities rigorously and to date, its achievements exceed those envisaged in the Price Waterhouse report.' From an independent accountant, that

is a notable tribute. I would have been severely critical, as
no doubt you would, had the BBC at least not achieved
what was envisaged. I am glad they have done better. We
have set ourselves an even tougher efficiency target of 12
per cent. However, all my experience teaches me that when
projecting future revenues it is wiser to be pessimistic than
optimistic. Since John Birt became Director-General, he has
injected a new dynamism into our approach and attracted
high flyers into the top echelons of the BBC. What he has
achieved has been in the teeth of resolute opposition concentrated on personal attacks on the governors, me but
mainly on him. The policy did not start with John. It started
with the appointment of Mike Checkland. That is why
much of the opposition is directed on the governors and
myself. It was perfectly clear to me when I joined the BBC,
although never outlined by any ministers at any levels, what
the BBC needed and what I had to do. It never occurred to
me that these measures would not be extremely difficult
and evoke hostility. I underestimated both.

We have now reached a vital issue. If as a result of the
Touche Ross inquiry the BBC is given less than the RPI for
any of the final three years of this charter it will be seen by
the BBC and outsiders as a failure by the government to
endorse our policies and a defeat for the forces of reform
within the BBC. If we are given the RPI for the remaining
three years it will be a vindication of all I and my colleagues
have tried to achieve. With all the force that I can command
I cannot impress upon you how strongly I feel about this.
There is no demand for a reduction in the licence fee and
many polls suggest that we should go for an increase. The
charter negotiation is the place and it will be the time to
judge how effective we have been and what the future
should hold. Only Michael Cocks [the newly appointed
Vice-Chairman, of whom more later] has seen this letter
and he agrees it. This is a critical moment in the BBC's
affairs. The seal of approval on our policies for the last six
years will set us on the road to continue and reinforce them
with all the benefit that will flow to the audiences. An

apparent defeat will demoralize the staff and create discord and difficulties. I cannot say more.

Several years later, discussing this letter, I was asked whether it was my intention to resign if my advice was not accepted. No Chairman, it was pointed out, had ever written so bluntly to the government. I don't know if that is true, but the thought of resignation had not occurred to me. I believed I had the confidence of the government and we deserved the RPI link. My six years' experience as Chairman had taught me that if I made a strong case, the government accepted it. And they did so on this occasion.

Talking to Robin Butler, the cabinet secretary, I commented once that I had had to spend my first six years at the BBC prodding management to do what they didn't want to do, and my last four stopping them doing too much. If Mike Checkland had been reluctant to act, John Birt sometimes, I felt, was too precipitate.

Nevertheless John tackled overmanning and wasteful expenditure with gusto and courage. A good example came when Margaret Salmon told me at the governors' meeting that John was intending to put through a major reconstruction of staff rates. This had not been discussed with any of the governors, one of whom was Bill Jordan, an exceptionally able, decent and powerful president of the AEUW. There was no way he would agree to that without discussion. Margaret and I arranged it so that she was able to come into the meeting to outline the plan and explain how many of the staff would either leave or lose money. Though I had not warned him, Bill, of course, raised the issue. After some discussion he turned to me and said, 'You have great experience in these matters, Chairman, and you know that it is always wise to have a little reserve in your back pocket.'

'Absolutely, Bill,' I said. 'What do you suggest?'

'Well, £5,000,000.' (It was a big scheme.)

'You can't do that,' said John, 'it's not in the budget.'

'It is now,' I replied.

No reorganization was too ambitious for him to undertake.

There was a wholesale transfer of resources from staff to pro-gramme-making which I applauded. He also cut back on studio duplication in the regions. Again I was broadly in favour, though I questioned whether if some centres were too much reduced they would lack a critical mass that enabled them to make decent programmes. In short, if there are only three or four senior producers in one centre, there are simply not enough to spark originality and flair.

But John not only addressed the obvious problems, he also looked ahead. The BBC was one of the first public institutions to have its own website. It was also among the first in the broadcast-ing industry to recognize the potential in digital. I totally sup-ported this, admired John's foresight and initiative, but worried in case the shadow of Annan's judgement proved, once again, prophetic. There was always a danger of spending too much on new initiatives and starving our existing production.

The governors made sure our own house was in order. We saw through the codification of the governors' role in the hope that it would stop wrangling with the Board of Management (it didn't but I had to try). Moreover, we enshrined the principle of accountability in the conduct of everything to do with the BBC. It sometimes caused arguments. Accountability, I was told by staff more times than I care to remember, was the enemy of innovation. 'It depends what you mean by accountability,' I would reply. 'If you mean just following the audiences, then you are right. What I mean is doing what you think right and then explaining afterwards why you have done it.'

To establish this within the BBC, the governors set up a formal complaints' procedure whereby viewers' and listeners' points of view were tackled seriously first by a specialist com-plaints' department and, in the final analysis, by a sub-committee of governors, chaired by our new Vice-Chairman, Michael Cocks, a former Labour Chief Whip who had taken over from Joel in 1993. There was a row over his appointment. John Smith, the Leader of the Opposition, wanted Tessa Blackstone, head of Birkbeck College in London and an ally. When he protested to me about the choice of Lord Cocks, I pointed out that it had nothing to do with me. He needed to speak to the

Secretary of State. But Michael Cocks was a good choice. He was rough and tough and wasn't afraid of standing up to whomever, whenever he thought he was right and they were not.

Among the guests that Sue and I invited every year to the Proms were Jim and Audrey Callaghan. In 1993 he commented to Sue about Michael Cocks who had served as his Chief Whip. 'I'm sure Dukie will not need this advice,' he said, 'but if he takes Michael into his confidence, as I did, he will find no more loyal supporter in the world. If he doesn't, I have never known anyone who knew better where to place a stiletto.'

John Birt did occasionally give me cause to wonder, though I preferred to put it down to his steep learning curve. Early on, the BBC broadcast a series about Margaret Thatcher's premiership, to coincide with the publication of her memoirs in 1993. John organized a BBC lunch to mark the occasion and invited Lady Thatcher and many of her kitchen cabinet – Woodrow Wyatt, Bernard Ingram, Charles Powell and others. From the BBC, he only included Robin Oakley, our political editor, and Peter Jay, our economics editor. I was worried about this lunch, on two grounds. One, the guest list, seen from the outside, would carry a strong whiff of political bias – if not creep. It would appear to compromise the independence of the BBC. Also, if John was going to entertain Margaret Thatcher it should have been his top advisers and his colleagues at the table, not hers. We should be demonstrating our strength. John just wouldn't see my point of view. He has many fine qualities, but admitting others may, on occasion, be right is not one of them.

Funnily enough, years later when I was in the Lords I found myself opposite David Lipsey, whom I remembered on the staff of the *Sunday Times* when I was Chief Executive. He said to me, 'May I ask you a question? What do you think was John Birt's greatest fault? I have to add he is a great personal friend of mine.'

'Well, David,' I said, 'if you really are asking me, I will tell you. He is very clever, very hard working but he has very poor judgement.'

'Oh, I think that's most unfair.'

'What do you think, David?'

'He will never accept anyone else's advice.'

'But they are exactly the same thing.'

John and I, I came to realize, were of a completely different cast of mind. Two opposites can work together wonderfully well – or they can fall out. I was determined it was going to be the former. We shared a vision of where the BBC should be. That should have been enough to overcome our differences of style and approach. For the most part, I was delighted with what he was achieving. He was making such a favourable impact on the government that Virginia Bottomley, the Secretary of State for Health, invited him to run a teach-in for top NHS managers.

There were, however, problems. One lay in his reluctance to make a decision. He liked every issue to be argued in long memoranda, which he would often take several weeks to read before reaching a conclusion. Often, too, there would be two or even three new versions. This was not my style. I believed in fast decisions and immediate reactions on nearly every issue except the most serious. I kept my diary free for anyone who wished to see me. His was planned three weeks in advance. He liked a structured day, but this led to slow and long-postponed decisions. It also led to great resentment in the ranks at all levels as they waited week after week for the verdict.

A good example was Radio 5 Live. Liz Forgan came to see me to explain the idea which she and Jenny Abramski had dreamed up to solve the awkward question of our fifth network. They had no evidence from focus groups and no pages of research to back up their hunch, although a working group under Patricia Hodgson and Phil Harding had been discussing what to do with the ailing Radio 5. Liz told me that it was running into difficulties with John and his management.

'I'm coming to you Dukie,' she said, 'to support my proposal.'

'What is it?' I asked.

'We turn Radio 5, to be called Radio 5 Live, into a live news and sports network. John wants it only to be news with no sport.'

'They must be mad,' I said. 'It's a brilliant idea. The combination of news and sport on radio will be a great seller.' (Rereading my notes I see I had once mused on this combination myself, although I had forgotten that when Liz put it up.) 'I'll back that and the governors will back me. Go ahead.'

With my support, and that of the governors, who also liked the title Radio 5 Live, Liz's proposal got the green light. Our head of PR had asked after the governors' meeting whether I would announce the plan to the journalists waiting outside Broadcasting House. No one from the management was prepared to speak publicly (except Liz, who wasn't allowed to). 'Certainly,' I said and breezed out and told them: 'You're all journalists. You all know that nothing sells newspapers like hard news except possibly hard sport. This will be a great success.' They weren't convinced either but some of them saw the point.

That is the story of the birth of Radio 5 Live. It has, of course, been one of the greatest media launches of the last twenty years. It was very cheap; no research, no focus groups – just three people, with long experience of the minds and attitudes of readers and listeners. Shortly after we had launched it, I was driving back from East Anglia where I had been visiting the BBC studios in Norwich. I heard on Radio 5 Live Prime Minister's Question Time, followed by the second half of a cup replay match. I just laughed. It was riveting. It couldn't fail and it hasn't.

In February 1995, when the government published its white paper on the charter renewal, we had every reason to celebrate. It endorsed everything we had hoped for. We had achieved what I had outlined to Sally Magnusson all those years before. The recipe for our success had been made up of four vital ingredients: to establish our political independence; to maintain an impartial, accurate news and current affairs department; to make, broadcast and maintain programmes of quality right across every genre; and to establish accountability as a way of demonstrating our prudent care in the use of public money.

The House of Commons dealt with the white paper in an hour. The future of the BBC no longer seemed a live political issue. The public likewise hardly blinked, though there were a few minor points still to be clarified. After all the headlines over the years, the BBC appeared to be out of the woods. John Birt held a champagne reception to celebrate. In his victory address, he told those present that he couldn't have achieved what he had if I hadn't been standing beside him. Many, like Tim Bell (our PR adviser), found this a little surprising. There was no reference to the governors, who had picked John and supported him through considerable adversity – much of it self-induced. There was no reference to his able and supportive colleagues, Bob Phillis, Will Wyatt, Margaret Salmon, Rodney Baker-Bates, David Hatch, Patricia Hodgson, Ron Neil, Howell James, Sam Younger, Liz Forgan, Michael Jackson and Nick Elliot; an exceptional bunch.

Denis Thatcher, a shrewd observer, and himself a genius at avoiding the limelight, once said to Sue of my spell at the BBC: 'He has done a superb job. Changed the BBC, never had an honour, never sought any public recognition, just done the job.' That was kind. Perhaps the comment that pleased me most was in an unlikely place and from an unlikely source. I was walking down the aisle at Westminster Abbey after Harold Wilson's memorial service next to Robert Sheldon, the senior and highly respected Labour MP and long-time chairman of the Public Accounts Committee. He said, 'You have every reason to be proud of your achievement. You have single-handedly saved the greatest cultural institution in the world.' It was lovely to hear, but only 50 per cent right – a good score for a politician. I had not done it single-handedly. I had been hugely helped by the loyalty and support of the governors, the Board of Management and many people down the line. We may have set the agenda, but they did the work.

The white paper did not, of course, end the debate. There were still a few outstanding issues. The new charter was going to be for ten years not fifteen, as before, but this was something I had privately proposed, despite opposition within the BBC. The pace of change in the broadcasting industry was so great and accelerating so fast that I thought the normal fifteen-year charter would be too long. Ten years would be a reasonable span and would give whichever government was in power time to assess the situation before it was too late to make changes.

Only ten days before the white paper had been published the government had decided not to propose the privatization of Radio 1. This had long been on the cards. The appointment of a new controller, Matthew Bannister, made the case that Radio 1 had to take on a new identity with more live music and a strong speech-based element. He sacked long-established DJs and watched the ratings tumble by six million.

Another hitch arose when John wanted to extend his power over appointments. His proposal was that he would select a single candidate to be put forward to the Board of Governors. It was a position of power that would be accorded to no chief executive of any public or private company, large or small, unless he owned it. I had this quietly altered to read that the governors would take advice from the Director-General over appointments, but would not feel compelled to accept it. It was not long before I felt I was proved right. Having enthusiastically supported the appointment of Matthew Bannister as controller of Radio 1, with the results I have mentioned, John then promoted him in 1996 after I had left, to be Managing Director of Radio. It was no surprise to me when he suddenly moved on. Looking back on my notes on the Radio 1 appointment board I see only two people were doubtful. Ken Bloomfield, the Irish governor, and me. Sometimes experience brings judgement.

The white paper also proposed that the BBC should become, in global terms at least, a multimedia commercial enterprise, with World Service Television and its spin-offs. This necessitated us setting up a separate board – to ensure that a clear distinction was made between domestic output, paid for by the licence fee, and international services. In truth there was some overlap. Domestic programmes were shown on World Service Television, while the effective marketing of what I believed to be the second-best brand name in the world – the BBC being just behind Coca-Cola – meant we could raise sufficient revenue to augment the licence fee and expand our home output.

This was especially vital if we were to compete effectively against Sky and ITV for sporting rights. My major failure in my dealings with government was not to get them to agree a list of sporting events which had to go out on terrestrial channels –

where everyone could watch them. Moreover, as the other channels pushed up the prices – in Sky's case as a loss leader to force sports fans to get their satellite dishes – the BBC's resources were strained. It is an on going problem and I continue to have concerns about the ability of the corporation, funded by the licence fee, to match the amounts advertising-based channels can bid. Major sporting events are national occasions and the audiences should be awarded national television coverage.

With the charter safely in the bag, it was the turn of Scotland to entertain the governors. It was to be a very splendid occasion at a new hotel in Edinburgh. We got a whopping discount. I was delighted.

I was shown up to my suite – lavish, with a huge bathroom and a wonderful Victorian bath with the original claw feet, well clear of the ground. Long and deep. I sank into it to enjoy a good soak before the hosting and the speech to come. When came the moment to get out, I couldn't. My legs are a bit of a snag. The right is missing below the knee and the left is paralysed from the knee down, so I have no movement in that ankle or foot and I can't walk without a caliper. My normal system is to drape my left leg over the side of the bath and lever myself out with my shoulders. This bath was too deep. I tried several times and failed. I looked for the bell. It was miles away, on the other side of the room. So was the telephone. I was stuck in this immense bath and I couldn't get out – and there was no way of attracting attention. Time was fast slipping by. The guests must already be arriving.

I lay in the bottom of this bloody bath and thought, 'Well, I'm supposed to be intelligent, there must be some way out of this.' Quite suddenly into my mind slipped the image of a seal. God knows why. 'How does he cope? I know, he flops out. I'll give it a go.' So I turned onto my stomach, hauled myself up to the level of the bath's rim, gave a huge heave, with my useless legs behind me, and did a massive belly flop onto the floor. It worked. Unhurt and triumphant, I crawled to a chair.

Overall, with a new charter assured, the BBC was slowly regaining its confidence, but at the same pace my worries about John Birt were growing. His problem, rightly analysed by George

Russell, was that allied to the best brain and programme expertise was too little managerial or financial know-how. The reasons
why we had chosen him as Director-General remained valid,
but he clearly needed advice. That is the responsibility of the
Chairman – rightly defined as: to appoint, support and, when
necessary, fire the Chief Executive.

What is required, in very difficult jobs, is a combination of
hard-bitten experience in top management, a shrewd commercial sense to cut through the hype and, above all, an understanding of people and an ability to engage their confidence and
support. John's disadvantage was that he had reached an
extremely important job with little management experience. He
had been a producer – and a very fine one – and he understood
supremely well the art of television for which he had an
undoubted flair. Checkland left a bit early. We hoped that John
would have a year to learn the job (not that he saw it that way).
We all tried to support him – his colleagues on the Board of
Management and the governors and his friends – but we were all
rebuffed. I wanted to help John. Indeed, it was my job to do so.
He was my choice. I had backed him, sold him to the governors
and also to the government as the one man capable of doing the
job. But he had to take the staff with him.

I tried to approach this softly. It wouldn't help either the
BBC or me if we fell out. We needed, both of us, to compromise. Knowing when to compromise is a vital factor in good
management.

I tackled it in three ways: first, I enlisted Arthur Brittenden,
a man of great personal charm and experience – now a senior
executive in Tim Bell's public relations company, of whom we
were clients. Just the person, I thought, to give John some
advice. Hopeless. A three-hour conversation and he got
nowhere. Arthur tried to persuade him to go round the offices
and explain to the staff what he was trying to do, meet them
informally in groups with no set questions. John refused.

I then took John out to lunch myself and told him delicately
that he must get closer to his Board of Management on whom
he was dependent. There were murmurs of discontent at his
style of management as authoritarian with little relaxed debate.

He reacted very badly. All his board were happy and content, he told me. Yet within the next few years all, except Margaret Salmon, had left.

Margaret was very close to him. She was a very able head of personnel and a good, blunt Yorkshire woman. I particularly raised with her my view that John, lacking the managerial training, didn't really understand the management of money and budgets. 'You are quite right,' she said, 'but I have got the matter in hand, and have sent John off on a course which should put him on the right tracks, even though he doesn't realize what is happening. And it is very important that he shouldn't. He's very proud and would not like to think we were trying to shore up a weakness.' Sadly, I saw no signs that the course worked.

The problem with John is that while he is a very good guided missile, on autopilot he is just as likely to hit his own troops as the enemy. In the summer of 1994 I was presented with evidence of this. John gave an extraordinary speech in Dublin attacking his own staff. He was tired, he said, of the posturing of interviewers on television and radio and would like to see more reflection on issues and less disputation. I had no problem with the general thought – I had previously had much sympathy for newscaster Martyn Lewis's campaign for more good news on bulletins and told him so – but it was the fashion in which John did it that took my breath away. To choose a public platform in another country to attack his colleagues was not tactful.

At once he was faced by a furious backlash from within the BBC in defence of the likes of John Humphrys and Jeremy Paxman. He backtracked rapidly and apologized which only made matters worse. He seemed to me to be frightened of the senior news staff ever after. Despite his love of position papers and long mulling over of issues, John could not think round corners. 'Odd sort of fellow, he seems to me,' said Peter Carrington, the former Foreign Secretary, 'very good at drawing straight lines I should imagine.'

Such episodes forced me to question John's judgement as a manager, but I also had concerns about his political judgement. In 1995 he saw no problem with the broadcast, days before the local elections in Scotland, of a *Panorama* programme which consisted of a long interview with John Major. It inevitably resulted in a violent protest from the Labour Party who said it would influence voting in Scotland. They had a very good point. Labour took the matter to the courts where we lost. I was not surprised. The next thing I heard was that the management had decided to appeal to a higher court in Scotland against the judgement. It was a Monday night and the judges were all dining together.

'Who on earth is deciding this?' I asked Michael Stevenson.

'The Director-General,' he replied.

'He must be insane,' I said. 'Does he really think that on a Monday night, we can go scratching around Edinburgh, pulling high court Scottish judges [always a prickly bunch] out of black-tie dinners to censor the verdict reached by one of their members? We will lose the case.'

'The management think we won't.'

'Well, that's their opinion.'

We lost the case. We looked complete idiots. John was rebuked by a group of the governors for the way he handled the matter. The following week, Tony Blair had scheduled a special Labour Party conference for four hours on Saturday afternoon to discuss the future of Clause Four of its constitution. It was an integral part of his determination to alter the Labour Party – and very controversial. I then heard that the Director-General had agreed to broadcast this conference live in its entirety, while our rivals were showing sport or films all afternoon. A party conference would have been a total turn-off. I asked to see the Director-General and expressed my doubts. 'We have to change the schedule, John. We will be attacked by the Conservatives and they will win just as last week we were attacked by Labour and they won. Impartiality doesn't mean taking one side one week and then the other the next. It is about not taking sides.'

'We can't change the programme,' he replied. 'It's all agreed with the Labour Party and we've cooperated in choosing the camera positions with them.'

To go ahead would grievously damage the BBC's reputation for impartiality. In my view it certainly cast a shadow over John's political judgement, let alone his eye for programme appeal. I discussed it with Michael Cocks, Bob Phillis and Michael Stevenson. 'You three have got to get hold of this programme and screw it up – radically reduce the length, stuff it full of Liberal Democrats and Conservatives to offset the Labour bias.' This they did and saved the day.

Whatever my concerns about the Director-General, my main job – the charter renewal – was complete. So in the spring of 1995 I saw the Prime Minister in the Cabinet Room. I told him I had decided I would like to retire about nine months early, immediately the charter was signed. It was the right moment to go. John Major was kind enough to say he hoped that I would stay forever. At that moment, a message came that he had to go to the House urgently to vote. 'Come on, Dukie,' he said, 'we'll go together and carry on the conversation.'

He shot out of the room calling for two cars. We went in the lead one. 'This,' I said, 'is a bit of a thrill for me. I've never shared a car with a prime minister before.' To which he quickly rejoined, 'I doubt whether any prime minister would ever share a car with the head of the BBC either.' At the Commons we stopped outside a little door with a staircase which leads directly into the Prime Minister's private room in the Commons. Up we went, me wondering how many prime ministers had used this secret entrance over the years and for whom. On the way, he had said he wanted to tell me himself that the cabinet had decided to keep the Royal Marsden Hospital open. (A wise decision with hindsight – to improve the care of cancer patients throughout the country, the present government now says we need more Marsdens.)

I saw the Prime Minister again, a few months later, to tie up all the details of my retirement. I said that I had given the announcement some considerable thought. I had been appalled that, every time there was a vacancy near the top of the BBC, it became open season for the journalists to speculate, criticize and disrupt the morale of the whole organization. 'Why don't you, Prime Minister, announce the name of my successor on the day of my retirement instead of the customary two-month delay? I shall lose out on a few hopefully admiring valedictory articles but you will deprive the journalists and the BBC of weeks of damaging but riveting speculation.' 'Splendid,' he said, 'we'll do that.' It worked a treat.

Having settled the issues with the Prime Minister, I then went to see John Smith. In retrospect, this was a poignant meeting. I didn't know him well but liked him. I outlined the objectives we'd achieved for the BBC and my views about how it should be developed in the future. He was a Scotsman and the Labour Party was heavily dependent on Scottish votes. I thought, like the famous Irish rugby football captain, I would get my retaliation in first. So I quickly said I was going to tackle Scotland. I have long been on record saying that the whole media is far too London biased and London based.

'So what are you going to do about it?' he asked. I said I planned to give BBC Scotland more rope – more money, more control over their programmes and more air time for their own Scottish programmes. 'Good,' he said, 'I'll back you on that.' Then he paused. 'But my goodness, Duke, if they don't make good use of it, I'd pull that rope in bloody quick.' I was fascinated. There he was, a Scotsman, likely to be Prime Minister, dependent on Scottish votes but clear-sighted and tough. He leapt to his feet. 'Sorry, I've got to go now and try and snatch a few Liberal votes at the Christchurch by-election.' He died suddenly the next week. A great loss.

I then had an hilarious meeting with Paddy Ashdown. It was all going swimmingly when his face suddenly changed. 'I have to tell you,' he said, 'my party and I were very angry at how disgracefully you handled the European elections [where the Liberals had done badly]. We attribute our poor performance entirely to your biased reporting.'

Not my view. I made some quiet demur.

'No, no,' he said, 'we feel this so strongly that my colleagues have advised me that I ought to have cancelled this meeting with you.'

'That would have been a bloody stupid thing to do,' I replied, 'because then we couldn't have talked about it.'

His features were fierce and determined.

'Give me the evidence, Paddy, and I'll look at it.'

Suddenly his expression changed and I could see in his mind

that he was deciding that he had done enough to go back and tell his colleagues, 'My goodness, I gave that chairman hell.' He never said as much, of course, but a broad smile crossed his face.

'Come on,' he said, 'let's have a cup of tea and a good gossip. Will you need any help later down the stairs?' A lovely man.

My final interview with a party leader as Chairman was with Tony Blair. Once again I went through the BBC policy, our aspirations and our achievements. He was particularly anxious to hear what I could tell him about Rupert Murdoch which was plenty. His secretary came in twice – always a sign of overrunning. As the interview drew to a close, I slipped in my little test.

'Of course, I'm very fortunate to have such a good Director-General as John Birt.'

'Oh yes, I make it my business to keep in very close touch with John.'

Just what I feared. In my opinion, no Director-General or Chairman of the BBC should be in very close touch with the leader of any political party. But it was a friendly and enjoyable hour. As I left, I said, 'Well, Tony, if there's anything you want to know about the BBC or any queries you have, you have only to ring up. You have my private telephone number and I will reply to you just as I would reply to the Prime Minister.' I then added, on the spur of the moment, quite unpremeditated, 'Incidentally, in all my nine years as Chairman, I've only seen the Prime Minister four times and on each occasion, as today, I followed up by seeing the Leader of the Opposition within a fortnight.'

'What,' he asked, 'Neil and John?'

'That's right.'

He looked astonished but I felt I had made my point.

We were quite successful during my chairmanship in securing honours for some of the most talented staff at all levels in the BBC. I was particularly pleased when in 1995 my strong recommendation that John Drummond should get a knighthood was accepted. As controller of Radio 3 and director of the BBC Proms, he had contributed colourfully and constructively to the national artistic scene. I was delighted too when Terry Wogan, as an Irish citizen, was given the appropriate recognition. Terry and I enjoyed a wonderful relationship. He consistently took the piss out of me on his morning radio programme, claiming that I was permanently drunk and lived in a hovel. This delighted my family – especially my wife and daughter who frequently rang each other up and said, 'Have you heard what Terry said about Daddy today?' The reaction of others was more starchy but I believed there was nothing wrong with an organization where a talented employee could take the mickey out of the chairman over the airways. But there is more to Terry than a superb broadcaster. He came to the Marsden to open a ward for me. We did the formal piece – each mocking the other – and then I asked him to go round the ward but said I would leave him on his own. One of our cancer experts told me afterwards that he had taken many very distinguished people round wards but no one had had such an effect on the patients as Terry. He sat on each bed and lightened the heart of every patient.

I never lost sight of the World Service. After the Kuwait war, there were, not surprisingly, some bruised feelings among some of the Arab states, which emerged when I had dinner with one of their ambassadors. After telling Nicky Gordon Lennox, a governor and a distinguished ex-ambassador, about this, and Sam Younger, the World Service's very able managing director at the time, we embarked on a bold strategy and invited all the Arab ambassadors to come and have lunch with us at the BBC. To our delight, sixteen came. Nicky told me that to get sixteen Arab ambassadors together at a luncheon in the BBC was a totally unique occasion. To do so, moreover, and have a discussion of our various difficulties virtually without a cross word, was really quite a contribution towards our relations in the Middle East. They have never forgotten that lunch, and frequently refer to it when I meet them around London. It was a great tribute to the BBC and of course, totally independent of the government. I don't even know that they knew about it – I suppose they must have heard.

Slightly more unusually, I was asked to entertain the President of Azerbaijan. Always willing, I dispatched the invitation. Though I was mildly disturbed when a briefing pointed out how suddenly and frequently his political opponents suffered unfortunate and usually fatal accidents. Nothing daunted he arrived, accompanied by two enormous countrymen with large and sinister bulges under their armpits. We climbed into the lift with Sam. After a few seconds, it jammed and stayed jammed. The armpits were loosened. The President was testy. It seemed to last for ever and I prayed fervently for release, which came eventually, but the subsequent conversation was stilted. Not one of our best efforts.

Once my retirement date had been decided, I made a mental decision that I would not do anything in the months left to me which would tie the hands of my successor. For the most part, it was an easy policy to follow, but in the summer of 1995 I had a major clash with John Birt over his plans to relocate radio news and current affairs to a new centre at White City. I had already shown my opposition to such a plan in Michael Checkland's period. I believed in the importance of Broadcasting House in central London. Moreover, radio and television news are different beasts, following the same agenda, but with their own styles and production values.

At the governors' meeting just before Christmas 1994, we were presented with a plan for a new building at White City, but were not told what was to go into it. We assumed it was part of the ongoing rationalization of the BBC property portfolio. Instead, what became apparent in the spring of 1995 was that John was planning to use it as the base for a merged radio and television news service. There was no reason why television and radio should not share the collection of the original copy. That made economic sense. I had discovered that sometimes on events we had eight or nine different BBC journalists reporting on them. What they could not merge, in my view, was the production and presentation of the subsequent story.

The new White City building was going ahead fast because funds seemed to be allocated for it in small but regular tranches, each coming just under the maximum over which John had authority without recourse to the governors. Many felt the whole plan was wrong-headed. Politicians and, for that matter, actors, were always willing to drop in to Portland Place for a quick broadcast, but travelling out to White City was another story altogether. I knew several people who told me flatly they wouldn't do it.

John's plans were bitterly opposed by Liz Forgan, Managing Director of Radio, but he took the position that he would not discuss it with her unless the head of news and current affairs was present. Liz appealed to the governors. She put up a powerful case and I was convinced she would win the day, but I had done my homework badly and one governor, Bill Jordan, couldn't come at the last moment. John had been lobbying hard behind the scenes, threatening, I believe, to resign if he did not get his way. The final vote was tied. I could have used my casting vote to block the plans, but with my retirement imminent and Liz demanding a decision, I reluctantly agreed to let John go ahead. Liz Forgan resigned – a great loss to the BBC and one compounded by the manner in which her severance package was handled. She was talented, funny, adored by her staff, all of whom supported her. Moreover, she had been conspicuously loyal to John. I was surprised that the governors did not take more into consideration the fact that every departmental head in radio was on Liz's side. Had I not been leaving, I would have overruled the governors and demanded a new debate with all the governors present. As it was, I mishandled it.

Suddenly a situation arose which prompted Downing Street to suggest that I postpone my retirement by a couple of months – a *Panorama* programme in November 1995 to be devoted to an interview with the Princess of Wales. I had no notice of this until an hour before the public announcement. This episode darkened my last months at the BBC.

I still do not know how this interview arose but apparently Diana insisted that it should be surrounded by complete secrecy in order to give her time to tell the Queen who was in New Zealand. Until she returned, neither the Palace nor the governors would be informed. Clearly this was not the real reason as the Queen was easily accessible by telephone in New Zealand and had anyway been back in England for several days before the Palace heard that the programme was about to be announced.

It was a highly political interview touching on the succession to the throne. In promoting it the BBC appeared to abandon any

pretence of objectivity. According to Ben Pimlott in his book
The Queen, there was a sense of betrayal at the Palace which felt
it had a special relationship with the Corporation. This event
certainly broke all the rules or conventions about the relationship
with the BBC and for that matter the press. It also broke all the
rules about the relationship of the governors with the Board of
Management whose responsibility it was to keep the governors
informed in advance of any major programme initiatives.

The BBC gave the forthcoming programme massive publicity, adding on every occasion that my wife was a lady in
waiting to the Queen. The clear implication was that the
governors had not been informed in advance of the programme
because neither she nor I could be trusted with the information.
The Secretary of the BBC raised that issue three times with the
Director General but no action was taken.

This event crystallizes one of the fundamental issues that
governs the conduct of the media. Which takes precedence:
standards or sales? It is a question made more difficult by
knowing that if you elect for standards, you may give a scoop to
the opposition. No doubt people will argue about the propriety
of this programme for many years. Some 23 million viewers
watched it, but was that sufficient recompense for breaking faith
with all the long-accepted agreements with the Palace and the
governors? Immediately before the programme was aired, and as
he was about to go abroad, John Birt was asked why he had not
told the chairman – or if he found that difficult, the vice-
chairman. No answer.

There are two types of scoop – one which is the result of
painstaking research and hard work by the journalists and the
other which comes gift-wrapped. In this case it was royally
wrapped. Those are the dangerous ones: 'beware the Greeks
bearing gifts'. The donors have their own objectives, but the
medium loses control over its own output while still having to
accept responsibility for the content.

To my mind – a view shared by some, but not all of the
governors – this was a direct rejection not only of our traditional
relations with the Palace but of the standards we were trying to
uphold as the hallmark of the BBC. Among many critics Phyllis

James and William Rees-Mogg strongly condemned the BBC for transmitting this interview. John was reprimanded by a group of the governors, though this was a decision and occasion to which I was not party. But I did write to the Queen's private secretary on behalf of 'the very many members of our staff who do not believe that this programme was our finest hour'. I received a courteous letter in response.

There it was: old history now – an issue of judgement about which no doubt many will argue. It was indisputably a riveting programme for which Diana had clearly been well-coached and which was subsequently regretted. It certainly attracted a huge audience. If it had been referred to me, I would have insisted that we followed the rules and told the Palace about it, although I could not have or would have interfered with it. For me it is all about the BBC, the Standard Bearer, in an increasingly diverse market.

The postponement of my departure by two months was of no moment. The farewells were multitudinous and moving. The staff at the BBC gave me a wonderful leaving party, where my health was proposed by Kate Adie (not, as is more customary, by the Director-General). I was proud and flattered that she did it. She is a superb reporter, courageous, undaunted by difficulty and determined. She said that there were two words to associate with the office of chairman: diplomacy and defence. She discovered a third 'D' word. Debt-free. 'A man shall cease to be chairman if he shall become either of unsound mind or bankrupt' (a quote from the charter). The last, never in doubt. The first, constantly.

She went on: 'In the matter of defence, attacking the BBC is an enshrined national sport. Defending the BBC is a full-time occupation. As you are all aware, we, the staff of the BBC, are engaged in full-time anarchy, setting off each morning to corrupt, enrage and deprave. This is the confirmed view of those who write to the chairman.

'It has been his job to cast his eye over us, take a different view, and to write back; and to have a quiet word in the ear of those – especially the powerful – whose breakfast cornflakes are ruined by Humphrys. Thank God, say the staff. For the chairman for defending us and because we all, despite the wheel of politics and fashionable practice, still love the BBC and owe much to those who uphold it and defend it. So thank you, Chairman.'

As I said my goodbyes around the regions, I was more than touched by the warmth and affection with which I was received – and the wit. In Birmingham, our old friends, the resident cast of the *Archers* whom Sue and I had often visited, performed a marvellous skit. 'What on earth was an Oxford-educated ex-Guards officer and a member of the Queen's Royal Household doing at the BBC?' they asked. 'Certainly, it's time they left' – and with it they gave me the car number plate which I have in my dining room, DUK IE. Will Wyatt at the television dinner said, 'Dukie is not known to be abstemious, but in the land of the legless, I suppose the one-legged man is king.'

In Scotland, Terry Wogan gave me a marvellous speech about us, not forgetting, of course, the drunken chairman and his packing case. For the first time, I went to Murryfield, home of Scottish rugby. It was a thrill. England won.

Perhaps for me, of all the many goodbyes, the most moving was the present of a solid-silver salver on which every governor's signature had been engraved with the following inscription:

Presented to Duke Hussey by the BBC Governors on 13th March 1996. In affection and gratitude for steadying the BBC, changing it and securing its future.

Epilogue

Since I left the BBC, apart from one speech in the House of Lords, I have very carefully refused all invitations to comment, write or speak about the Corporation. I am a great believer in once you go, go. And that is what I have done. Yet it seems odd to finish off this personal story of most of my life without some small reflective epilogue.

Clearly the critical event in my life was being wounded and the six years in hospital that followed. That in itself had an unusual and psychological effect on me because, although I was not ashamed of my war – at least I got close to the enemy, too close in retrospect – I felt I had not done enough. So many of my friends had been so much more involved.

My whole attitude to that and therefore to my life was changed by the publication of the article about my experiences as a prisoner-of-war in the *Daily Telegraph* in 1998 which I referred to at the beginning of, and which directly led to, this book. Some time after it appeared came an article about courage, written by Ronnie Taylor, the adjutant in my battalion, in the *Guards Magazine*. Five people were picked out – four, all awarded the Victoria Cross, including my company commander, Bill Sydney, for outstanding courage in the face of the enemy, and the fifth, myself, for, 'individual courage of a different kind . . . in the same German attacks which yielded a VC for Sydney, Hussey was most horribly wounded and taken prisoner. Many times he was told he was about to die. His spirit alone sustained him.' I was much honoured and humbled by this. It changed my conception of my life. My war had not been the disaster I thought it was.

Of course the nature of my injuries – spine, both legs, hand – has affected my lifestyle but, curiously, in a positive way. It presents me with a daily challenge. I set myself targets on what I plan to do, and particularly to keep fit, trying to walk or swim for at least forty minutes when possible. Normally I reach them because I haven't got the guts to admit that I have failed. So in a weird way it has been a stimulus, not a handicap, and has strengthened me through an interesting and enjoyable life.

It is five years since I left the BBC and I look back on it with great admiration and affection but with some concerns which it seems appropriate to air here. When I left, the governors hosted a farewell dinner for me at the National Portrait Gallery on 13 March 1996. Because it seems a good summary of what we achieved I am including an excerpt from the speech I gave which, I hope, is still relevant.

> The last ten years have been a bit of a rollercoaster – but the peaks were much higher than the troughs were deep. I thoroughly enjoyed it and learnt a thing or two. One is, there are some people who dislike the BBC all the time. Rather more dislike us some of the time. There is nothing we can do about the first and not a lot about the second. People will always remember the bits with which they disagree. They forget the bits they like – the great stream of splendid, uncontentious material we transmit, art, nature, history, sport, comedy, drama, news and current affairs and documentaries – but they are why 94 per cent of the population listen to us or watch us every week.
>
> There have been huge changes at the BBC in the last twenty years and they were necessary. For example, Alastair Hetherington, who was BBC controller of Scotland in the late 1970s, once told me that back then when he wanted to spend £800, already agreed within his budget, he had to inform fifty-eight different people in London before he could go ahead. John McCormick, who holds the job today, tells me that figure is now down to nine. That's real progress. On the other hand, coming from the Manchester *Guardian*

where, as on *The Times*, no board paper was allowed to be more than two pages, Alastair was amazed to find at the BBC there were expected to be five pages. We will go down on our knees today if we've got one paper with less than twenty.

The great triumph has been winning the charter. We have given the BBC ten years in which to adapt itself to the new broadcasting scene. Such a result was unthinkable ten years ago, when our very continued existence was under threat. Of course an able management, under Mike Checkland and then John Birt, has made a tremendous contribution, but the driving force has been the governors who set the strategy and chose the team to implement it – not always, I'll admit, without some controversy.

I love the BBC. It's always been part of my life and when you think of the wonderful programmes we continually transmit on television and radio, you cannot be anything but proud. I am particularly glad that Sue Birtwistle is here, producer of *Pride and Prejudice*. I have a particular interest in that, because, although I didn't interfere in programmes, I can take credit for banging on to the BBC about the need to restore the old great classical serials for which we became so famous. The result was *Pride and Prejudice* (I had nothing to do with the choice) and when I left, BBC Television gave me, as a memento, photographs of all the Georgian buildings that had been used in that wonderful production. Sue is an archetypal example of the best of the BBC. We have a wonderful, dedicated and talented staff. They need to be inspired and led with elan so that their talents can bloom as hers have done.

As I leave, I have a few worries. We talk about extending choice – providing something different. Our system of funding can only be justified by offering an alternative to independent television and radio, by impartiality and high standards and production values which will clearly delineate us from our opposition. I do not believe we always achieve this in every area. Radio is certainly more distinctive, but it was certainly careless to mislay both David Hatch and Liz

Forgan in the same year, depriving the management of a hefty hunk of experience, talent and humour.

We need to work on that mysterious factor X which enables football teams, armies and businesses to win battles against all odds. It's usually called morale. I think we need a few more laughs and less relentless debate, faster discussion and more independence down the line.

Winning the charter is an accepted public triumph. An equally important but hardly noticed one is to have clarified and established our – your – authority as governors as the sole regulator across the whole of the BBC's activities, setting objectives, monitoring and adjudicating on the outcome. This is more important than you think. Only recently, with great courage from Virginia Bottomley and help from Michael Cocks and George Russell, we have frustrated an attempt to remove the responsibility for impartiality from the governors and regulate it to the Broadcasting Standards Council. That would have been a total disaster. If we, the governors, cannot ensure that impartiality, complain and if necessary take strong action, if our output does not achieve that impartiality, we will not maintain our privileged status.

When I became Chairman, the governors used to spend at least ninety minutes at each fortnightly board discussing recent programmes. I felt that was too restrictive and discouraged it, but now we hardly talk about them at all, except for board papers on specific strands. I blame myself for this. The programmes and the staff who make them are the core of the BBC's business. I strongly adhere to the principle I laid down on my arrival – that we would not preview programmes as had been done earlier that year, but equally, we should never sacrifice our right to do so. We are responsible for the output and the tone of that output. If we get our programmes right, no one can touch us. If we get them wrong, everyone can.

I've got a present for you all – a paperback by Penelope Fitzgerald which I read recently. I wrote to tell her how moved I was, how I laughed, how I cried and how I was exasperated at the BBC and its funny little ways. I hope you will enjoy it. She wrote back to say that all her characters were based on real life, under the impression that they would be dead by the time it was published! Unfortunately they all turned out to be indestructible and wrote to explain her mistake.

Indestructible is what I hope the BBC will be, in the interest of the millions of listeners and viewers who share with us the belief that it is part of the nation's history, heritage and fabric. We would be a poorer country without the BBC. It is in your hands. If things go wrong you will get the blame. You will not of course get the credit, if things go right, but you will have earned it. Good luck!

Throughout my time at the BBC, I made clear my view that, in the future of broadcasting, there would be no shortage of channels. The shortfall would be in the quality of material on those channels. The increasing competition, not just here in the United Kingdom, but across the world, is going to lead to larger and larger consortia. It would not surprise me if one of the major British broadcasters lines up with one of the American companies and calls it globalization.

The potential expansion – or foreign domination, whichever way you like to put it – of British companies is one of my concerns. This is the core of the BBC's problem. It is up against huge commercial companies, but unlike them it is accountable to Parliament (not the government) and above all to its audience who are compelled to pay £105 a year for the privilege. And privilege it is. The BBC has never understood, to my mind, that they are not separate from the considerations that affect the rest of the country. Life is hard and can be cruel. There are very few people who reach the top who have not at some time walked into an office with a good job and walked out a few minutes later, without it. It happened to me.

The problems for the BBC become more urgent and more timely because of the way in which the media have developed in the last few years. Lord Callaghan, in a superb speech on 3 November 1987 which I quoted earlier (I was so impressed that I asked for his notes to which I now refer) remarked: 'Democracy can only exist if there is a constant stream of information. Politicians, governments, the press, radio and television all share responsibility to provide a pure stream of information.' But 'the media not only *record* news, the electronic revolution enables them to *make* news and *decide* what is news' [my italics].

To a certain extent, of course, that has always been the case since the first newspapers in the eighteenth century. But the power of television, the selection by television operators of what is news, and the reluctance of any major newspaper or broadcasting channel to stand apart from the accepted popular agenda all maximize the problem. The very system of funding the BBC and its unique governance carries with it the implication that it should have the courage to set its own agenda. It should extend choice, not mirror what is already available.

In this new world, there has to be a place for a powerful media influence in the pocket of no individual proprietor or interest group or advertiser, an organization which does not give paramount weight in choice of programmes to what will earn the most money from subscription or advertising but which instead offers schedules to tempt audiences and to uplift their interest and understanding. Above all, the BBC has to maintain its position as a standard setter in the industry.

Sir William Haley, when Director-General, said: 'All the problems of the BBC stem from its power.' That is true. Back in 1929 the chairman of the Conservative Party sent the BBC's first chairman, Lord Clarendon, the following message, 'The immediate cause of my writing is the widespread resentment aroused amongst members of the Conservative Party by Mr Dickinson's talk. We have repeatedly been told by the BBC that every possible step is taken to secure complete fairness for all parties. I should be neglecting my duty if I did not ascertain what arrangements are being made to secure impartiality for all three parties. It is clear that the balance is very heavily weighted on the side of socialism.' Nothing has changed.

So the BBC will never be free of charges of political bias, but in my experience those problems can be handled. Of course I was leant on by politicians, but once I'd made it clear that I would uphold the BBC's independence, I was left alone. I saw my job as a trusteeship to preserve a unique part of the country's heritage. Many of those who worked alongside me saw it in the same way. They had low salaries but high ideals and devoted their life to public service broadcasting.

There have been changes there in recent times. When I left the BBC I thought that it was in danger of spending far too much money on consultants, too much time on consulting and too much energy debating endlessly on decisions. Leaders must be prepared to make decisions and take the responsibility for them. The wanderings of the journalists originally based in Portland Place, particularly in radio, to and now from the News Centre in White City must make them feel that the Grand Old Duke of York was an amateur out for an afternoon hike.

Greg Dyke, the current Director-General, is tackling the problems with resolution and good humour. But what of the governors? When I left the BBC, I thought we had established them as the ultimate power within the BBC. An unkind critic might say that they have subsequently stood supinely by while one Director-General did one thing and his successor did the opposite. They would make a good chorus for the musical version of *The Vicar of Bray*.

It is important, though sometimes difficult, for the Chairman and the Director-General always to work closely together. The Director-General is hopefully a proven expert in his craft. The Chairman is an outsider, hopefully with some worldly wisdom and experience. It is a set-up which might be designed to result in a personality clash, and it usually does, starting with Lord Clarendon and John Reith. (Reith left because he had a row with Clarendon, who remained.) Nevertheless I believe that something as important but as introspective as the BBC does need the challenge of experience.

So what now? I do not think that, with the world of broadcasting expanding globally, the BBC can face its financial future with total confidence. It is a minnow in these waters and must not end up as once-proud British makes like Riley and Humber did in the global car-making market after Ford and General Motors started throwing their weight around.

I see that from my notes as early as 1990 I was worrying

about the future finances of the BBC. There are only three ways
by which it can be financed: the licence fee, advertising or worst
of all, in my mind, by direct government grant. On the whole, I
have no doubt that the licence fee is the best because it gives
the BBC the most opportunity to develop according to its
cherished and unique principles, but I seriously wonder how far
the great British public can be increasingly taxed for the privilege. The recent licence fee deal was a good settlement and
sufficient, I am assured, to cover present output. Yet its burgeon-
ing digital channels, I believe, take the BBC remit too wide. Its
world reputation is built on its national channels and it is on
those national channels that its continued world reputation will
depend.

The finances of the BBC are opaque and shrouded in mystery. However financially able they may be, it is not practical for
the governors to intervene except on questions of generality or
major issues. To delve into detail creates an impossible situation
for both governors and management. The BBC management has
a long record of telling the governors as little as they possibly
can about the details of expenditure. No management is innocent of that [I have not been myself]. But, bearing in mind the
importance of the BBC in the body politic, more clarity could
yield more efficient governance. I wonder whether the National
Audit Office could be of assistance here. They have the twin
virtues of total independence and outstanding expertise in this
type of problem. For the BBC the continual pressure and concentration on the timing and size of the next licence fee is
debilitating. I would like to see this sword of Damocles, which
hangs over the BBC, removed. Too much depends on whoever
happens to be in the key political appointment at the time.

A recommendation on the licence fee from the National
Audit Office would carry great weight and be difficult to dispute.
I also wonder, and with much hesitation suggest, that a moment
may come when it is thought appropriate to merge the two
regulatory authorities – the governors of the BBC and the
Independent Television Commission. Broadcasting, whether
television, radio or digital, is a vastly important medium, not just
in this country but all over the world – where, incidentally, our

World Service is gratefully accepted in most places [but not all!] as a supreme example of independence and high standards.

Any such suggestion will invite huge opposition, but I am beginning to think that broadcasting could be strengthened by a single voice at the top. It would, of course, be hugely difficult and demand a chairman of outstanding ability, tact and determination, supported by a board which would combine men and women with a strong and dedicated commitments to the arts and quality, alongside colleagues with a healthy regard for the merits of financial discipline and profit. The present Board of Governors, like many of its predecessors, has on it individuals of outstanding ability who find it difficult to carve out their roles as distinct from that of the management.

This dichotomy results not just from the power of the BBC but also from its constitution. The BBC is more than a constituent part of our national life. It is a national heritage. It is not a business and should not be run as such. I myself urged the BBC to make much greater use of their existing assets, so I am in no position to complain, but the current expansion of the BBC, I suspect, will stretch its intellectual and managerial resources beyond their natural limits. It is, in fact, becoming a business. That may be its predestined future but, if it is, it cannot claim or expect the special treatment that the award of a licence fee gives it, and the unique system of governance that the governors provide. Will the BBC – the British Broadcasting Corporation – become ABC – Another Broadcasting Company?

These are the fears of someone committed to the BBC's heritage, but who see that it is now faced with a world so different from that in which it was started. I am not saying that these arguments are conclusive or that I actually agree with them. All I am suggesting is that it is worth considering how far the BBC can stand alone and still maintain the great traditions of quality, performance and output which have made it renowned all over the world.

A new joint board watching over the future of British broadcasting in its entirety could establish total political independence and might be a more logical and effective method of governing an industry which, in many different ways, affects the life of every British citizen. So that is the BBC. Good luck to it and all who work for it.

From 1950 to 1985, I was, of course in newspapers, rising from a copy boy to a chief executive. The final and absolute defeat of the unions by Rupert Murdoch has liberated the newspapers from appalling and frustrating restrictions. Sadly, one result has predictably been bitter increased competition and probably, though not yet, a reduction in the number of newspapers. As always, competition has resulted in a dramatic fall in standards. Newspapers are certainly more bawdy, but then that is a streak that reaches back to Chaucer. We may deplore the tacky but this is the twenty-first century. What I mind far more is the appalling inaccuracy of journalistic reporting right across the national newspaper output. That is a matter to which, I think, the Press Complaints Commission could direct more attention because there could be a danger that the newspaper industry exercises power without responsibility which, as Stanley Baldwin famously remarked, has been the prerogative of the harlot down the ages.

Meanwhile, in my life, it is a relief not to have the constant pressure of a big organization. On the other hand, it is a sore trial not to have the comfort of Carole, my very good secretary, and Alan, my loyal and enchanting driver. So I get myself in the most frightful muddles. But it was a great honour, which I much appreciated, to become a member of the House of Lords. I am fortunate to be on its 'Euro A' committee, looking at the finances of the European Union. The weight of paper is formidable, but, undaunted, we publish reports on our various subjects which are widely studied throughout the EU.

The House of Lords committees are extremely distinguished and valued, less in this country than they should be. When I first joined, I was petrified. Most, though not all, of the members had been brought up in the dialectical mode of parliamentary discussion and debate, so the approach was to extract information by question rather than by discussion. I found this very difficult at first and was terrified to ask a question, but one day I came back looking very happy, like a little boy who'd been told by the headmaster that he'd bowled rather well.

'What are you so pleased about?' said Sue.

'Lord Dahrendorf said I had asked a very intelligent question today.' My cup was overflowing.

Otherwise, I listen to many debates but as a cross-bencher, I do not often vote. The atmosphere and the surroundings are superb and persuasive. I suspect the new members – though I am one – will slip more easily into the way of life than they anticipate. Debates are often illumined by peers of wide experience and nearly always conducted with good humour and good manners.

The courtesy of the officials is unrivalled. There was a splendid occasion once when Phyllis James and I were, after a debate on the BBC, having a drink with her daughter. Unfortunately we were in a bar, the Bishops', into which only peers or peeresses in their own right are allowed. This was pointed out by a beautifully mannered 'doorman' in his morning coat and white tie, who offered to escort Phyllis's daughter to another bar which did not have such exclusive rules for entry. So off they went, only to return four minutes later. 'I'm afraid,' he told us, 'Baroness James's daughter is not allowed in there either unless accompanied by a peer or peeress.'

We immediately left and started off in a little procession down the long corridor, Phyllis striding ahead, in her characteristically stolid manner, the official and I hobbling along in the background. Halfway down the corridor, he paused, turned his head over his shoulder and said, 'I hope you will excuse my saying this, my Lord, but I bet you have been thrown out of a lot better bars than that in your life.'

This vignette seems to me to encompass much of the charm and character of the House of Lords.

What else do I do? I am not short of charitable activities. I am much involved in the Wells Cathedral School and BLESMA, and am patron of the Somerset British Legion and also of BAPO, the association of prosthetists and orthotists. As I have one on each leg I was an easy touch. I am also chairman of two small but interesting companies – one in financial management, the other in a high tech construction business. I know nothing about either, but this is useful as, rather like the Euro committee, you approach the problems from a different and perhaps unusual angle.

Above all, I have the good fortune to have my family around me. This legendary delight of old age is in no way exaggerated.

This book started at Anzio in February 1944. It finishes, surprisingly, at the German Embassy in London. On 29 July 1998, I opened a letter from the German Ambassador, Gebhardt von Moltke, in which he said he had read with sympathy and admiration the article about my war-time experiences and imprisonment in the *Daily Telegraph*.

He had learned that I would soon be celebrating my seventy-fifth birthday and said that it would give him great pleasure if he could contribute on this occasion with a dinner in my honour at his residence in London. A date was agreed for September. I was moved and surprised by this invitation. The ambassador had even supplied a distinguished guest list, including many people mentioned in the preceding chapters. Among the guests were Sue and my two children, James and Katharine.

The evening was touched with sadness because that night, 13 September, Frank Gillard, who was eagerly looking forward to the event, died suddenly. Nevertheless, as I subsequently wrote to the ambassador, it was a memorable occasion described by several guests as unique.

As I had started this book in the hands of German soldiers at Anzio under fire from our own troops, it seems appropriate to end it at the German Ambassador's excellent table. I will quote a few closing paragraphs from the speech I made on that night.

All over the world, wherever there is malnutrition, war, hardship and suffering, you will find the Red Cross. They certainly contributed to saving my life. So did the Catholic nuns of Saint Vincent de Paul who nursed me so devotedly. That I was an enemy made no difference. I was a patient. Every night we could hear our bombs falling nearby. To them, Ambassador, we listened with mixed feelings but that did not influence the nuns. Human compassion, sympathy and care accept no boundaries, military, territorial or political. I was well treated by German soldiers, doctors and nurses. In war, terrible things are done. No country has a monopoly of good or evil. Equally, on all sides, there are examples of courage, compassion and a faith in Christian values.

The ambassador comes, of course, from a distinguished and historic family. His cousin, Helmut von Moltke, stood up to Hitler on principle and was executed for his courage. He was described by George Kenyon, the American diplomat, as the greatest person morally and the most enlightened in his concepts who he had met on either side of the battle lines. I mentioned this in my speech.

He was one of the few Christian martyrs of our time. A few days before his execution, he said to his judge, 'I stand before you, not as a Protestant, not as a landowner, not as a nobleman, not as a German, but as a Christian, nothing else.' The memory of his courage and faith illumine those years. The rehabilitation of Germany after the war was a legacy he, his colleagues and their successors bequeathed to their country, which now plays a vital role in the Europe to which we all belong.

I was very fortunate to meet those who shared von Moltke's values. I know we all in this room share the pleasure that our two countries are friends and allies again as in the years before the twentieth century they usually were.

Ambassador, thank you again for this evening, on behalf of all your guests for which we all and no one more than I, are deeply grateful and which illustrates so vividly the values in which your cousin believed and for which he died.

Index